Fighting to Learn

Fighting to Learn

POPULAR EDUCATION AND GUERRILLA WAR IN EL SALVADOR

JOHN L. HAMMOND

Rutgers University Press

New Brunswick, New Jersey, and London

Portions of this book have previously appeared in different form in "War-Uprooting and the Political Mobilization of Central American Refugees," *Journal of Refugee Studies*, 6 (1993), 105–22; "Popular Education in the Salvadoran Guerrilla Army," *Human Organization*, 55 (1996), 436–445; "Organization and Education among Salvadoran Political Prisoners," *Crime, Law, and Social Change*, 25 (1996), 17–41; "Popular Education in El Salvador: Lessons for College Teachers," *Review of Radical Political Economics*, 29, no. 3 (Summer 1997), 103–111.

The map of El Salvador has been adapted courtesy of NACLA Report on the Americas.

Library of Congress Cataloging-in-Publication Data

Hammond, John L.
    Fighting to learn : popular education and guerrilla war in El
Salvador / John L. Hammond.
       p. cm.
    Includes bibliographical references (p.) and index.
    ISBN 0-8135-2525-X (cloth : alk. paper). — ISBN 0-8135-2526-8
(pbk. : alk. paper)
    1. Popular education—El Salvador—History—20th century.
2. Critical pedagogy—El Salvador—History—20th century.
3. Literacy—El Salvador—History—20th century.   4. Insurgency—El
Salvador—History—20th century.   5. Peasant uprisings—El Salvador—
History.   6. El Salvador—Politics and government—1979–1992. I. Title.
LC196.5.S2H36 1998
370.11'5—dc21   97–43068
                                                           CIP

British Cataloging-in-Publication information available

Manufactured in the United States of America

*To the popular teachers, who share what they know
with their compañeros, and with me*

CONTENTS

I went to cover the war and the war covered me.
—Michael Herr, *Dispatches*

PREFACE

Through most of my adult life I have been active in politics and have tried to integrate my political involvement with my academic work. Most of my prior research has been on topics that interested me because of their political relevance. That is why I became interested in El Salvador, too, but there I discovered something more: what I learned also bore on my work as a teacher. Studying popular education not only presented challenging intellectual problems and political relevance, but also caused me to rethink (often) what I did in the classroom.

During my first trips to Central America, focused on other topics, I nevertheless fell into the habit of asking people—especially peasants—how they had learned to read. The answer was always a *story*. It was never just "I went to school and I learned to read." Sometimes that was what the story came down to, but in the telling it became clear that for them it was no ordinary accomplishment; it represented victory in a struggle. More often, the story was in fact much more complicated: picking up little bits of knowledge here and there, buying a book on a rare trip to a big town, learning for the first time in a refugee camp.

Learning was an effort—not only a mental effort, but a strain on the resources they had to live on. And because they knew how hard it was, they were proud that they had done it. Being able to tell a story about themselves was an expression of empowerment. To see oneself as the subject of a story is not that far from (in Spanish, in fact, it is etymologically identical to) seeing oneself as a subject of history.

I found their pride inspiring—the pride of people who had learned, and even more, the pride of teachers, usually of limited education themselves, at sharing what they always called "the little bit they knew." As an educator I was thrilled to find people to whom education meant so much. Many of my students at home take it for granted. The pride itself is also thrilling: it is always a pleasure to meet people who are enthusiastic about their accomplishments. The tone of voice changes when they talk about learning and teaching, and their excitement shines through.

Their generosity and commitment were all the more striking because of the duress of war. They lived through it not only with forbearance and dignity but, it seemed, with their determination and community spirit strengthened. In their communities, education is a collective project and they carry it out even though they are utterly lacking in material resources and buffeted by war. By comparison, austerity at my institution does not look so bad. In contrast to the mean-spirited attacks by public officials here, however, I was pleased to find that education there is still treated as a social responsibility.

I owe a great debt of gratitude to many people in El Salvador who made my research possible. They housed, fed, and transported me, let me observe their work, and let me into their lives and their communities. Many of them show up, pseudonymously, in the book; many more do not. I give special thanks to the people in six organizations, who in different ways helped me to see and understand popular education and El Salvador: the National Federation of Agricultural Cooperatives (FENACOA), Segundo Montes City (earlier the refugee community in Colomoncagua, Honduras), the Non-Governmental Human Rights Commission of El Salvador (CDHES), the Inter-Association Literacy Committee of the Eastern Zone (CIAZO), the Community Development Council of Northern Morazán and San Miguel (PADECOMSM), and the Coordinating Committee of Communities and Repopulations of Chalatenango (CCR).

Doing field work is fun and games; writing is something else. I have had extraordinary support, criticism, and encouragement from Laura Kramer, who invited me to talk in public about popular education for the first time; read the articles which preceded the book, all the chapters as they were written, and finally the whole manuscript (often with heroically fast turnaround); encouraged, advised, scolded, and persuaded me (sometimes) to unleash a draft before it was ready for anyone's eyes but my own. Our writing partnership has brought me great satisfaction. To all colleagues: live like her.

Many others have helped by reading what I wrote. For careful attention to the entire book manuscript, I thank Bob Arnove (who also offered friendly advice and encouragement to a novice student of popular education at an early stage), Leigh Binford, Meg Crahan, Marc Edelman, Mark Kesselman, Hector Lindo Fuentes, Susan Lowes, Jack Spence, and Lise Vogel. Others gave valuable comments on parts of the manuscript or preceding articles: Terry Arendell, Charles Bahn, the late Hal Benenson, Josh DeWind, Joe Esposito, Bill Fisher, Jean Franco, Ann Garvin, Gerry Handel, Maria Lagos, Patty Parmalee, Maggi Popkin, Martha Soler, Sarah Towle, and Eric Wolf.

In discussions, Rina Benmayor, Gerry Handel, Paul Hoeffel, George Martin, Mike Perna, Peter Shiras, Jean Weisman, and George Yúdice provided insights and helped me over problems. At Rutgers University Press, Martha Heller offered enthusiastic support and astute criticism. The members of my study group—Renate Bridenthal, Hester Eisenstein, Lenny Gordon, Paul Montagna, Ellen Schrecker, Carole Turbin, and Lise Vogel—read and commented on my work; we also discussed many issues that turn up in one way or another in this book, and learned from each other.

My association with *compañeros* in the Central America solidarity movement, especially in the Committee for Nonintervention in Central America, New
York CISPES, and Voices on the Border, made it possible for me to integrate
my scholarship with my political activism in support of the people this book is
about. As I have discovered before, writing a book in the context of a political
movement helps one to keep working. Many of these people and others made
phone calls on my behalf to the Sixth Brigade and the U.S. Embassy on one
momentous occasion. I particularly want to remember the concern on that occasion of my friend the late Pat Peppe. I know how much he would have contributed to this book if he were still here.

Beth Cagan, Steve Cagan, Bill Hutchinson, and the Marin Interfaith Task
Force made possible some unique experiences. Lisa Katzenstein and Marcia
Lifshitz fed me speakers for my classes and set up meetings with Salvadoran
popular movement activists visiting New York. I learned by experience in the
Institute for Popular Education with Lina Cartei, the late Eleonora Castaño
Ferreira, João Paulo Castaño Ferreira, and Claire Picher, and in Lee Knefelkamp's
class at Teachers College.

Of an army of transcription typists, I thank Sandra Palacios and Maria
Prieto in particular for their steadfastness. Hugh Byrne, George Vickers, and J.
Michael Waller provided important documents. (Mentioning Mr. Waller, whom
I have never met, reminds me to make the usual disclaimer that none of these
people bear any responsibility for the use I have made of their help.) Norman
Clarius and Suzanne Siegel of Hunter College Interlibrary Loan can find any
book, anywhere. Tim Crouse, Joanna Foley, Ana Golici, and Fred Rosen helped
me select and prepare the illustrations, and Joshua Lapidus prepared the map.
Hunter College, the City University of New York, and the PSC-CUNY Research
Foundation provided essential support, financial and otherwise, and an environment in which I could continue trying to figure out experimentally what popular education is.

I have learned from popular education (among many other things) that
things don't always fit into small, labeled packages. If I thank someone for reading a draft, someone else for setting up a meeting, and someone else for getting
me a document, I do not mean to leave unrecognized that many people helped
me in a variety of ways, including their enthusiastic interest in the project.

ABBREVIATIONS

AMS	Association of Salvadoran Women
ANDES	National Association of Salvadoran Educators (teachers' union)
BPR	Popular Revolutionary Bloc
CDHES	Non-Governmental Human Rights Commission of El Salvador
CIAZO	Inter-Association Literacy Committee of the Eastern Zone
CCR	Coordinating Committee of Communitites and Repopulations of Chalatenango
COPPES	Committee of Political Prisoners of El Salvador
CRIPDES	Christian Committee for the Displaced
CUNY	City University of New York
ERP	People's Revolutionary Army
FAPU	United Popular Action Front
FECCAS	Salvadoran Christian Campesino Federation
FENACOA	National Federation of Agricultural Cooperatives
FMLN	Farabundo Martí National Liberation Front
FPL	Popular Liberation Forces
FTC	Rural Workers' Federation
FUNPROCOOP	Foundation for the Promotion of Cooperatives
NGO	Nongovernmental organization
ORDEN	National Democratic Organization
PADECOMSM	Community Development Council of Northern Morazán and San Miguel
PCS	Salvadoran Communist Party
PNA	National Literacy Program
PPL	Local Popular Power
PRTC	Central American Revolutionary Workers' Party
RN	National Resistance
UNHCR	United Nations High Commission for Refugees
UTC	Union of Rural Workers

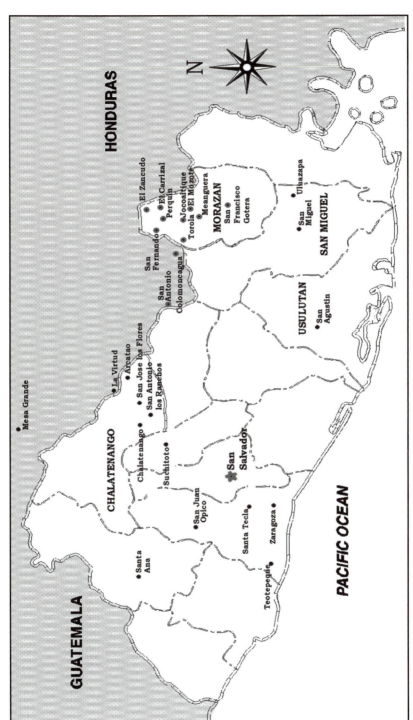

El Salvador

Fighting to Learn

CHAPTER 1

Introduction

––––––

Chebo was a volunteer literacy teacher who met a group of adults from his community, Apulo Amatitán, for two hours five nights a week. One afternoon in July 1990, he finished work at four o'clock and had to walk an hour and a half to catch the bus. At home he wolfed down his supper standing up, donned a sport jacket, and left for his six o'clock class.

He began by showing the group a poster-size photograph of two men in straw hats walking down a dusty road carrying machetes. The same photograph appeared in the students' *cartilla* (primer), *Alfabetizando para la paz* (Literacy for Peace). He invited them to "reflect" on the photograph: who are these men— are they students, workers, men who are loafing? What are they doing? Are they happy or sad? His smooth delivery in front of the classroom showed his complete confidence in his material and in his relationship with his students.

Chebo, more formally Eusebio, belonged to a fishing cooperative on Lake Ilopango, close to San Salvador. One of its best educated members (he had completed sixth grade as a boy), he had been invited to take several special training courses in fish cultivation and cooperative management. The cooperative was affiliated with the National Federation of Agricultural Cooperatives (FENACOA— despite the inclusive name, it was only one of several such federations). When the Ministry of Education created a program to conduct literacy classes in rural communities, FENACOA sent volunteers to train as teachers. Chebo was recruited in 1985. The cooperative then invited its own members and other illiterate people from the community to join the class. The ministry gave each of them a cartilla, a notebook, and a pencil.

In this poor community, the free school supplies were not a trivial incentive. The structure provided by the formal program was a further incentive for the class in Apulo Amatitán. But classes ended when funds ran out at the end of the year. They began again in 1989, when FENACOA joined a new nongovernmental literacy program for grassroots organizations. Through the federation, Chebo was recruited once again.

On this night fourteen people were present, seven men and seven women. Most appeared to be between twenty and thirty years old. The atmosphere was informal—they called the group a "literacy circle," not a class. They entered into an animated discussion of the photograph: The straw hats meant that the two men were going to be out in the sun; the machetes meant that they were going to work—or maybe to look for work. They were *campesinos* (peasants).

"That's the interesting word we're going to look at," said Chebo. "Who are campesinos?" Answers rang out: "We are people who live in the *campo* [countryside], outside of the capital city." "We are people who cultivate the earth." "And what can we grow?" Chebo asked. "Corn." "Beans." "Coffee." "Sugar cane." "Vegetables." Students competed with each other, naming some fifteen different crops.

"We see how many different things we know how to grow," said Chebo. "Do we grow them all?" "No," a man answered, "because we can't work without money." Others joined in: seeds and fertilizer are expensive, and it is hard to get credit. "We only grow corn," said one.

When Chebo started teaching, he felt inadequate because of his poor education.

> I was afraid. I was afraid they might criticize me. I didn't know if I was going to say good things, or if they would like me. I had never spoken up in a meeting. At the beginning we had forty-five people— it was full (since then we've divided the circle in two). Besides, there were twelve-year-old kids and sixty-year-olds. All kinds of people. So I thought if some of them liked me, others wouldn't. But little by little these people came to understand me. I told them I wasn't a professional, just someone who wanted to teach them the little bit that I knew. I might even mispronounce words, I said, but they shouldn't be surprised because that's the way I am and I can't change even if I'm going to stand up in front of them.

Chebo had clearly overcome his fear. He conducted the lesson with assurance and enthusiasm. He pushed the discussion forward by asking who had land, and where. No one in the group owned land. One man rented a field fourteen kilometers from his home, the closest piece of land he had found. Another had rented three *tareas* (less than half an acre) because that was all he could afford.

Some had not rented land at all. They had found none available; or they could not afford the seeds and fertilizer to plant, and they could not get credit. "A lot of us are displaced from the war," said one man. People fleeing the bombings in their villages moved to safer areas of the country. "We just grab empty land that belongs to the state. But we have no papers for the land so we can't get credit."

The lively discussion went on for half an hour. Only then did Chebo bring the group around to reading and writing. He wrote the word *campesino* on the

Figure 1. *Campesinos* (peasants). *Alfabetizando para la Paz.* CIAZO, 1990.

board and asked them to divide it into syllables. "Cam!" someone shouted, and Chebo wrote the first syllable on the board. "Pe!" followed; then "si!" When he asked for the fourth syllable, someone said "sino" and he offered a gentle correction.

Then they constructed the "syllabic families" of the word by varying the vowel in each syllable. When he asked for the syllabic family of "cam," students offered "cum," "com," and "kem." "No," he said, with a sly smile, as if he were about to reveal an inscrutable mystery. "It's not *kem*, it's *cem*." They went on to "cim," "pa," "pi," "po," "pu," "sa," "se," and so forth.

They recited the syllabic families in unison several times. Chebo interspersed comments to amplify their understanding: he discussed the lip movements necessary to pronounce the sounds; he pointed out that a woman from the countryside is called a *campesina*. Then he asked for volunteers to read the syllabic families individually. After five people had read them off, he called for a round of applause.

The meeting concluded with a discussion of why they thought it was important to learn to read. Many illiterate people don't join the circle, they said, for a variety of reasons: they say that they are too old, that their eyesight isn't good enough, or simply that it won't do them any good.

Others, however, don't have time because of economic pressures. In this fishing community, Chebo told me later, "lots of men take their wives to help them fish. If a man hires a boy to help him, what they catch isn't enough to feed his family and pay the boy, so he takes his wife. They spend the whole night, and leave the children deposited in someone else's house." Others work during the day, but at night they have to haul water, look for firewood, or do other household tasks.

Still, the students believed it was important to learn to read. For very practical reasons: "Sometimes you need to sign something, and if you can't read it you don't know what you are signing." "You can't get credit to buy seeds if you can't sign your name." A man said, "In a store, they may overcharge you." A woman offered, "Sometimes a woman, no matter how poor she is, wants a new dress and can't afford it. But if she knows how to read she can get a pattern, measure the cloth, and make it herself." Chebo added that cooperatives had to have people who can read and write to assume responsibilities in the organization. Discussing the value of learning led them to raise a question that had come up before: "Can we get a diploma or a card to prove that we have learned to read? You need it when you look for a job."

With his six years of schooling, Chebo did not regard himself as a great intellect; in fact, he took eight years to complete six grades because he was held back twice. Despite his experience teaching, he was modest and uncertain of his skills. He was not kidding when he referred to "the little bit that I know," but he offered to share it out of generosity and commitment.

Teaching, he said, is as much a matter of human relations as of technical knowledge. "In the training we learned to be tolerant and to have a certain patience with adults. Their opinions sometimes—one person says one thing, another says something else, but good or bad, you have to learn to respect their ideas." What gave him the most satisfaction from his literacy circle were these human relations—"sharing with all the *compañeros*[1] there. I chat with them: 'What did you do today? Are you working? Why didn't you find work?' When I feel wiped out, I don't feel it until I get home. [While I'm there] I forget that I have problems for a while." Summarizing his work, he said, "You put love into it."

Doing Popular Education

Chebo and his circle were doing popular education. This book tells their story. It is the story of thousands of campesinos in El Salvador who educated themselves and their children on very scarce resources and in the middle of a war. *Educación popular* means education of, by, and for the *pueblo*—organized by people in their own community, outside the control of the official education system. During the war that wracked El Salvador from 1980 to 1992, communities organized popular education in zones controlled by the Farabundo Martí National

Liberation Front (FMLN), in contested zones, and (though less commonly) in cities and relatively peaceful rural areas as well.

This book will describe what went on in literacy circles and more formal classrooms and in the communities that created them. I make five main points about popular education. First, carried on in conditions of scarcity, it was limited by poverty, war, and the lack of education and experience of those who taught. Second, it nevertheless achieved some significant successes, because it was guided by a vision of education tailored to those circumstances, a vision summarized by the very name "popular education." The third and fourth points grow out of that vision. By linking intellectual development and personal growth, third, popular education developed skills and fostered confidence in people whose lack of education made them uncertain of their abilities. Fourth, it established close links between education and other practices and goals not normally considered part of it—community organization, political struggle, and social transformation. Finally, popular education was a crucial factor in the Salvadoran war. It developed the political consciousness of the campesinos who became the insurgency's base, and it contributed to the outcome, which, while not a complete victory, was a substantial political and military success.

Poverty and War

First, both the war and the extreme poverty of the communities where it was fought imposed daunting hardships. Popular schools lacked the most basic supplies—books, notebooks, and pencils, not to mention buildings and desks. The teachers themselves were poorly educated—many had only a year or two of formal schooling—and they lacked experience; they had to improvise as they went along. The war constantly interrupted their work, not only when combat fell nearby, but when tasks of organization and defense took priority over classes.

But the setting of education in poor communities and in a war zone also created an opportunity. The will to teach and learn grew out of the commitment to struggle together for economic justice and dignity. The communities were locked in a vastly unequal combat, one that required using all available resources, especially human resources, to the maximum. Because most people had grown up without access to education, those resources had to be developed.

An Emancipatory Vision

Education was effective, second, because it was guided by a unique vision tailored to promote learning in circumstances of poverty and conflict, one that turned those deficiencies to advantage. That vision comprised four important elements:

- The claim that political content is an appropriate—even essential—part of education, and that political commitment can motivate people to get educated. Popular educators argue that any educational process is necessarily political.

- A pedagogy that encourages active participation and the development of critical consciousness. In this process of *concientización* (consciousness-raising), poor and oppressed people discuss and reflect on the conditions of their life and thereby analyze the nature of their oppression. The process of learning to read and write must help people to identify situations as oppressive and to take action against them. The use of concientización as a pedagogical tool is derived from the teaching methods of the Brazilian literacy pioneer Paulo Freire.
- The integration of schools with community life. Schools depend on the active support of their communities and should serve those communities. They should instill in learners not only the necessary skills, but the will to participate actively as well. Those who volunteer to teach are performing a social duty. Though they may lack academic training and skills, their political consciousness and dedication are more important. They identify with the learners, and the learners with them, because they come from similar backgrounds.
- The principle of universal access. Everyone is not only entitled to education, but capable of benefiting from it. Those who grew up without schooling can learn as adults. During the war, popular schools extended education widely in the zones of conflict, providing new schools where there had been none before, higher grade levels than official schools had offered before they were closed, and (though less systematically) adult education. Learning was an obligation to the whole community. Because they had the opportunity, everyone was expected to learn.

In this emancipatory vision, the goal of popular education is to create a new society. Its pedagogy is intended to mirror and foreshadow in its methods the cognitive liberation and cooperative spirit educators hoped would prevail in that new society. Learning itself is a mutual process. Those who taught also learned, and those who learned also taught, as they enthusiastically acknowledged.

The vision represented aspiration as much as reality. Education suffered many deficiencies. Teachers were often only a step ahead of their pupils, and many uneducated campesinos resisted taking the opportunity to learn that was offered them. But even if the practice fell short of the ideal, the ideal offered more than just empty abstractions; it provided meaningful objectives that teachers and learners strove to realize.

Learning and Empowerment

One element of the vision was indeed a reality. Education was closely integrated with the rest of life: the life of the individual learner and the life of the community as a whole. Popular education drew strength from these identifications, helping it to overcome the shortage of resources. On the one hand—and this is the third main point—learning empowered people. It provided integral development by cultivating practical skills, intellectual growth, and self-confidence. People learned in order to affirm themselves and declare their dignity; they also learned because they had to know how to read and count. Education served a technical function; but it also had larger social purposes.

Most of those who learned and taught had grown up as campesinos, held down not only by the exploitative agricultural system but also by the disdain in which urban Salvadorans held them. Lacking education, political power, and confidence in their capacity to act, they had had drummed into them a deep sense of inferiority that they had to overcome before they could envision fighting their oppression. As they learned, they discovered previously unsuspected abilities and found occasions to use them. Cognitive skills were important, but they were not the only thing. Literacy circles provided a platform for speaking out and convincing themselves that they were entitled to do so.

Education and Community Life

The fourth main point is that a close relation existed between education and the communities that promoted it. Education was not an isolated activity, but part of people's common life; it expressed their collective commitment and was undertaken as a community project. It was a central part of community organization, and played a major role in the political struggle they took up.

But it took work—in the community and in the classroom. Community leaders had to win the support of parents and other community members to provide labor and material resources to keep the schools running; they also had to overcome the resistance of some who thought that learning or sending their children to school was not important. Teachers had to work with limited skills and virtually no supplies or equipment. Learners had to overcome not only the habits of illiteracy but the sense of futility engendered by self-doubt.

Education and political engagement reinforced each other. Political leaders knew that they needed educated people and saw education as a recruiting ground; they therefore supported it and invested political resources in it. Participants in the educational process (we would say teachers and learners) contributed to political activity by integrating political lessons into their pedagogy.

In the integration of the school with the community and in the pursuit of diverse pedagogical goals in a single educational process, popular education differed from most formal systems, including the official Salvadoran educational system. Most schools define their goals narrowly and technically, on the bureaucratic assumption that by specializing and differentiating themselves from other institutions they achieve greater efficiency. As I will show, however, the very lack of differentiation was an important strength of popular education.

Popular education occurred on three levels: elementary education for children; literacy and basic education for adults; and paraprofessional training for popular teachers themselves and in other skills such as health work and running cooperatives. It went on in several social settings; the most important were the guerrilla army, refugee camps in Honduras, jails for political prisoners, and communities in the guerrilla-controlled zones. Differences in organization and physical conditions made education vary with the setting.

When community organizing was forced underground at the beginning of the war, government repression could not reach into the guerrilla army, refugee camps, or prisons (where political prisoners organized their cellblocks and won significant control over their daily life). These constituted protected spaces where education could continue. Refugees and prisoners, and sometimes even combatants, had an excess of free time; the desire to fill it made studying a welcome diversion. Prisoners and refugees could define studying as an act of defiance to oppressive authorities. In the refugee camps and civilian communities, unlike prisons and combat units, there was little turnover in membership, and people lived in families; they could plan education programs for the long term, and most adults wanted their children to get an education. Each site therefore offered distinct conditions, some that facilitated popular education and others that hindered it, despite the common elements of war, poverty, and political struggle.

Women were more active than men. Working as teachers allowed them to put their talents to public use, something they had rarely had any opportunity to do. Becoming active outside the home, however, sometimes led to conflicts with their spouses. Popular educators came into contact with well-educated people from outside their communities: in the guerrilla army, they worked with combatants from urban areas who had secondary or university education; in the refugee camps, foreign volunteers supervised the popular teachers; in the civilian communities in the war zones, politically sympathetic professional teachers working for nongovernmental organizations gave the popular schools technical assistance. Popular educators and professionals learned from each other; many of the outsiders said that they learned more than they taught. Yet campesinos often deferred to them and expected them to take the initiative, creating a contradiction: even among people working together to build a society that would eliminate social inequality, unequal social origins affected their collaboration.

The Political Impact

Finally, popular education became a crucial factor in military mobilization and affected the outcome of the war. It not only empowered people and gave them the confidence to act; it was an important part of the rural organizing that led up to the war. It also contributed to the morale and organization necessary to sustain for more than a decade a struggle against forces vastly superior in numbers and equipment. The insurgency did not win a victory; but it did achieve a stalemate and significant political concessions. Popular education brought military and political skills and belief in the prospect of a better future to poorly educated combatants and civilian supporters.

Campesino Life and Learning

The learners in Chebo's circle, as they themselves said, were campesinos. Though Apulo Amatitán is only half an hour's bus ride from San Salvador, the capital city, it is rural. Many people work in construction or factories, but they also farm and fish in nearby Lake Ilopango, and houses are grouped in the small clusters characteristic of rural areas. It is significant that they call themselves campesinos even though they live in the shadow of the city and work in the urban economy. In El Salvador, growing up in the countryside marks one. In this country whose economy still depends primarily on agriculture, probably a majority of the people identify as campesinos, and for them that term represents a culture as much as it refers to their rural surroundings or their source of livelihood.

But their life as poor cultivators underlies their culture. Their poverty is due to the extreme concentration of land ownership in the hands of a tiny oligarchy and the despotic political methods by which that oligarchy maintains its wealth. In societies dependent for their wealth on the labor-intensive cultivation of export crops, landowners typically achieve dictatorial rule to assure their control of the labor force and maintain that control either directly or by means of a loyal military (Moore 1966; Rueschemeyer, Stephens, and Stephens 1992). El Salvador's history illustrates this pattern in extreme form.

With the highest population density of any country in the Western Hemisphere, El Salvador is land-poor; but land scarcity generally depends less on its absolute amount than on its distribution. In 1961, according to the best available estimates, 28.0 percent of the economically active population in agriculture was landless (that is, did not farm any land, either their own or owned by someone else). In 1970, among rural families with access to land as owners or tenants, the 33 percent with less than .7 hectare (one hectare = 2.5 acres) farmed 1.3 percent of the total farmland; at the same time, only 3 percent of all farms were larger than 35 hectares, but that 3 percent occupied 67 percent of the farmland (Seligson 1995:62–63; computation based on Weeks 1985:112). Many families had enough land to produce some or all of their food, but no surplus, so to meet their other needs they migrated to work as day laborers in the three-month-long coffee harvest. Landlords profited from this dualism, as the division between subsistence farming and large-scale production for export is called, because they could hire field hands who could grow some of their own food, and therefore could work for far less than a full-time living wage.

The system was maintained by an extensive coercive apparatus, but one that changed its character over time. During the depression of the 1930s, the bottom fell out of the world market for coffee, which was virtually the sole source of El Salvador's export earnings. Reductions in wages imposed by coffee growers provoked a major uprising in 1932, called by the Communist Party under its leader Farabundo Martí. The uprising, concentrated in the western coffee-growing region of the country, was quickly suppressed, but in reprisal the army went on a rampage through the region, rounded up the Indian population in the main squares of the towns, and shot them down. At least ten thousand people, and possibly more than thirty thousand, were murdered in what is known as *la matanza* (the massacre; Anderson 1971; Pérez Brignoli 1995).

For more than fifty years thereafter, a series of military governments ruled El Salvador, enforcing the dominance of the landed oligarchy by deploying military and paramilitary forces in the countryside. They maintained the outward forms of democracy by holding regular elections, but assured their victory by massive fraud. Though military reformers emerged periodically, hardliners always reasserted themselves (Montgomery 1982; Walter and Williams 1993). Nor did incipient industrialization after World War II affect the political balance; agricultural export earnings continued to be the major source of the country's wealth and the oligarchy's power.

Coffee remained the principal crop, but beginning in the 1960s the world economic boom raised demand for new exports—cotton, sugar, and beef. Production of the first two expanded in the 1960s, and cattle ranching likewise increased in the 1970s. While the agricultural economy boomed, however, the life of the campesino, never prosperous, only got worse. Campesinos who had formerly rented land for cash or in exchange for labor services saw owners reappropriate it to devote to production for export. Vast extensions on the fertile coastal plain were planted in cotton or allowed to revert to range land.

The campesinos were pushed off. Between 1961 and 1971, the landless increased from an estimated 28.0 percent to 38.1 percent of the economically active population in agriculture, and the landless and land-poor (those farming less land than the minimum necessary for subsistence) totaled 60.1 percent in 1971. (Though there are no good data, the proportion must have continued to increase through the 1970s with the expansion of cattle ranching.) As the production of agroexports soared, production of food (that is, corn, beans, and other crops for domestic consumption) actually fell, and in the early 1970s an estimated 74.5 percent of children were malnourished (Brockett 1988:76–84; Seligson 1995:62–63; Williams 1986).

El Salvador's neighbor Honduras had a much lower population density and relatively abundant land. Many Salvadorans emigrated to Honduras to escape starvation. By 1969 three hundred thousand of them were squatting on infertile state-owned land along the Salvadoran border and scratching out a meager living. The 1969 war—though presented in First World media as the Soccer War, supposedly caused by sports rivalry between the two countries—was largely due to this quiet invasion, and when it was over, the Salvadorans were expelled to return to the poverty they had fled their homeland to escape (Durham 1979).

Salvadoran campesinos are not only poor economically; they are poorly educated. No government has seriously tried to provide education for them. The illiteracy rate among the rural population in 1975 was reported to be 48.9 percent for men and 57.2 percent for women; in 1978 62.1 percent of those who earned their living in agriculture were reported to be illiterate. In 1970, 60 percent of the rural population aged fourteen and over had never attended school

(Moncada-Davidson 1990:283; Pérez Miguel 1994:641; *Statistical Abstract* 1987:148). The longstanding neglect of basic education in rural areas reflected the subservience of Salvadoran governments to the landowning class whose prosperity depended on having a rural population so poor that they would continue to provide cheap farm labor. Getting educated would open up other opportunities for them.

Many rural communities have no schools, or did not have them when today's adults were growing up, because they are too small and spread out. Rural schools, where they existed, commonly offered only two grades. Even if there was a school nearby, children could not always attend. School was free, but many families could not afford to keep children clothed and buy them school supplies. More important, they often depended on the children's labor—their help in the fields could make a real difference, especially if they joined their parents working for cash in the coffee harvest. In the words of a character in *One Day of Life*, Manlio Argueta's gripping novel of rural life and repression in prewar El Salvador, "Already when [my brothers and sisters] were seven years old, they were going to pick coffee, cotton, and cacao. That's the decisive age: you either go to school or to work" (1983:132).

Those who attended found that the rural school system treated them with disdain. Rural teachers rarely came from or lived in the communities where they taught. Teacher absenteeism was high—many teachers went home for the weekend, traveling on Mondays and Fridays. The curriculum, imposed by a centralized education bureaucracy, was—and still is—remote from the lives of the pupils (Dewees et al. 1995; Pérez Miguel 1994).

In 1968 El Salvador undertook a major educational reform. Walter Béneke, the minister of education, had been ambassador to Japan, and was so impressed with Japanese education that he was determined to reproduce it in El Salvador. The planners of the reform acknowledged the defects of the traditional system and showed some awareness of new proposals being discussed elsewhere in Latin America, including experiments in popular education, to give students a "clear and critical consciousness" and to use education to promote economic development (Escamilla 1981:128).

Nevertheless, the reform did little to make basic education more widely available. Instead it concentrated on urban areas, the secondary level, and high-technology fixes: educational television and diversification of the high school curriculum. In 1977 the ministry announced a program to combat illiteracy, but it was merely symbolic: it reached only 1.5 percent of its goal in 1978 and 2.5 percent in 1979 (Clippinger 1976:76; Mayo, Hornik, and McAnany 1976; Nóchez and Pérez Miguel 1995:510; Pérez Miguel 1994). The major teacher training institute in the country, the Alberto Masferrer Normal City, was closed when the war broke out in 1980, its teachers accused of fomenting subversion. Its campus (unlike most higher education institutions in El Salvador, it had student dormitories) was taken over as an army barracks.

Campesinos' lack of schooling not only prevents them from acquiring skills and seeking opportunities; it contributes to widely held stereotypes that dismiss them as inferior.[2] People of rural origins identify as campesinos: the men and women in Chebo's class, discussing the word campesino, all unhesitatingly said "we" even though they lived close to the city. Being a campesino offers a cultural identity that has both positive and negative connotations. Working the land and being self-sufficient give many of them a quiet dignity.

They know that many Salvadorans despise them, however. The oligarchy maintained its grip in part through a culture that presumed its natural superiority and challenged the competence of the uneducated to exercise democratic responsibility. These beliefs were widely accepted by the population at large, giving the oligarchy what Antonio Gramsci calls ideological hegemony. In 1929 Alberto Masferrer, a leading intellectual and early advocate of land reform, sardonically characterized the attitude of the Salvadoran elite, "Actually, there is no misery in El Salvador: The people go barefoot because they enjoy going without shoes, caressed by the fresh air; the laundry woman who earns four colones a week can save one-fourth of her earnings; and the child who comes to school without breakfast is convinced of the virtue of fasting" (quoted in Montgomery 1982:47). As recently as 1995 a current affairs periodical from the Central American University in San Salvador referred to the common bias that "axiomatically define[s] campesinos as people incapable of intelligently deciding what is best for their interests" (*Proceso* 1995). Campesinos are as aware of this bias as intellectuals are. Herminio, a campesino who fled with his family to Honduras in 1980 to escape the army's massacres, explained the repression: "They always hated us as campesinos."

Rural culture itself did not value education highly. Children who were going to follow in their parents' footsteps and remain on the land could expect little payoff from schooling. Chebo's students, integrated into the urban economy, knew that learning could pay off. All of them probably sent their children to school. But for many who were further outside the mainstream, it was still easy to dismiss the importance of education.

Even so, campesinos internalized the dominant culture's disdain for them and attributed their inferiority to their lack of education. Being illiterate was a source of embarrassment and self-blame. Hardly unique to Salvadoran campesinos—in the English language, "social judgment is . . . powerfully built into the term *illiterate*. . . . The word also carried the connotation of 'unpolished', 'ignorant', or 'inferior'" (Bailey and McArthur 1992:498)—this sense of inferiority made them feel that to be ignorant is to be dumb, and that their deprivation was in some incomprehensible way their own fault.

Campesinos were poor, uneducated, economically deprived, and politically repressed; they were victims of prejudice and their own self-deprecation. A knowledgeable and sympathetic observer, the Jesuit priest and social psychologist Ignacio Martín Baró,[3] found that these conditions left them passive and fatalistic, too intimidated to imagine attempting to improve their lot (1973:486–488).

Peasant Mobilization

A new political consciousness arose in many Salvadoran campesinos during the 1970s. It led many of them, together with others from the towns and cities, to build a political movement that went on to wage a guerrilla war in the 1980s. They fought the Salvadoran government to a standoff for more than a decade despite massive military assistance from the United States. Popular education contributed to the rapid and dramatic change in their consciousness that made that struggle possible. The basic cause of the war was poverty and inequality, aggravated by economic changes in the 1960s that made starvation a real threat for many. But deteriorating economic conditions would not have led to war if campesinos had not first overcome the fatalism and passivity instilled by poverty and repression, become convinced that they were entitled to a better life, and organized to assert their rights. This new consciousness gave them the capacity to respond. Popular education was both a cause and a manifestation of the dramatic change.

The twentieth century has been a century of peasant wars (Wolf 1969; Paige 1975; Skocpol 1982; Wickham-Crowley 1992). The term "peasant war"[4] usually connotes not only a particular social base but also certain patterns of recruitment and tactics. Combatants are largely rural cultivators who are poorly educated and exploited—that is, consigned to poverty by coercive or market mechanisms (or both) that prevent them from enjoying any significant surplus from their production (Wolf 1966:9–10). They are not conscripts; rather, they are recruited through solidary communities. They espouse—or at least their leaders espouse—an egalitarian ideology that promises triumph over exploitation. In other words, a peasant war is fought not just *by* peasants (by social origins, after all, the tsar's army was a peasant army; so is the Salvadoran government army) but in defense of their interests. And they fight a guerrilla war, emphasizing small, mobile units, lightning actions rather than engagements between concentrated troops, and close contact with a civilian community that keeps them supplied.

The scholarly debate on the conditions for peasant mobilization turns on three main questions: what structures of rural propertyholding and employment make peasants most likely to revolt; what historical conditions trigger a rebellion; and what ideological and strategic resources are available to peasants. I will briefly examine the second and third questions. What has been called the "moral economy" view argues that the conditions of poverty and exploitation in which peasants live make them very conservative, averse to risk, and therefore resistant to change; and that if they do revolt, they do so to recover what they regard as unjustly usurped prerogatives. In this view, only a severe disruption endangering their very survival, coming from outside and usually associated with the encroachment of capitalism in the countryside, can explain peasant revolt. This same viewpoint holds that despite these limitations, once they reach the point of revolt peasants require no special organizational resources because the capacity to revolt is latent in their normal behavior—their "everyday forms of resistance" (Scott 1976, 1985).

The "rational peasant" approach presents peasant revolt, like peasant behavior in general, as an act of individual self-interest. Peasants revolt when a rational calculation of their expected utilities promises an advantage, or when guerrilla movements offer them incentives such as territorial defense, land, medical care, and education. In this view, peasants do not have the intellectual or material resources to carry on a guerrilla war on their own, so they will only revolt if a political movement from outside identifies a group of peasants as a potential social base, organizes them, and offers suitable incentives (Goodwin and Skocpol 1989:492–494; Popkin 1979; Wickham-Crowley 1987:482–485).

Neither of these arguments adequately explains the war in El Salvador. Though mutually contradictory on most points, both ignore the emergence of a new belief system that was essential in mobilizing peasants for war. Consistent with the moral economy view, the way of life of Salvadoran peasants was under assault with the economic changes of the 1960s and 1970s. But peasants were not merely reactive; they acted when a new understanding of injustice, rooted in liberation theology, gave their grievances legitimacy and offered them a revolutionary alternative.

The rational peasant view correctly recognizes that mobilization and rebellion are not latent in everyday behavior, but require agitation, recruitment, and organization. But it does not recognize the importance of the beliefs and community commitments of those who are mobilized. This view construes the term "rationality" too narrowly. Individual calculation of self-interest can never explain willingness to risk death. The rational peasant view holds that peasants are only mobilized by a revolutionary movement brought to them from outside—almost as pawns. In fact, although the insurgent movement came to the Salvadoran countryside from outside, the peasants who joined it acted as protagonists and actively collaborated in building it. Their participation depended crucially on their membership in solidary communities. And they had to overcome a pervasive fatalism to believe that participation would not be futile. The most important studies of the insurgency of the 1970s and 1980s in El Salvador (and elsewhere in Central America) are unanimous in emphasizing the ideological transformation that underlay it and the active role of peasants in building and shaping the movement (see Berryman 1984; Brockett 1988; Cabarrús 1983; Montgomery 1983; Pearce 1986; Vilas 1995).

Salvadoran peasants did not respond homogeneously. Agrarian changes were felt differently in different regions of the country, and people embraced the new ideology most strongly in those parishes where church activists organized Christian base communities. The response even differed strikingly between neighboring communities (Cabarrús 1983; Kincaid 1987). But the reaction was broad enough to fuel an insurgency, overwhelmingly campesino-based, that waged twelve years of war and fought the government to a standoff.

To be sure, the war exacted its heaviest toll on the campesino population. Many were killed; others were bombed out of their home villages and fled the country or swelled the refugee settlements and shantytowns of the larger towns and cities. Most of this book is about those who were directly under the gun, but no one was exempt. Even in areas far from combat, campesinos saw their sons literally abducted to serve in the army, while the sons of the wealthy were left free, despite a theoretical obligation of universal male military service. Everywhere, those who were suspected of guerrilla sympathies or were active in civic and community organizations could be arrested and tortured or simply "disappear" at the hands of death squads. Even though the war aggravated their already impoverished living conditions, in popular education the campesinos had learned that they were capable of confronting these injustices.

Literacy and Political Struggle

Illiteracy and the struggle to overcome it are an important cultural and political theme in the literature and life of poor people throughout Latin America. Many believe that "the rich have always wanted us poor people not to learn many things, so as to keep us ignorant" (as Julio Portillo, former secretary general of the Salvadoran teachers' union, put it). Many people assume the reason others are more powerful is that they are more educated and skilled.

One way the wealthy take advantage of the poor is through their ability to manipulate the legal system and the bureaucracy. Many poor Salvadorans felt that ignorance put them at the mercy of others who were out to get them. Again from Argueta's *One Day of Life*, "My mama said it was bad to live in ignorance because that way it was easier for them to cheat you; you'd be more at the mercy of intelligent people" (1983:141). Organizers often urged campesinos to learn to read "so they [an undefined 'they'] can't cheat you."

For those who manage it, on the other hand, getting educated is a personal triumph. It also breaks down the social barrier separating them from their presumed superiors. Many accounts of the mobilization of poor people elsewhere in Latin America point to learning to read as a significant event, often a turning point in their biographies (Levine 1992:3; Wasserstrom 1985).

Education has become an important tool of Latin American movements for social and political change. To acquire knowledge is to acquire power, or at least it is a necessary first step. Popular education fosters specific skills, personal growth, and critical consciousness among the poor and oppressed. Learning empowers poor people because they prove they can do something they were always told was beyond them. Reform-oriented political movements have promoted popular education in the cities and the countryside (Fink and Arnove 1991; La Belle 1986:169–250; Torres 1989; van Dam, Martinic, and Peter 1991). In the more developed countries of the continent, popular education does not focus on literacy, because the majority of the population, even the poor, have access to elementary schooling. In a country such as El Salvador, however, the fundamental dividing line is between those who have some education and those who have none at all. Popular education therefore necessarily focuses on literacy and basic education.

Many Latin American revolutionary movements have promoted education during their struggle to seize power; where they succeeded, they have continued to promote it to transform society. After the Mexican revolution the government expanded rural schools and staffed them with militant teachers eager to spread revolutionary ideology and challenge the reactionary influence of the church. When Carlos Fonseca, cofounder of the Nicaraguan Sandinista National Liberation Front, encountered some compañeros giving military training to Nicaraguan campesino combatants, he told them: "And also teach them to read." Shortly after the triumph of their revolutions, the new governments of Cuba and Nicaragua organized nationwide literacy campaigns (Arnove 1986; Barndt 1991:33; Carnoy and Samoff 1990; Fagen 1969; Hamilton 1982:136–137; Hellman 1994:51; Miller 1985).

The purpose of revolution is to liberate people, and learning is part of that process. For a revolutionary struggle to be successful, moreover, people of limited resources must master a variety of skills to carry out military, political, and organizational tasks. So militants have made education part of their revolutionary struggle both to realize the universal emancipation to which they aspire and to meet practical needs.

In El Salvador too the political-military organizations that fought the war practiced popular education. As I have emphasized, it served multiple purposes. Its manifest purpose was to teach people skills, first of all reading and writing; but it was also pursued for the broader goals of personal growth and political organizing.

Where the lack of education consigns people to inferiority, education almost necessarily serves to give them a sense of their own worth and abilities. This was especially important in El Salvador because so many people internalized the blame for their lack of education. Learning took them across a fundamental cognitive and social divide, giving them confidence and making it possible for them to attempt to transform their world.

Finally, popular education was an organizing tool. Creating literacy circles—and, later, schools for children in areas where the government closed official schools because of the war, or where they had never existed—was an important act of community organizing. The classes themselves became a training ground where people learned new skills and, even more, where those who conducted the classes proved their capacities, often moving on to other, more responsible positions. Popular education, therefore, meant much more than merely teaching cognitive skills. It meant developing all the resources necessary to fight.

Experiments in Learning

One of the first people in Latin America to argue that literacy training could be a powerful political weapon, and to provide a teaching methodology designed for poor people, was the Brazilian educator Paulo Freire. Freire developed a new method of literacy education in northeastern Brazil, the poorest region of his country, in the 1950s. He proposed what he called (in the title of his best-known book) the *Pedagogy of the Oppressed* (1970), a pedagogy for poor people that made learning part of the process of liberation.

Freire claimed that his method would stimulate poor and uneducated adults to learn by engaging them politically. The approach was widely adopted across Latin America in the 1960s and 1970s, and became influential in adult literacy education there and elsewhere in the Third World. It was never adopted wholesale; it was applied partially and modified in practice by people who learned it informally or through brief formal exposure. Most of the poorly educated volunteers who conducted literacy circles in communities never saw a written training manual, nor did they know the name of the man widely identified as the founder of popular education.

Freire's method is designed to accommodate the needs of people who lack both education and the confidence to express their own views. He criticized traditional education, which he called "banking" education because it assumed that teachers could "deposit" knowledge in students. Instead, he called for "problemposing" education. Adults would learn successfully, he argued, only if they analyzed their poverty and found ways to overcome it as they learned (1970:58–74).

Throughout the Spanish-speaking world, children, and illiterate adults, learn to read by forming syllabic families. They learn the five vowels, and some cartillas start with a long word that contains all five vowels (such as *educación*). Then they combine these vowels with a consonant: The "family of m" is "ma, me, mi, mo, mu." In the early months of first grade, children sit in class reciting "ma, me, mi, mo, mu" in chorus.

Because Spanish (like Paulo Freire's native Portuguese) is phonetic and relatively free of double consonants, a large part of the vocabulary can be created by combining these two-letter syllables. They are the building blocks for words, and learners set about finding words that can be made out of the syllables they have learned. From the family of m, the new reader can produce *mamá*, Meme (a man's nickname), and even sensible complete sentences like *Mi mamá me mima* ("My mother pampers me"). They can already feel the pleasure of reading even before learning the next consonant.[5] Old-fashioned first readers were called syllable books (*silabarios*) and the first grader went through the syllable book to master all the consonants and learn how to combine syllables into words.

But Freire argued that syllabic babbling is less inspiring for adults than for children, and that the learning process has to be motivated by something more real to them. Popular literacy teaching therefore uses material derived from the

real lives of poor people. A cartilla presents a small set of words chosen to include all the letters of the alphabet and the most common consonant combinations (in Spanish, this can be done with about seventeen words), but which also
reflect important aspects of campesino life: work, poverty, the family, and the
possibility of cooperation as part of a community.

As in the traditional reader, each lesson is organized around a single word.
The word is illustrated on a page of a cartilla. Before studying the word in its
written form, learners "reflect" on the concept it names by examining the picture and discussing its significance for their lives. Through reflection they come
to a clearer understanding of the causes of their poverty and deprivation, and
become aware that these are not facts of nature or due to the will of God. The
words are called "generative words" because they generate the syllabic families
and because they generate reflection, which is meant to instill the desire to learn
the word in its written form by arousing interest in the concept it embodies.

Reflection proceeds by dialogue. Learners participate actively rather than
absorbing passively as in the usual classroom. "In educating adults, to avoid a
rote, mechanical process one must make it possible for them to achieve critical
consciousness so that they can teach themselves to read and write" (Freire
1973:56). The process of critical reflection, in other words, is a process of emancipation. People come to exercise their intellectual potential—and the conviction that everyone has that potential is basic to popular education—and as they
do, they become aware of the social forces that constrain them and prevent them
from being free. Education is not just the acquisition of skills; it is the development of the whole person, through which people come to exercise their capacity for independent and critical thinking.

Yet adult learners often lack confidence in their abilities and are reticent
to speak out. A lifetime of oppression has ground into so many of them the belief that they are unworthy to hold and express opinions. They have been told
that their ignorance is their own fault and that they are not capable of learning.
They must overcome those internalized prejudices, recognize that they have a
right to a sense of dignity and a decent standard of living, and affirm their legitimacy to be heard. Taking part also motivates them to master reading and writing. A broad understanding of their social world is thus both an end in itself
and a means to the learning of skills.

Beyond that, Freire argued, learning should be an instrument for raising
consciousness—a process he called *conscientização* or (in Spanish) *concientización*. Through reflection and dialogue about generative themes, learners bring
to the foreground the knowledge they already possess to analyze the nature of
their oppression. Concientización does not occur through an educator's presenting a fully formed ideology. Instead, learners must actively examine their own
life situation. Their consciousness must emerge from their own experience and
understanding. Educators and learners develop consciousness mutually; they are
"equally knowing subjects." The educator learns from the learners and is "constantly readjusting his knowledge" (Freire 1985:51, 55). A teacher who offered

a prepackaged ideology and expected learners to absorb it passively would only reproduce the authoritarian "banking" pedagogy (Freire 1970:77–81; 1985:49–50). Most literacy teachers in Freire's pioneering Brazilian programs were politically mobilized university students (Beisiegel 1974:170–173), and Freire warned against their trading on their superior education and status to impose their views on new learners.

Concientización means more than just the development of cognitive awareness; it also means the recognition of an ethical obligation. (The term *conciencia*, which can be translated as "consciousness," also has the connotations of conscience and commitment.) For Freire the ultimate goal of concientización is to inspire people to strive to change their world. He conceived of education not as merely the mastery of a repertory of skills, but as an instrument for social change, a means to achieve personal liberation and to create a new society. The critical consciousness education cultivates should enable learners to take action to solve the problems they identify through reflection. The oppressed identify a contradiction between themselves and their oppressors that requires that "the concrete situation which begets oppression must be transformed." Reflection is "not a call to armchair revolution. On the contrary, reflection—true reflection—leads to action" (1970:35, 52).

Revolution is therefore a necessary outcome of concientización; and revolution is only genuine when it arises from the consciousness of the oppressed themselves: "While no one liberates himself by his own efforts alone, neither is he liberated by others." "It is absolutely essential that the oppressed participate in the revolutionary process with an increasingly critical awareness of their role" (Freire 1970:53, 121).

Freire's pedagogy has inspired literacy programs throughout Latin America—and elsewhere in the Third World—since the 1960s. He himself worked outside of Brazil for more than fifteen years. He went into exile after being jailed briefly by the military government that unseated President João Goulart and took power in the 1964 coup. In Chile until 1969, he worked for the government of Christian Democratic president Eduardo Frei organizing literacy education. In 1970 he went to the World Council of Churches; based in Geneva for ten years, he advised literacy programs in some of the newly independent Portuguese-speaking countries of Africa after 1975 (Gadotti 1994:35–47).

In Latin America his ideas and methods were spread mainly by the church, which was undergoing dramatic changes in the 1960s and 1970s, inspired by the Second Vatican Council and liberation theology. Progressive church workers who sought to involve the poor majority of believers in the institutional church discovered that many of them did not know how to read, and few were accustomed to thinking critically. Freire's pedagogy, they hoped, would lead people to learn and participate more actively.[6]

The method provides several pedagogical techniques designed to encourage participation, minimize any association with traditional schooling, and bridge the hierarchical gap between teacher and learner. Not only is the discussion of practical experience the basis of each lesson. Groups of learners are called "culture circles" (or more commonly in El Salvador, "literacy circles") rather than "classes." They play games, designed both to serve specific learning objectives and to break the monotony for adults not used to sitting still. Frequently the entire group sits in a circle, to minimize social distance, and the teacher is supposed to be treated not as an authority but as a member of the group. Many have verified in their own experience the principle that everyone is a teacher and a learner—everyone learns from everyone else. People who come to popular education with much higher levels of education than the new learners with whom they work say that they learn far more than they teach. In popular education, people learn together.

In his writings, Freire prescribed elaborate preparations for a literacy campaign, with linguistic research to tailor the choice of generative words to a particular community and careful selection of images, which he called the codifications of generative words, that would stimulate reflection and dialogue (1973:51; 1985:91–93). In fact the church workers who adopted Freire's program and spread it through Latin America usually took shortcuts. They did not learn by studying Freire's books, which present the methods in all their complexity. Instead they learned through practice at church-sponsored training centers, linked in an international network, which spread Freire's pedagogy even before his writings became available. From these centers, church workers went home to reproduce what they had learned. Armed at best with mimeographed handouts to remind them of the basic steps, they applied the methods creatively in response to local conditions rather than reproducing them mechanically. The same techniques have been discovered independently and adopted gradually and experimentally in many different places.

It was through the church that popular education was brought to El Salvador. From newly created Christian base communities grew a movement that brought to thousands of poor Salvadorans a new consciousness during the 1970s and inspired them to revolt beginning in 1980. They made education part of their struggle, and learned together during the war. If many of the pioneers of popular education in El Salvador were consciously applying the Freirean model, however, most popular teachers were unaware of it. They approached their task pragmatically, with little knowledge of any theoretical base. They improvised and learned from experience before they had any formal knowledge of popular education. When some popular educators were eventually trained in Freire's methods, they found ratification of what they had discovered independently and guidance to improve their practice.

Chebo followed some of Freire's prescriptions without knowing their origins. He did not use the word concientización, but he confirmed that it heightened the motivation to learn, because he had first taught literacy without it. When he was trained by the Ministry of Education, he was told just to teach people to read and write. The cartilla included words that had little meaning for the people in his class, such as *pala* (shovel). "We don't use the shovel. When we go to the field, we take a hoe, or a machete. No one cares about getting a shovel. The hoe, yes; it helps you produce, and when you come back from the field you've made ten pesos."

Chebo was sure that people learn better if they do not just read but reflect on what they are reading. "There's more participation; they have more time to think and give their opinions. The purpose is not just to teach them to read and write, but to get rid of their fear that what they have to say isn't worth anything. They learn to reflect, to think about what to do or why things happen. Before, it was just getting them to learn the word."

Salvadoran practice, then, diverged from the Freirean model in part because popular educators were ignorant of it. But more importantly, poverty and war both demanded creative responses. As people struggled valiantly to cope with material shortages, their methods derived from improvisation as much as from the lessons of theory. Education flourished because it was practiced not as an isolated activity, but as part of the communities' larger political project.[7]

Popular education's adaptations to poverty and to the war that racked the country from 1980 to 1992, and its place as part of the political struggle of the communities that practiced it, made the Salvadoran experience of popular education unlike any other. Contrary to Freire's prescription, popular education was less a cause than an effect of politicization. As I have mentioned, the Salvadoran vision of popular education called for integration both between learners' cognitive development and political consciousness and between education and its community setting. Freire strongly emphasized the first pairing; it is the heart of his pedagogical scheme. But he paid scant attention to the relation of education to the community and the effect of social conditions on the organization and conduct of education. In chapter 8 I consider in more detail the relation between the Freirean model and Salvadoran practice, and argue that the former must be amended to take account of the effects of the community setting. For reasons I will make clear, this is in my view the most important lesson of the Salvadoran experience for popular education elsewhere.

In this study I examine classroom practices: methods for teaching children and adults, the linking of basic skills training and political education, and the training of inexperienced and poorly educated people to teach. I also examine the relation of education to community organization: the close connection between education, community, and political action; the cultivation of practical skills that served the war effort; and the mobilization of community support.

Between 1988 and 1993, I made eight field trips to El Salvador, each lasting about a month. (Not all of them were devoted primarily to research on popular education.) I observed classes for adults and children, participated in teacher training sessions and planning meetings, and experienced the life of the communities where popular education was practiced.

I conducted 130 interviews with people at all levels of popular education: newly literate adults, popular teachers, professional teacher trainers, and political cadres; former political prisoners; refugees and returnees; civilians and members of the guerrilla army.[8] The interviews, averaging forty-five minutes to an hour in length, were taped and transcribed. Each informant provided basic information on background, educational history, and experience as a teacher, learner, or organizer of education. The interviews were open-ended and followed no fixed protocol, because each informant's experience depended on the setting in which it had taken place. For the most part, then, I allowed the informant to determine the specific topics covered.

I came to study popular education through my activism in the El Salvador solidarity movement, and it was as an activist that I was able to enter the zones of conflict and meet informants who represented all of the important sites of popular education. Since I met them through political contacts, they were not a random sample. The political basis of my access to them undoubtedly affected our interaction, an issue I discuss in chapter 9.

This book discusses the development of popular education in the decade that led up to the war and then during the war itself. In chapter 2 I describe the Christian base communities where popular education began in the 1970s. With the inspiration of the Second Vatican Council, church workers moved into poor communities, especially in rural areas, and encouraged peasant and community organizing. When new organizations promoting demands for just and equitable treatment were repressed, many activists gradually opted for armed struggle and brought the lessons of popular education with them.

The next two chapters cover popular education at the beginning of the war, under rather special circumstances. When repression drove organizing underground, popular education could continue only in what I call protected spaces. Political prisons, refugee camps, and the guerrilla army constantly felt the pressure of the war, but the Salvadoran government could not penetrate them to persecute education directly. Chapter 3 is about the education of guerrilla combatants, most of them young campesinos with little or no previous schooling. I show that learning to read, getting trained in combat skills, and developing their consciousness contributed strongly to their combat effectiveness. Chapter 4 discusses education among political prisoners and refugees. Both were kept confined against their will, and idle time weighed heavily. Prisoners and refugees organized instruction and the majority of those who were illiterate on arrival succeeded at learning.

The next three chapters describe popular education in rural communities in the war zones. Chapter 5 shows that community schools were part of a broader organizing process and that the effectiveness of education was due largely to a reciprocal relation between community support and the orientation of education to meet community needs. Pedagogy in the teaching of children and adults is discussed in chapter 6. Classroom practices drew on both popular education methodology and teachers' intuitions. Teachers had to overcome the limitations of their educational background. They volunteered to teach out of political commitment and they were rewarded with social recognition. This reward structure had disadvantages, but it was suited to mobilizing limited community resources. Chapter 7 is about the training of teachers to convey, in the classroom, material they had never formally studied. It also shows that despite social distance and habits of deference toward the well-educated people who trained them, both groups struggled to achieve equality.

I present a theoretical summation of the entire book in chapter 8. I discuss in more detail the image of their work held by popular educators and others in the communities where it was practiced. I reexamine the theories derived from experiences of popular education elsewhere. The Salvadoran experience suggests that those theories must be modified to take into account the central importance of the community context. Finally I return to the impact and show that popular education of combatants and civilians was a decisive factor in the relatively successful outcome of the war.

In chapter 9 I offer a personal epilogue relating the importance to me of my encounter with popular education. I discuss my field experience, especially the political and methodological issues of access to the zones of conflict and interaction with informants there. I also discuss the effect of my study on my work as a college teacher. Popular education has influenced my teaching. Teaching poor and working-class students in an urban public university and teaching poor campesinos to read are as different as the different social contexts suggest they must be, but what I saw there has its application here.

Though popular education was remarkably successful, it was nevertheless limited. It often fell short of the ideal held by practitioners outlined earlier in this chapter. The effort to educate was hampered by factors beyond their control—poverty, war, and the poor education of most participants. But some problems were of their own making. Not everyone who came into contact with popular education was a model community member, combatant, or pupil. Despite the aspiration to universality, not everyone learned. Despite the ideal of equal treatment, men and women had different roles, and men were freer to carry out organizational tasks. Peasants deferred to people from urban and high-status backgrounds. Some local political leaders abused their authority and made peremptory demands on community members. Not everyone participated with heart and soul, and some did not participate at all.

The effectiveness of popular education must be gauged not only by its own ideals, however, but in comparison to the availability of education previously and in relation to the resources available. By both standards, success at educating, mobilizing communities, and putting into practice an ideal of equality was significant. Some people, as volunteers, taught grades higher than they had ever attended. Others who had had no opportunity as children or had not taken advantage of it learned as adults. Many were mobilized to support schools with resources and labor. Though relations were never completely equal, people interacted across traditional social barriers and testified warmly about how valuable they found the experience. Even if popular education did not attain its own highest ideals, it was nevertheless effective.

People practiced popular education despite their material poverty and their lack of schooling and experience. Poverty, oppression, and the war not only made popular education necessary but strongly affected the form it took. Despite those limits, however, learning became a major part of the Salvadoran struggle. The experience shows that it is possible to overcome material and cultural deficiencies—and even to turn them to advantage—by educating in a way that is attentive both to political oppression and to the community context in which people struggle to learn.

CHAPTER 2

The Christian Origins of Revolt

———

$\mathcal{D}$uring the 1970s a political movement arose in the Salvadoran countryside that led to the decade-long revolt of the 1980s. Innovative churchpeople inspired by liberation theology formed Christian base communities in rural parishes, and from these a new political consciousness emerged. Though the new teaching and practice were not initially promoted with a social revolution in mind, they encouraged believers to question the established order and to struggle for social change. The campesino population was receptive to new ideas because the agrarian transformations of the 1960s had produced a subsistence crisis for many. Campesinos organized, peacefully at first, to demand their rights, and when their claims were rebuffed they fought a guerrilla war. Their movement turned into a revolt in large part because repression drove it underground.

In this chapter I show that the new church doctrine, brought from abroad, found its greatest influence in El Salvador among the rural poor, and that its tenets implied that education and organizing are inseparable and essential. I analyze the significance of education as an organizing practice, first in the parishes and then in peasant organizations formed to redress economic grievances. Finally I discuss the politicization of the movement and its turn to armed struggle.

Popular education permeated all these activities and formed the consciousness that motivated campesino organizing, political action, and finally rebellion. Its purpose was not just learning to read. Acquiring the skills of the classroom was integral to becoming politically conscious actors, because learning both gave people confidence in themselves and enabled them to perform political tasks.

The Rise of the People's Church

The Latin American church had long been closely tied to the oligarchy and the most conservative sectors of society. In the 1960s some churchpeople challenged that link. When the Second Vatican Council (1962–1965) called for the modernization of the church, clergy and members of religious orders in Latin America interpreted its call as demanding identification with the cause of the poor and a profound change in the church's social teaching and practices.

The Latin American bishops met at Medellín, Colombia, in 1968 to consider how to apply Vatican II in their region. In their concluding statement they endorsed the main tenets of liberation theology, already anticipated in the work of some Latin American theologians during the preceding decade. Liberation theology teaches that God acts in history, that all human beings share a dignity that deserves to be honored in the present life, and that people must act to put God's will into practice. The bishops acknowledged the cry of the poor for liberation; they commended "poverty as a commitment," a voluntary identification with the poor, to priests and members of religious orders; and they called for "joint pastoral practice" (*pastoral de conjunto*), a shorthand expression for greater involvement of lay people in church affairs. The document's chapter on education, which called for a "liberating" education, reflected the influence of Paulo Freire (Consejo Episcopal Latinoamericano 1979:46–49, 103–106).

The bishops' pronouncements at Medellín inspired new ways of doing church work. Clergy and lay activists tried to make the institutional church more democratic. The liturgy was conducted in Spanish rather than Latin; it was set to music inspired by popular genres; lay people took a more visible role in conducting it and in carrying out the church's mission. The Vatican Council had redefined the church as a collegial rather than a hierarchical institution, and taught that lay people should not just receive the church's teaching and sacraments passively but should become active agents.

Many priests, nuns, and seminarians answered the call to identify with the poor and join them in the struggle for social justice. In El Salvador, Father José Inocencio (Chencho) Alas was one of the first. Alas left a comfortable upper-class parish in San Salvador to go to Suchitoto, a rural town fifty-one kilometers to the north, as parish priest in 1968. His new parish included some twenty-five neighboring villages, which, together with the town of Suchitoto, had a total population of forty-five thousand.

Alas quickly realized that if he ran the parish in the traditional way—saying mass, hearing confessions, and attending the sick—he would have no time for anything else. But he thought that, "in light of the new theology that was being developed, liberation theology—though they didn't call it liberation theology yet—and within the message of the Second Vatican Council and the Conference of Medellín in 1968, it was necessary to work with a group of campesinos who could celebrate the word in the communities, give communion, and organize the communities."

His ideas were not fully formed—as he said, liberation theology did not even have a name yet. He began by asking each of the twenty-five villages to elect a leader to attend a training course for delegates of the word. Nineteen sent representatives, all of them men. Alas taught them a course on the theme of community, in which he invited them to interpret the Bible in the light of their own lives. When they had completed the course, they conducted weekly services in the villages of the parish and taught catechism classes to others, and Alas said mass in each village once a month.

   Other priests and nuns likewise left elite parishes and private schools in the cities to live and work in poor communities, especially in the rural areas but also in urban slums. They tried to breathe new life into their parishes. The first step was to recruit a few lay people who appeared to be potential leaders. These people made a commitment to study and be trained for special responsibilities as delegates of the word (they were also known as catechists or celebrants of the word). They joined what was called a Christian base community,[1] a small group of lay people who came together for study and social action within a parish.

   They began by studying the Bible. A small group—perhaps fifteen or twenty people—would meet regularly with the priest to read and discuss the Bible and examine its relation to their own lives. José Alas began by working with the villages of his parish; German Montoya began in the town. Soon after his ordination in 1970, Montoya became the parish priest of Uluazapa, a town near San Miguel. "The first thing I did was have meetings in the neighborhoods; there were four neighborhoods. First [I asked] about what they knew about the church. What did they know? Nothing. So we started meeting on Wednesdays and I gave a Bible class. I explained the Bible from their point of view."

   Study groups read the Bible not as a source of inerrant truth but as a manual for living that offered inspiring stories and role models (cf. Levine 1992, 138–139). The story of the exodus would bring up the idea of liberation; sharing of goods by the apostles suggested the theme of community. They practiced concientización, applying the Bible to the study of injustices committed against them—sometimes in conjunction with literacy education, sometimes not. Popular education and concientización were an integral part of the new pastoral practices. Church training institutes founded throughout Latin America to promote the new pastoral orientation adopted Freirean pedagogy both to promote education and as a methodology for group organization. They made little distinction between education and organizing. Learning skills, analyzing social structure, and organizing for change were seen as part of a single process.

   Even when it is introduced into communities by outsiders—priests, seminarians, or nuns—concientización cannot be a top-down process; if it does not come from the subjects themselves it will not take hold. To overcome the paternalism inherent in their status as well-educated outsiders, those who called the group together made strenuous efforts to give the lead to the members of the communities themselves.

   Priests strove to break down the prevailing assumptions about the hierarchy. Many people saw them as virtual magicians, dispensers of the sacraments that would get one into heaven. Traditional priests always wore a cassock; they derived much of their income from fees for baptisms, marriages, and funerals.

Priests who identified with liberation theology wore street clothes, even blue jeans, and they did not charge for the sacraments. Many of them were supported by foreign orders or had paying jobs as teachers; but more importantly, they refused to treat the sacraments as a commodity or a means of livelihood. When a parishioner asked him how much he charged for baptism, German Montoya would reply, "Baptism is a sacrament which God has given us to bring us closer to him, to participate in the church. It has no price in money. You can give a donation to the church. Remember, that donation isn't for the priest; it's for the church."

As the priests became less magical, God too came closer to real life. Adelinda, one of the first delegates of the word in the parish of Aguilares, later remembered how her views changed. "Before, we had participated in the women's congregation, which went to church once a month for a sort of vigil. The movement was called Daughters of Mary. We had a vision of God very much in heaven, up there; a very punishing God. With the [new] mission we discovered that God is in each one of us, and that He has made a choice for the poor. So our commitment is not just to go to church, but to celebrate, to proclaim [*anunciar*], and to serve the community." The new teaching, in the characterization of Father Miguel Ventura, parish priest of Torola, Morazán, declared that the Christian "is being saved in history, not after death, and [finds] salvation in community. In other words, there are many elements tending to base faith on salvation of the person within history, and on salvation in a communitarian dimension."

When José Alas discovered that his recruits in Suchitoto were shy in his presence and waited passively for him to explain things, he decided to give them lessons in public speaking. "These classes consisted simply of someone standing up and trying to give a little speech. At the beginning it was practically impossible, because they didn't know what to say. It was terrible: after three minutes they just sat down. At the end it was terrible, because there was no way to stop them."

Many had to struggle to overcome their passivity, and they only increased their participation slowly. But the practice presumed that everyone had something to contribute and everyone, including the priest, could learn from everyone else. If the outsiders worked effectively and the parishioners stuck to it, many of them became acute analysts of the Bible and its relevance to their social condition. As Alas said, there was no way to stop them.

Most rural parishes were large, consisting of a central town and surrounding villages and hamlets (in El Salvador, the rural districts are called cantons). Some cantons were close by, with easy access to the central town, but others were in remote corners of the mountains, inaccessible by road. The priest could only visit each village of a parish occasionally. Lay leaders, however, conducted weekly "celebrations of the word," worship services with Bible reading, hymns, and reflection. As lay people, delegates could not say mass, but in a few places they distributed the consecrated host to those who wished to take communion.

Through these activities the church maintained a presence in areas underserved by the clergy and came closer to the lives of isolated campesinos: they encountered it more often, and the encounters had a new meaning.

Many new lay activists came from poor backgrounds. They had little education and no professional training. Nevertheless, when they conducted worship and catechism in their home villages on their own, they acted independently of the clergy, and put into practice the knowledge and skills in which they were being trained. By assuming these responsibilities, they expressed their commitment and affirmed their right to play an active role in the church.

These new teachings were put into practice across Latin America, but unevenly (Berryman 1987; Cleary 1985; Levine 1992; Levine and Mainwaring 1989; Montgomery 1983; Smith 1991). In some countries the bishops favored the new orientation; elsewhere they were divided or unsympathetic, but an important minority embraced it and its far-reaching social implications. Central America became one of the areas where the effects of liberation theology were greatest. But even there the church was divided: while some bishops endorsed it enthusiastically, others were hostile.

In El Salvador the new pastoral practices were initiated under Luis Chávez y González, archbishop of San Salvador. Though not so well known as his successor Oscar Romero, Chávez y González was archbishop for nearly forty years (1938–1977). He was politically conservative but nevertheless receptive to the message of the Vatican Council and Medellín. By encouraging younger clergy to respond to it, he laid the groundwork for changes in the Salvadoran church.

In 1968 Chávez y González created the Foundation for the Promotion of Cooperatives (FUNPROCOOP) to stimulate rural cooperatives. In 1970 he called a conference, the National Week for Joint Pastoral Practice, to promote innovations in the spirit of the Medellín conference. He actively recruited priests of rural origin (though not necessarily from the poorest families—to enter the seminary they had to have gotten basic education first). He encouraged them to study abroad. José Alas studied the new pastoral model at the Latin American Pastoral Institute in Quito, Ecuador; so did Father Rutilio Grande, who as parish priest of Aguilares was to become the first of many priests murdered by paramilitary forces (Cáceres Prendes 1989; Montgomery 1983; Peterson 1997; Richard and Meléndez 1982).

For clergy to immerse themselves in poor communities meant a departure for the church, whose pastoral care for the poor had often been only perfunctory. But those who went to the countryside did not have clear political objectives. They certainly did not intend to foment revolution. Though they were making a conscious option for the poor (and a radical break in their personal lives), they did not fully anticipate what that meant.

The social implications of the "option for the poor" were not self-evident. Two alternative visions could be derived from it: one focused on development or modernization, the other on liberation. The first aimed at social and economic development in the spirit of the papal social encyclicals and the Alliance for

FIGURE 2. Catechist in celebration of the word, Chalatenango. *Photo by Steve Moriarty.*

Progress. (Reform-oriented Salvadoran Catholics in this tradition had founded the Christian Democratic Party in 1960.) In this vision, "development" implied choosing programs based on technical criteria and implementing them from above without the participation of the people the programs were supposed to help. The second vision called for liberation from below. This view held that poor communities could only free themselves from oppression through their own action.

Aguilares, like neighboring Suchitoto, was among the parishes where base communities set down the deepest roots. Thirty-five kilometers north of the capital, Aguilares is the center of a sugar-growing region. Virtually all campesino men cut cane in the sugar harvest every year, but many also either owned or rented land to farm on their own. In 1972 Rutilio Grande, a Salvadoran Jesuit, went to Aguilares as parish priest. The Jesuit order, which had sent many foreign priests to El Salvador and which had founded the Central American University in 1967, chose the parish for a pilot organizing project in which other priests and Jesuit seminarians joined a team led by Grande.

Their goal was to bring all the laity into active participation in the church, but in stages. The parish team worked most closely with a few actively committed parishioners, recruited to become delegates of the word. They were to "multiply" the teaching by spreading it to their fellow villagers. The delegates continued to study with the priest. They also went to special conferences with delegates from other parishes at church retreat centers.

Adelinda remembered that the biweekly sessions in the parish of Aguilares covered three main topics. First, delegates studied church doctrine, usually focusing directly on the Bible or on texts such as the Medellín resolutions that were informed by liberation theology. Second, they discussed "national reality." They learned about poverty and the social structure of El Salvador from a standpoint inspired by the Marxist analysis of exploitation, and studied the national constitution, equally subversive because it proclaimed a democratic government and respect for human rights. Third, they learned techniques of popular organization, including group dynamics and how to plan and conduct meetings.

Learning to organize, they also learned a sense of their responsibility and how to relate to their peers, according to Adelinda:

> What is a good leader or a bad leader. We talked about the *cacique* [boss], the authoritarian, the paternalist.
>
> *And are there a lot of* caciques *and paternalists among the campesinos?*[2]
>
> Yes, there's a lot of that. And we talked about how one needs constructive, healthy and fraternal criticism from the community to keep growing, and to be concerned to win the acceptance of the community, and their confidence, and to be a spokesperson for their concerns and needs and at the same time take them new things, new ideas, and to understand that the successes and failures of the work are our responsibility.

These courses prepared them to spread the mission throughout the parish. They conducted celebrations of the word in the outlying villages and hamlets. They also organized. In Adelinda's canton of Amayo, delegates organized a women's group, a youth group, an education committee, teams to work on community improvements, and a theater group. They conducted classes, often repeating lesson plans worked out with the priest and the delegates from the other villages of the parish in the Saturday meetings. Candidates for further training as delegates were recruited from these discussion groups. Participants were expected to expand the organization by passing on what they had learned. In principle no one was only a learner or only a teacher—everyone was a "multiplier" who learned and then taught what he or she had learned.

The visit of the priest, though no longer the only—rare—church activity in the cantons, became a major event to which the delegates' other activities looked forward. José Alas said mass in every village in Suchitoto once a month, normally on a weekday evening. He usually did not preach a sermon. Members of the congregation read the gospel of the day and a contemporary reading—a news article, a passage from a papal encyclical or Vatican Council document—because, as Alas explained, "today's deeds also have elements of revelation, not just what is in the Bible." Then the worshippers divided into groups to discuss the readings. After their discussions, someone from each group stood in front of the whole congregation to report the group's conclusions.

Alas said mass—in a two-hour service, from eight to ten o'clock—in a different village practically every night, getting home at eleven or staying overnight in the village, especially in the rainy season. "But I was young then, so I could do it," said this man whose energy was still boundless twenty-five years later.

Many delegates went to special conferences at church retreat centers with delegates from other parishes. There were seven church-sponsored study centers in El Salvador in the early 1970s. Delegates came to these centers to take courses that lasted an entire week, and sometimes as long as four weeks. They covered in greater depth the topics taught in training sessions in the parishes: Christian theology, national reality, and organizing techniques. The centers also offered intensive courses in agriculture and health care (Binford 1996:82, 98; Montgomery 1982:103; Peterson 1997:55–58). Many delegates became health promoters, learning first aid, preventive health measures, and treatment of common diseases. Health care, and the training of lay people to provide it, occupied a place next to education in the priorities of Christian activists. Both were basic needs that went unfulfilled in many communities. Like education, health care was emphasized not only in the base communities but later in the zones of guerrilla control during the war.

The new pastoral orientation was not adopted in all parishes. Base communities were created only where priests and parish workers from religious orders actively promoted them. Many priests and lay people rejected the innovations, as did most of the Salvadoran bishops. Some regretted the abandonment of traditions and resented the intrusion of social questions into church life, and others who had derived prestige and authority from their stake in traditional parish organizations saw the base communities as competitors (Williams and Peterson 1996).

In the face of these divisions, base community activists asserted the new orientation's legitimacy. They insisted that the church should welcome the commitment, autonomy, and participation of lay people and fulfill its obligation to act on behalf of justice in the world. Increasingly, they considered themselves a separate tendency within the institutional church, calling themselves the "people's church."

The emphasis on reading the Bible and discussion materials made literacy a virtual requirement for delegates of the word. Most of the first parish activists—those who volunteered or were chosen by their communities to be delegates—had gone to school for at least a few years. But some were completely illiterate, and there were others whose skills had decayed because they did not use them often. Meetings and conferences provided an occasion for reinforcement. Study texts were read aloud, often more than once, before people began discussing them. Texts in comic book form became a popular genre.

Beyond initial learning, fluency in reading and writing is mostly a matter of practice and reinforcement. For people who read seldom and with difficulty, encounters with the written word became exercises in reading and writing—not onerous exercises, but a normal part of training and working as a delegate. Those with only rudimentary skills improved with regular practice in discussion groups, organizational activities, and conducting worship. Héctor, a catechist from San Fernando in the department of Morazán, explained that the process of helping people with reading was not separate from the process of discussing and preparing the lessons the catechists were expected to multiply in the cantons. (With a sixth-grade education, he was one of the better-educated delegates.)

> Many compañeros might have only gone to first or second grade, and it was really hard for them to understand what was going on [*la realidad de ese momento que se vivía*]; the violations of human rights, for example, which were hard for anyone to understand. In the workshops they got more practice. In the community, too, we took extra time so that if any catechist compañero got behind, the rest of us helped him out; so that when he went to work in the community, he wouldn't make too many mistakes.
>
> *Then you didn't have classes, but the compañeros helped each other out?*
>
> That's right. There wasn't a special literacy effort like there is now.

Popular education did not separate content and methods. People learned the skills as they learned the material, as they came to understand "what was going on."

One of the main manifestations of poverty in rural areas was the lack of educational opportunity. Well-educated church workers who went to rural parishes were already convinced that education was necessary for intellectual and spiritual growth, so discovering its lack in poor communities reinforced their political and theological convictions and gave impetus to literacy and education projects. More people who had never been to school or were only marginally literate joined base communities. So delegates with only a few years of schooling held regular classes to teach them.

Part of the genius of the new pastoral movement was that it both made people feel the need for literacy and brought them the means to meet it. They could not study the Bible and carry on pastoral activities without it. Literacy was therefore a Christian's duty. As German Montoya put it, knowing how to read "was an obligation. Baptism is a serious commitment. Joining the group was like renewing your baptismal vows. This was an obligation. It wasn't a question of 'I want to learn to read.' No. Christ says, 'You have to learn to read.' It's a demand of your faith. You have to learn to read." Not only a duty, literacy was also an assertion of dignity by people widely despised as campesinos and blamed for their own ignorance. Ultimately it became an instrument of struggle as well. Still, general literacy campaigns were not a high priority at the beginning. The process focused on forming leaders, and it very quickly became more political and turned to organizing and pursuing grievances.

The Christian Community and the Worldly Community

The new pastoral practices were open-ended. Outsiders who brought them to the parishes had no clear goals. Studying church doctrine, learning organizational skills, and promoting activities in the parish were seen as ways for campesinos to improve their lives and solve their own problems. As they met and discussed the gospel in relation to their lives, members of a community inevitably began to consider community issues and community needs. They first tried to find solutions by cooperating among themselves, not by challenging propertyholders or authorities.

In Uluazapa, German Montoya organized a pastoral team for each neighborhood of the town. Each team met for Bible study. "Once, in the class itself, we started talking about what they needed in that part of the village. 'Wouldn't it be nice if they put a streetlight on the corner.' 'And why haven't we put one there?' 'The mayor says there's no money.' So, 'Why don't we make contributions, little by little, and one of you keep the money.' 'But how do we know no one will steal it?'" Suspicion was almost automatic and was one of the many barriers that made it difficult to cooperate on even the simplest tasks.

Uluazapa was in the diocese of San Miguel, which was not as hospitable to the new pastoral practices as the archdiocese of San Salvador. José Eduardo Alvarez, bishop there for more than two decades, was a military chaplain with the rank of colonel. Like most of his colleagues in the Salvadoran hierarchy, he did not favor liberation theology and the new form of ministry. But the younger priests in the diocese studied at the Jesuit-run seminary in San Salvador and returned home with new ideas. The diocese had two church conference centers, the Centro El Castaño and the San Lucas Campesino University, founded under Alvarez's predecessor. They offered regular courses until they were closed in the 1970s. The diocese included the department of Morazán, the northern part of which was to become one of the strongholds of the insurgency in the 1980s.

The base communities in the parish of Torola in Morazán, encouraged by Father Miguel Ventura, experimented with working their fields collectively. Without pooling the land—some farmed land they owned, others had to rent—they shared their labor. According to Octavio, a campesino from Torola, "One day we would go weed one man's cornfield, the next day someone else's, and sometimes when someone had just a little, we could do someone else's the same day." The idea of collective work had arisen, he said, "because of the poverty we lived in. Sometimes a compañero had a sick wife, or sick children. He couldn't go weed his field. The cornfield was going to weeds. So we thought, let's go help that compañero out." They also worked land owned by widows or other poor people who could not work it themselves, and some small owners offered parcels of land rent-free on which the collective groups grew food to be given to the poor of the community.

Collective cultivation of hemp, an important local cash crop, played a special role. According to Ventura, campesinos who were completely landless or whose land was insufficient to support their families frequently fell into a form of debt peonage. To get a loan from a landowner or to rent a tiny tract on credit to grow corn, a man often had to agree to work in the landowner's coffee harvest the next year at very low wages. Producing hemp collectively freed the poorest campesinos from dependence on wealthy landowners for credit.

Working together was an expression of the collective spirit that animated the base communities. Many from Torola or neighboring San Fernando (in the same parish) recalled the experience. The delegates of the word were not the only ones who worked collectively; others who were not active in the pastoral work joined them. Octavio insisted that the idea had not come from a priest, or any outsider, but had arisen among themselves. Collective work, he said, "was very helpful for getting along and understanding that we could solve our problems." Héctor, a catechist from San Fernando, also felt that the value of working together was more than just increased production. "More important, the idea was to discover the values of the person through working collectively." According to Ventura, "Lots of the people of northern Morazán remember the strong solidarity that existed among the campesinos in the 1970s." By encouraging such new experiences of cooperation, base community activists extended their influence beyond their own membership to others not so involved in parish life.

To be delegates was especially a new experience for women. It was unheard of for women to speak up in public and become active outside the home. Many husbands found this hard to accept. According to Heriberto, a young catechist in the parish of Teotepeque,

It was a very hot topic for [the women]. A woman who understood things would say to a friend, "Look, it's important that if we are equal to them, then we can decide too, we can struggle just like them, we can work just like men."

In all the meetings the problem was the men. When you asked the women something, they said no, the problem was that the man didn't let her go, that the man was jealous, that he would get angry and whatnot.

Even men who were themselves committed and active resented their wives' devoting time to the community or were suspicious when their wives came home late at night. Adelinda said that her husband

was very responsible in the work and always tried to support me, as long as I was in the community. But when I left my home and my children to work in other communities he was very opposed.

Sometimes you went away and stayed overnight?

Yes. He was very opposed. We talked a lot about why he was opposed if I accepted having him work in other zones, and took care of the children [when he was away]. He said he was afraid for my safety but I thought that was just an excuse. It's not the same thing to talk about commitment and liberty as to practice it. . . . This was something that we talked about a lot in the campesino organization. In my husband's case, it was very hard for him to accept. But in the end I didn't agree to go back home, because work was needed elsewhere. . . . So I said I had the right, and the ability, and I had to share what I had learned with other compañeros. And that it was just something he had to get over.

Not all men got over it. Many remained opposed to their wives' participation. Their resistance was a problem for couples and hampered the pastoral work as a whole.

Urban Youth Groups

Christian base communities were also organized in urban parishes, especially in the capital city, seat of the archdiocese, which under both Chávez y González and Romero was much more open to new forms of ministry than other dioceses. Many high school students became active. Recruited through their parishes or from the church's private schools—many were from elite families—the youths formed study groups under the guidance of parish priests or private school chaplains. Many chose to "go among the poor": they regularly visited rural parishes and promoted education and community action. To some extent this was a teenage fad—the woman who became FMLN *comandante* Nidia Díaz later said that as students during the Holy Week vacation, "instead of taking off for the beach we went to the countryside." The experience nevertheless affected many of them deeply, including Díaz.

Matías belonged to a youth group from the parish of Zacamil, on the northern edge of San Salvador; the group visited several rural communities on weekends. Members taught catechism to the children, reading and writing to adults; and they held meetings to promote discussions of the campesinos' social situation. They just "tried to start the discussion off because the people had so many examples that they were the ones who really taught us about the injustices around land in that place."

Others worked in the city. Emilia taught a group of women from a San Salvador slum to read and write, and used the lessons for concientización. "For example, we had *casa*, and the drawing of the house, and we started discussing what a house means, and what kind of houses they had."

Others without a church base also did popular education. The University of El Salvador was a hotbed of leftist sentiment among students and professors— the government closed it several times between 1972 and 1989. When the school was functioning, students' courses included field work in poor neighborhoods in the city and rural villages, where they offered assistance and practiced the professions they were learning. The Revolutionary University Students (UR-19), a left-wing student group, promoted contacts between students, workers, and campesinos. Unions organized classes for their own members, taught by other members as volunteers, and some members of ANDES, the teachers' union, conducted literacy classes in the countryside.

Camilo, a law student, worked with some students of education to train rural teachers. Campesinos with a second- or third-grade education were teaching in villages where there was no government school; the students met with them on the weekends to bolster the campesinos' elementary education and to train them to teach their classes.

> We tried to show them how to organize some things that they hadn't gotten together yet. We reviewed the work they had done during the week and told them, "You did this this week; try to teach this next week."
>
> They came from different places. There were some who had walked five or six hours to get there.

All these efforts were directed at education and community organization simultaneously. Popular education did not distinguish between the two. Some outsiders who worked in rural communities sought out people with leadership potential for special training. Others tried to work with larger community groups and encourage them to collaborate to solve their communities' problems. Their goals, Matías said, were "practical: for people to learn to write and read, to communicate among themselves, to have more fellowship, so that with the support of the community they could resolve problems as far as they were able, like getting clean drinking water and electrification."

Urban youth, even from relatively poor families, were shocked by rural living conditions. Discovering the countryside and poverty for the first time, they also learned some things about themselves:

We had to learn to ride the buses. You know, in El Salvador the upper class doesn't take buses. So it was a learning experience for us. (Emilia)

One young compañera showed up with high-heeled shoes, as if she were going to teach in a classroom. And they set us to walking almost two hours. When I say two hours, you walk twenty or twenty-five kilometers up and down hills. This showed that compañera some of the problems, and may have disabused her of the idea that campesinos don't learn because they're dumb. But she liked this kind of program and worked there longer than a lot of us. (Camilo)

They had food for you, and how could they be giving you a piece of chicken and tortillas when they themselves didn't have enough? So we always said, "No, I already ate," and we tried to bring our own food. (Francisco)

The students were also impressed by the campesinos' eagerness and aptitude to learn, which belied stereotypes that they were stupid and incapable. According to Francisco, a university teacher, "the process wasn't top-down. Not only did they learn from us when we came to teach them something, but we learned too. They wound up teaching us more than we [taught them]." Here too, education and consciousness-raising went hand in hand. For Christian activists, discussion always began with the Bible. In Emilia's group, "we began with a lesson, like an epistle of Saint Paul, and opened the discussion: 'What is this? What does it have to do with our lives?' Then they started to discuss it: 'What I get from this is . . . ' 'This is what happened to me at work this week: they fired me, they didn't want to pay me my hours.' And little by little they discovered that in the gospel there are messages [about] their rights—that it isn't true that they have to be poor all their lives. So this sort of semi-theological discussion was the basis for them to create and carry out their own projects later."

The Bible was sometimes interpreted in novel ways, as Matías illustrated:

Someone would ask, "What do you think is God's will?" And "If we are all made in his image, why should there be differences between us?" Then, "What has someone else done that you haven't done who has more than you?" Then the creation of capital—where it comes from.

You talked about capital and labor?

Yes. If you read the Bible you'll find lots of references. For example, when Archbishop Romero told the oligarchy to share a ring or else they would lose a finger, that's in the Bible. We didn't use Marx's *Capital.*

The mutual good will and a shared political project did not completely overcome the differences that separated campesinos from their urban collaborators. People looked, dressed, and talked differently. More significantly, outsiders, even from the working class, were better educated and higher in status than campesinos, and assumed that they could speak for campesinos and tell them what to do. Many campesinos, in turn, deferred to outsiders unthinkingly. Urbanites struggled against their assumption of superiority and overcame it as they discovered how much they could learn from their campesino collaborators.

For many of these young people, working in Christian base communities was a transforming experience. Emilia said that her group cultivated a mystique, which involved both creating community and taking on a special mission as Latin Americans within the modern world:

> We considered developed countries to be developed technically, but humanly and politically they were more backward than we were. . . .
>
> The mystique was a completely deliberate part of our work. It meant including activities to build friendship and a sense of fraternity: it involved rituals, and conscious effort by a leader to be concerned about the personal situation of another leader, for example. So there was the conscious creation of a spirit of community; we weren't in this just because it was necessary to learn to read and write, but because we were creating something bigger. That's what it was, a mystique.

From Community Organizing to Political Action

The effectiveness of concientización became apparent as many campesinos achieved the confidence to speak up and assert themselves. In the United States we take overtly egalitarian social relations for granted, so we are unlikely to appreciate both how important and how unexpected this transformation was. Even if our egalitarianism is only superficial, it gives subalterns much more freedom to act than they have in a society that demands deference to social superiors. Many have noted the dramatic awakening of peasants and other poor people through community organization under various auspices, in El Salvador and elsewhere. "To those of us who have lived primarily in societies which place great emphasis upon individual autonomy, it is perhaps difficult to understand the kind of personal odyssey such people must undertake to modify time-honored patterns of submissiveness and obedience. And so it is equally difficult to understand how joining a soccer team or taking part in a discussion group at church may mark the first step on a journey that leads to great resolution and commitment" (Wasserstrom 1985:11).

Sister Joan Petrik, a North American Maryknoll nun who worked in El Salvador in the 1970s, observed the transformation firsthand. "When I first arrived in Tamanique, every time a child died the family would say 'It's the will of God.' But after the people became involved in the Christian communities, that attitude began to change. And after a year or so I no longer heard people in the communities saying that. After a while they began to say, 'The system caused this.' [Base community members] walk upright, their heads held high, with self-confidence" (quoted in Montgomery 1982:104).

Pooling resources to put up a streetlight or working in common to produce food gave people a new experience of collaboration and a sense that collectively they had the power to improve their lives. But they were still poor and could do only so much by mutual aid. Concientización meant coming to understand the causes of their poverty and in particular the growing landlessness that followed from the increased concentration of land tenure after 1960. Liberation theology provided Christians, especially campesinos, with a new way to interpret the crisis—by recognizing its source in the skewed distribution of land. The delegates of Suchitoto learned this when José Alas taught a course on baptism.

> Baptism, according to Saint Peter, makes us priests, kings, and prophets. So all the discussion about whether we Christians are really kings or not, whether an oppressed people are kings, and what are the oppressions we suffer in the political field and in the economic field—we came down very hard on the problem of land tenure, as a demonstration that our people are not kings. . . . And what it means to be a prophet, to denounce the structures of sin—which is part of liberation theology—and announce the kingdom of God. As a result, after two months, the campesinos said to me, "Okay, we've discussed land tenure and about being kings, but now we need a course on agrarian reform."

In Suchitoto, the struggle for campesinos' rights came to a head in 1969, less than a year after Alas arrived in the parish. Landowners commonly rented wooded plots to campesinos, who had to clear them before farming. A year later the owner, instead of renewing the lease, could use the newly cleared land for pasture, taking advantage of the campesinos' free labor. One Suchitoto landlord was notorious for this form of exploitation. According to Alas, "Campesinos worked for him and paid him [rent] to get a miserable harvest, and sometimes after they had prepared the land, he took it back before the family could plant their corn." He preached a strong sermon condemning the practice—but without mentioning the landowner by name.

Shortly thereafter, five campesino families went to a local justice of the peace with a claim to rent land that they had cleared. Alas appeared before the justice to support them. "The fact that a parish priest, the landowner, and the justice came together in the city hall to resolve a case about land had a tremendous repercussion [in the community], and a tremendous repercussion in my whole life," Alas said. Parishioners organized a demonstration in support of the campesino litigants.

Tension mounted over several weeks. The town council declared Alas persona non grata. The declaration had no official consequences, but it did not take much imagination to interpret it as a threat. Parishioners organized another demonstration in his support, to be held on a Sunday. The authorities responded to this uncommon boldness by sending the army and the National Guard to occupy the town and blockade the entrances, but hundreds of campesinos from the outlying cantons slipped in through backyards and coffee groves. To show his support, Archbishop Chávez y González came to preach at that Sunday's mass. His presence was sufficient pressure to prevent the troops from turning on the demonstrators, who learned a lesson in their own strength from the successful face-off.

Sporadic acts of protest gave rise to campesino organizations. They were founded to raise specific grievances; then they took on an increasingly political role and became part of the popular movement that took shape in the mid-1970s. The Christian Campesino Federation (FECCAS) was especially active in Aguilares, where canecutters went on strike against the La Cabaña sugar mill in 1973. FECCAS, founded in 1964 out of the same reform impulse that inspired the Christian Democratic Party, lay dormant until 1974, when delegates of the word took it over as a vehicle for their demands. At first it raised minor, local issues: slight improvements in salary for farmhands; hot rather than cold tortillas for lunch at work; the opportunity to rent small parcels of land at reasonable prices. But the very fact of organizing provoked tremendous opposition on the part of the landowners.

The revival of FECCAS grew directly out of the work of the base communities, and activists made little distinction between church work and organizing. The same person might be educator, pastoral agent, and political organizer. In Amayo, Adelinda said, many delegates of the word were also officers of FECCAS. "This was never a problem for the community because they were the ones who had elected us, democratically," she said. Education was a major part of FECCAS's work—in the cantons, in the parishes, and nationally. Some of the Jesuit seminarians who worked with Rutilio Grande in Aguilares trained its leaders. Educational meetings were held regularly in the cantons of Aguilares, led by the local FECCAS secretary in each community and the regional education coordinator, often with a seminarian collaborator. A seminarian who later became a guerrilla comandante under the name Javier Castillo described the topics they discussed: "national reality, the situation of the campesino and the rights of the campesino. Then, what was FECCAS? Why was it formed? What is it about? What does it offer? What doesn't it offer—because the FTC [the Rural Workers' Federation, product of a later merger of FECCAS and another campesino organization] always presented itself as a vehicle for the campesinos' struggle, not an organization which was going to give things to them." The organization had no money to subsidize these events. If a regional

FECCAS leader came to a local meeting, according to Castillo, "they gave him a meal and they all contributed to give him the bus fare—one peso—that he needed to go back home."

More elaborate meetings were held to train FECCAS's national leaders, often three-day meetings in a church conference center. Their training was patterned on the training of the delegates of the word, and dealt with similar topics: social analysis (under the heading of "national reality") and organizational skills like keeping minutes, keeping track of the resolutions of a meeting, and maintaining communication with the members of the organization at the base.

But these conferences were not only for training; they were strategy sessions. Under the cover of a church-sponsored conference, organizational leaders could come together from different areas to lay plans. They were therefore conducted by the organization's leaders, campesinos themselves, not by pastoral workers. Participants in these conferences went back to their parishes and taught the material they had learned, and those who participated at the parish level did the same in their cantons.

Education was thus linked directly to political action, as Castillo emphasized. "This educational experience was profoundly linked to the process of struggle, not something separate. So for the people in a course, the idea was to leave with more knowledge to continue the struggle, so they were really enthusiastic about participating."

Campesino organizations became part of a popular movement that was growing in size, boldness, and visibility only a few years after the beginning of the Christian base communities. Organizations also sprang up in urban areas. Some of them were based in the people's church, but more of them grew out of the secular left, which reemerged after a long period of quiescence following the matanza of 1932. Slumdwellers formed organizations. Trade unions, which had been hemmed in by legal restrictions and sometimes openly repressed since 1932, showed signs of life in the late 1960s. The national teachers' union ANDES (National Association of Salvadoran Educators), founded in 1965, took the lead in the reinvigorated labor movement. ANDES led three major teachers' strikes between 1967 and 1971. Because teachers were spread across the country, ANDES was one of the few national organizations with a presence in rural areas (Lungo 1987:44–73; White 1973:236; World University Service et al. 1981:13–14). Like the university-based organizations, ANDES members offered assistance to popular education in the countryside, and other unions held classes for their own members.

These popular organizations, as they were known, linked up with each other within and across sectors. FECCAS formed an alliance in 1975 with the Rural Workers' Union (UTC), which was especially strong in Chalatenango; the two later merged to form the Rural Workers' Federation (FTC). The United Popular Action Front (FAPU), formed in 1974, brought together organizations of campesinos, workers, and students and the Communist party. This was the first nationwide attempt to unite the diverse constituencies of the popular organizations. FAPU was short-lived, but the Popular Revolutionary Bloc (BPR), founded the next year, was at the center of popular protest for the next several years. ANDES and FECCAS were leading components of the emerging movement of popular organizations.

After decades of quiescence, the rapid growth and spread of these organizations was startling—especially to the oligarchy, which found any form of popular organization threatening. Tens of thousands of people regularly turned out for demonstrations in San Salvador. They came on buses from all over the (very small) country, despite the risk—demonstrations were often fired on by police or soldiers, with fatal consequences.

Moderate factions within the oligarchy and the military tentatively proposed reform. But the intransigents remained dominant and derailed all such efforts. In 1970 the national legislature invited representatives of labor, business, and other nongovernmental groups to a conference on agrarian reform. José Alas was delegated to present the church's position strongly favoring agrarian reform. Upon leaving the meeting he was kidnapped. An immediate and forceful protest by Arturo Rivera y Damas, auxiliary bishop of San Salvador, undoubtedly saved his life, but he was tortured and left naked in the mountains near San Salvador (Montgomery 1983:85–86). In 1972 an opposition coalition led by Christian Democrat José Napoleón Duarte ran in the presidential election, but the government organized a massive fraud campaign to secure a victory for Colonel Arturo Molina. In 1976 Molina himself proposed a very mild land reform program, but it caused such a storm of opposition among the oligarchy that the National Assembly voted it down. The oligarchy's clear refusal to permit change through either elections or paternalistic reforms pushed the popular organizations further to the left.

The oligarchy did not content itself with crushing reform efforts through political institutions; it also actively repressed those who proposed them. Repression was mild at first. Authorities controlled people's movements, especially in the countryside. At first, Camilo said,

> the repression wasn't so great yet, and didn't isolate campesinos as much as it did later. So we could take school supplies—not in very large quantities, but we could get in a small notebook, or twenty pencils, or a bunch of notebooks. We tried to bring in materials when the patron saint's day was approaching. When there was a festival, there was a bigger concentration of people, and they could take things in, and it didn't arouse the suspicion of the repressive forces to make them ask what you were carrying.

Héctor of San Fernando remembered:

> In 1976 repression started against the church. They started capturing catechists. Nationally, the first priest they killed in Aguilares was Rutilio Grande; and from that moment repression started in all the zones where people were talking about base communities.

By the late 1970s people from the city could no longer go to the rural areas at all:

> Repression grew, and our way of dressing in the city is easy to spot in the countryside. We tried to look as much like them as possible, but it was hard. In the city you don't get as sunburned, you don't usually wear a hat, so you comb your hair differently. So we had to withdraw from the campesinos somewhat. (Camilo)

> In 1979 and 1980, I withdrew from the countryside, because it was too dangerous for people from the city to move around in the countryside. They spotted you as someone who didn't belong there. And around that time we also abandoned the idea that the people from the city could tell the people of the countryside what to do. (Francisco)

Death squads targeted individual activists, and, increasingly, the church. ORDEN (National Democratic Organization), a paramilitary organization founded in 1967 by General José Alberto Medrano, head of the National Guard, used patronage to recruit campesinos to the death squads, which became more active as rural organization intensified. The death squads sought out delegates of the word and campesino leaders, often pulling them out of their houses at night. Organizers took to sleeping out in the mountains for safety. Some fled to the cities and found refuge in the parishes of the young people who had worked with them. But these parishes and their young people were victims too: in 1979 the National Guard attacked a retreat center in San Salvador and killed Father Octavio Ortiz and four young men, two of them teenagers.

Death squads were run clandestinely from the headquarters of the military and security forces. Many of their members were policemen or army or National Guard troops, dressed in civilian clothes but acting under the orders of their superiors. But those forces also worked openly, turning the entire countryside into a virtual war zone. In 1974 in La Cayetana, in San Vicente department, the National Guard massacred six campesino members of a group that had occupied farmland they had unsuccessfully offered to rent; in 1975 troops broke into two homes in Tres Calles in Usulután department and murdered the fathers.

Public demonstrations were mowed down. In July 1975, troops attacked a university students' march. The announced toll was six dead, but many more disappeared. In February 1977, General Carlos Humberto Romero was elected president in blatantly fraudulent elections. Popular organizations called a demonstration on February 28 in San Salvador to protest the fraud. The army and the National Guard fired on the demonstrators, leaving an estimated one hundred dead.

Some were captured and held in clandestine prisons. A 1978 investigation by the Inter-American Commission on Human Rights found numerous cases of arbitrary detention, torture, and inhumane living conditions in what it called "slave prisons" (Inter-American Commission 1979:65–122). Many who were kidnapped by death squads simply disappeared.

On March 12, 1977, Father Rutilio Grande of Aguilares was ambushed while riding in his jeep. He and two parishioners were murdered. He was the first priest killed in what became an escalating bloodbath. A clandestine organization, the Union of White Warriors, claimed responsibility and publicized the slogan, "Be a patriot! Kill a priest!"

FECCAS and UTC had been negotiating to rent parcels on large estates that the owners were holding idle, and had asked the minister of agriculture to intervene. Receiving no response, they occupied the targeted lands in several areas, including Aguilares, where FECCAS had always been strongest. The army and the National Guard responded in May with a sweep that militarized the whole Aguilares region. Some parishioners sought refuge in the church. On May 19 the troops broke in, sacked the church building, and rousted the people out. According to the government, seven were killed; according to parishioners, the toll was fifty. Later that year the Union of White Warriors issued death threats against all members of Grande's Jesuit order who did not leave the country within thirty days. (The Jesuits held firm.[3])

Oscar Romero, bishop of Santiago de María, became archbishop of San Salvador in February 1977, succeeding Chávez y González. Romero was known as a man of humane instincts, but a traditionalist; though he had been influenced by his contact with progressive clergy in Santiago de María, he felt the church should remain silent on political questions. Many in the people's church resented his appointment and had hoped to see Auxiliary Bishop Rivera y Damas named. But Romero was soon converted to support of the popular movement, in his preaching and with the archdiocese's institutional resources. The murder of his close friend Rutilio Grande a month after Romero assumed his new office affected him deeply. He responded to the murder vigorously, as he would to later attacks on churchpeople; in protest, he decreed that the only mass celebrated in the archdiocese the following Sunday would be in the cathedral, and he refused to attend government functions (Brockman 1982:1–29; Richard and Meléndez 1982:94).

The organizations that grew out of base communities increasingly took open political positions that challenged authorities and landowners. For many Christian activists it seemed only natural to move from Bible study to community organizing, and then to politics. Learning to participate, cooperate, and lead persuaded many campesinos that they could work to change their society and gave them the tools to do it. For many from middle-class backgrounds who learned about poverty in their country firsthand, political organizing seemed an inevitable step.

Others had their doubts. The Medellín conference had called on churchpeople to live among the poor and bring the gospel to them, but had not implied any specific social measures. Archbishop Romero identified wholeheartedly with the people's church and preached powerful sermons—broadcast by radio throughout the country every Sunday—but he continued to hold that the church, while it supported popular organizations, should stay above specifically political issues. Some of the clergy agreed. They tried to keep their independence and abstain from overtly taking political positions, which they saw as appropriate for lay people but not for themselves.

Even though Romero tried to keep the church above politics, his fellow bishops opposed him for being too engaged. René Revelo, in Rome as delegate to the Synod of Bishops in 1977, publicly denounced Salvadoran catechists for being influenced by Marxists; Pedro Aparicio, at the Latin American Bishops' Conference in Puebla, Mexico, in 1979, went even further, saying to the press that Romero himself was influenced by Marxist priests and that people whose disappearance had been denounced had in fact joined armed organizations (Brockman 1982:82–83, 148). In a 1978 pastoral letter Romero attempted to draw a line, asserting that the church should take no political stands but still recognizing the people's right to join popular organizations. Five bishops took the extreme step of publicly dissenting from the pastoral letter and claimed that Marxist-Leninists had infiltrated the church through popular organizations. Both Romero and his adversaries attempted to enlist the support of Rome (Berryman 1984:134; Brockman 1982:passim).

Nor was it just the hierarchy that was divided. Base communities had taken root mainly in parishes where clergy and other church workers promoted them, and even in those parishes some campesinos were recruited to the paramilitary ORDEN through a combination of patronage and anticommunist appeals (Cabarrús 1983:43, 102–104).

Despite these disputes, the people's church was the most dynamic force in ecclesiastical life in the 1970s. It challenged the church as a whole to serve the poor and provoked it to debate what kind of institution it should be. Activists in base communities and the peasant movement also provided the bulk of politically committed recruits to the guerrilla movement that was starting to organize.

The Move to Armed Struggle

For those identified with the people's church, repression made it hard to stay independent of politics. Many lay people and some clergy, as well as others from secular movements, concluded that peaceful political action was fruitless and that only armed struggle would be effective. They organized clandestine armed movements. The first two were the Popular Liberation Forces (FPL) and the People's Revolutionary Army (ERP). The FPL was founded in 1970 by dissident members of the Salvadoran Communist Party (PCS), including the Secretary General, Salvador Cayetano Carpio, who rejected the Communists' moderate, electoralist line in favor of armed struggle. The FPL inherited the Communists' anticlericalism and at first required all militants to declare their atheism (Harnecker 1993:64–65). The ERP was founded in 1971 by Christian activists, some formerly in the Christian Democratic Party.

These organizations were mainly known to the public for the murder and kidnapping for ransom of prominent public figures and foreign businessmen. The founders were from the cities, and most were university students. They knew very little about rural poverty, and they embraced armed struggle on theoretical grounds rather than out of direct acquaintance with injustice. But they also sought ties with popular organizations.

They rejected Che Guevara's *foquismo*, the doctrine prevailing among Latin American revolutionaries since the Cuban revolution, which held that "the insertion of a small nucleus [*foco*] of revolutionary fighters into the countryside would act as a spark for mass peasant rebellion" (Dunkerley 1985:89). Following Che's example, the 1960s generation of Latin American guerrilla fighters had initiated armed struggles in several countries without cultivating sufficient popular support; like Che, most of them were wiped out. The FPL adopted instead the Maoist thesis of prolonged popular war (*guerra popular prolongada*), according to which victory would require a long guerrilla struggle with the support of civilians in large areas of the countryside (Castañeda 1993:81–83; Dunkerley 1985:90; Harnecker 1993:220; Loveman and Davies 1985:397–399; Wickham-Crowley 1992:215).

Recognizing that the church-based organizations were already organizing campesinos for political struggle, the FPL addressed a Letter to Progressive Christians in 1975 that, without glossing over differences, invited cooperation (Harnecker 1993:65). As many leaders of popular organizations faced repression, they became receptive to recruitment by the political-military organizations. Overcoming the militant atheism of its origins, the FPL developed the closest ties of any of the armed groups to the people's church.

The ERP and the FPL established strong bases of recruitment and support in the areas they came to control during the war: northern Morazán in eastern El Salvador for the ERP, and eastern Chalatenango in the center of the country for the FPL. These two mountainous departments, bordering on Honduras, are among the poorest of the country. They provided many recruits, and many who did not join the organizations supported them covertly. Because the armed organizations recruited Christian activists and recognized the need to organize at the base, they took up popular education. They continued it in the guerrilla army and later in the communities of the territories they controlled.

Repression mounted through 1978 and 1979. More and more activists were murdered or disappeared at the hands of death squads, and campesinos in organizations felt directly threatened. According to Justino, a UTC activist in Arcatao, "Things got ugly, and we couldn't stay at home any more. For a while we only came home during the daytime. We didn't stay there because they came looking for us at night. Then came a time when we couldn't be there day or night, because if they didn't find us at night, they came looking for us during the day. So we had to flee our homes once and for all."

Popular organizations and armed groups stepped up their challenge. The armed groups staged confrontations with government forces and, despite their mutual ideological hostility, tried to come to terms that would establish operational unity. The Communist Party too formally abandoned its electoral strategy and began to prepare for armed struggle. Demonstrations were regularly fired on, but the popular organizations kept filling the streets, and people continued to go, wondering "How many will they kill today?" (as Juan José Rodríguez, who became the president of Segundo Montes City in Morazán, remembered some years later).

As the country became increasingly polarized, a group of young army officers tried to find a middle way. They hoped that moderate social and economic reforms could stave off the revolution that seemed increasingly inevitable. On October 15, 1979, the officers staged a coup. They brought to power a military-civilian junta and a cabinet in which representatives of the political opposition predominated. The new government promised democratic elections and agrarian reform (Mena Sandoval 1991:175–185).

But the reform-oriented officers did not control the armed forces, which were still dominated by hardliners. To test the intentions of the new government, popular organizations held demonstrations and demanded an accounting of missing political activists. The military and security forces continued to fire on demonstrators, killing more than one hundred people in the first week after the coup, and eighty more in a demonstration on October 29. Meanwhile, the death squads stepped up their clandestine activity.

Many of the reformers resigned from the government, protesting its failure to bring the armed forces under control. The military hardliners held onto power and installed a new junta in January 1980. The new junta did carry out part of the promised agrarian reform in March under heavy pressure from the Carter administration, which was eager to prevent any repetition of the Sandinista triumph in Nicaragua six months earlier. Agrarian reform expropriated very large farms, most of which were relatively infertile, but did not touch most of the smaller but more productive coffee plantations (Brockett 1988:153–154; Deere 1984:170–172). The reform did not seriously threaten the oligarchy's power base, and it did not halt the impending revolt. Repression—public, by the security forces, and clandestine, by the death squads—continued to mount. The most brazen death squad murder, of Archbishop Romero, shocked the world. He was shot as he said mass on March 24, 1980, the day after he directly called on Salvadoran soldiers, in his Sunday sermon in the Cathedral, to "Stop the repression!" (Brockman 1982:217).

As they prepared for war, the armed organizations overcame their divisions. In November 1980, the Farabundo Martí National Liberation Front (FMLN) was formed by the ERP, the FPL, the PCS, and two other political-military organizations, the Central American Revolutionary Workers' Party (PRTC) and the National Resistance (RN). The period from the 1979 coup to the FMLN's "general offensive" on January 10, 1981, was one of escalating terror and polarization that finally gave way to all-out war (Armstrong and Shenk 1982; Dunkerley 1985; Montgomery 1982).

The guerrilla army recruited many who had been politicized through activism in the people's church and then in the peasant organizations. For churchpeople already divided over the legitimacy of overtly political activity in the church's name, the question of armed struggle cut even deeper. But as repression became pervasive, many campesino activists felt they had no choice.

Other campesinos who had been less active also felt the threat of death squads and the marauding army. Repression is an inefficient instrument; while it can often intimidate people and quash overt opposition in the short run, it is also likely to increase latent opposition (Mason and Krane 1989:177–178). In communities where the people's church and the campesino movement enjoyed latent ideological support, some who were on the fringes joined the guerrilla army because it appeared to be the least dangerous alternative.

During the years immediately preceding the outbreak of war and during its initial phase, repression put a halt to all public organizing. Popular education had to be suspended in these communities. During the first several years of the war, it went on mainly in protected spaces where it could not be singled out for attack. Ironically, these safe areas included political prisons and the guerrilla army itself, as well as the swelling refugee camps. Later it was revived in civilian communities in FMLN-controlled zones. Though the war had relegated education to second place, it would become central to political organizing once again.

But the church was no longer its center. The death of Archbishop Romero deprived the base communities of their most important supporter. Of the activists who had not been murdered or driven into exile, many committed themselves to the armed struggle. Once war broke out, the church's role in grassroots activities diminished. When popular education resumed on a broader basis in the mid-1980s, it was usually promoted by community councils or popular organizations with no direct relation to the church.

The people's church was a major source of popular education and political militancy during the 1970s. Many early accounts of the spread and influence of Christian base communities in El Salvador and elsewhere in Latin America (mostly written by churchpeople, North American and Latin American) viewed them with great enthusiasm: they appeared to hold the key to a revitalized church and a transformed social order (e.g., Berryman 1987; Cleary 1985; Montgomery 1983; Randall 1983). Later research in several countries, however, showed that the effect of the base communities had been exaggerated. In fact, adherents were few relative to total church membership, base communities only flourished in particular locations and usually depended on the support of the hierarchy, and they achieved little measurable political change. These shortcomings were attributed in part to the base community methodology, which was overly intellectual and politicized and neglected the spirituality that appealed to more believers (the evangelistic success of Protestantism in Latin America in the last twenty years offers a dramatic contrast). In a base community in Brazil,

John Burdick found that the emphasis on study and analysis left many who had only limited literacy and intellectual skills feeling marginalized. According to the critics, observers projecting their own values and political views onto the "people" exaggerated the reach of the base communities (Berryman 1994:102, 204–209; Burdick 1993:75–80, 221–226; Crahan 1992:156, 164; Daudelin and Hewitt 1995; Levine 1992; Levine 1995:16–17, 21).

These conclusions, derived from studies in several countries, apply less to El Salvador than elsewhere. With Nicaragua, El Salvador was one of the countries where the people's church was most influential. Though never more than a minority in the church as a whole, it contributed significantly to those two countries' revolts. Many combatants and community activists entered the struggle through base communities, and many of the ideas and ideals that motivated the struggle germinated there. Even for El Salvador and Nicaragua, however, the claim must be qualified. With the armed struggle and, in the Nicaraguan case, the movement's transformation into a revolutionary government, activists broke away from their church roots, and the church's direct influence declined.

Popular Education: The First Lessons

Although Christian base communities became less important as sites of popular education during the war, the people's church laid a foundation for the future and developed the consciousness of those who went on to wage the struggle on new ground. In less than a decade Christian activists had found a new way of seeing themselves and the world. They had learned important lessons that continued to inform popular education throughout the war. First of all, they had recognized the need to start with education, because its lack impeded all their work. They had begun to reexamine relations between men and women, and learned something of what it takes for people of different social levels to be able to collaborate. Most important, they had seen the value of education for individual growth and political organization. Though issues of gender, class, and the relation of education to political practice were never completely resolved, their understanding of these lessons deepened as the war progressed.

The lack of education had to be confronted, because without it people could not participate effectively. Literacy was an essential tool for understanding the world, for personal development, and for performing organizational tasks. Dealing with illiteracy required organizing: organizing classes and organizing a broader struggle that gave people an incentive to learn. So those who promoted the new pastoral orientation and who were educated recognized that educating others was a necessary first step.

Though popular education proclaimed the equality of all participants, traditional distinctions of status did not disappear automatically. Men kept women down, and poorly educated campesinos were separated from upper-status, well-educated outsiders by the campesinos' habitual deference and the outsiders' skills and verbal articulateness, to which the campesinos aspired.

Throughout the subsequent struggle women continued to prove their abilities. Outsiders from privileged backgrounds, especially Christians, conscientiously adopted a standpoint of "accompaniment." A prominent theme in Archbishop Romero's preaching about the role of the church in organizing, accompaniment implied that the church supported but did not dictate the choices of the poor (Berryman 1984:340; cf. Berryman 1994:173; Brockman 1982:175–176). In practice it meant that those who came from outside listened to the campesinos and took them seriously—something many campesinos had never experienced before.

In that way outsiders offered encouragement but gave the lead to activists from poor communities who developed the confidence to define their own goals. Differences of interest or viewpoint often arose openly, and when they did, the poor asserted their position. Popular organizations followed principles that assured that people of higher status or education did not dominate but subjected themselves to the decisions of the group. It was an authentic learning process, as was demonstrated by the commitment, consciousness, and organization that grew out of it. The proof, according to comandante Javier Castillo, was that "in the FPL many [campesinos] became our leaders."

Those who worked with the poor found that they learned a great deal, not least that the campesinos with whom they collaborated *did* have something to teach them. Some who facilely assumed their own superiority (even though they benevolently offered it in the service of the poor) were genuinely surprised to observe the skills and knowledge of those whom they went to accompany. The popular education principle that everyone taught and everyone learned was a reality, not a pious wish. According to German Montoya, "In Uluazapa I learned theology from the people. . . . Uluazapa taught me to read."

This mutual learning, even from one's ostensible inferiors, entailed a broad view of education, not restricted to book learning or to what went on in the classroom. Indeed, when people who participated talk about education (in the base communities of the 1970s, and in the guerrilla army and the civilian communities of the 1980s), they often refer to the whole range of organizing rather than just literacy or training in skills.

This broad view of education was embraced for several reasons. First, it made for good pedagogy. Because many of the potential learners were uncertain that they had any *right* to learn, getting educated, educating oneself, or educating others inevitably entailed raising one's consciousness and becoming active. Second, the view that education encompasses the whole political process was embraced as a principle. Learning did not just mean learning to read, but learning to express oneself, to work with others, and to solve real problems. People saw education as a tool for struggle, not something to be pursued for its own sake. Finally, it was an observable fact that education and organization, education and struggle were one. Because education was inseparable from politics and struggle, it *did* expand people's consciousness and change their thinking. This broad understanding of education as an all-embracing process made popular education central to the insurgent struggle.

CHAPTER 3

Learning on the
Front Lines

---

*W*hen full-scale war broke out, community organization was driven underground. Popular education was only safe in a few places that were protected from government repression. The most important sites were refugee camps in Honduras, prisons holding political detainees, and the guerrilla army itself. It might seem paradoxical that combat zones were safe areas where the popular education that was repressed elsewhere could continue, for the fighting forces were under the most direct and intense attack. The presence or threat of combat brought constant interruptions. Ideologically, however, the war fronts were free spaces. The government could bomb and attack, but it could not interfere directly in education or single out for punishment those who participated in it.

During twelve years of guerrilla war, the FMLN worked to educate its mostly illiterate or barely literate troops. This chapter discusses the education of combatants in the guerrilla army. The FMLN invested considerable time and energy in the effort and called on combatants who themselves had very little education to be teachers. Soldiers in the guerrilla army were educated despite severe shortages and the constant presence or threat of combat. Education served both practical and ideological ends. It taught basic literacy and technical skills—both of which were useful to the military effort—and political orientation, regarded as reinforcing the motivation to fight. The FMLN's ideology, moreover, called for the elimination of inequality. Educating its troops put that ideology into practice, but at the same time revealed its limits. People of higher- and lower-level social backgrounds were treated differently, as were men and women (women accounted for nearly a third of the membership of the guerrilla army).

Revolutionary leaders insist on political education for combatants because they assume that it builds fighters' morale and is therefore an important determinant of combat effectiveness. Many scholars dispute that position, arguing that ideology contributes little to combat morale among soldiers in general or among peasant combatants in particular, and that their morale in any case makes little difference to the outcome of war, which is instead determined by macro-political conditions at the state and international levels (Goodwin and Skocpol 1989; Keegan 1976:46–52; Wickham-Crowley 1992).

But some recruitment conditions and combat tactics place a premium on the morale of the individual soldier, as in the French revolutionary army, raised by the *levée en masse* and specializing in the bayonet assault (Lynn 1984). Martin van Creveld argues that the typical war since 1945 has been a guerrilla war in which "a small, weak force confront[s] a large, strong one [and therefore] will need very high fighting spirit to make up for its deficiencies in other fields" (1991:174). In the Salvadoran case, the morale of the combatants was inspired by political education and contributed significantly to the military effectiveness of the FMLN.[1]

Education and Guerrilla War

During the war the FMLN attempted to teach all of its troops to read and write. Many of its campesino recruits had never been to school, whether because there was no school close enough, because they had to go to work in the fields at a very early age, or because, without a culture of literacy, parents saw no need to educate them. Combatants who had studied were mobilized as teachers: some from urban areas had had access to secondary education, and a few had been professional teachers or university students. But many campesinos taught others to read even though they themselves had only a few years of schooling. People of all levels of education in the FMLN shared the popular education assumption that *conciencia*—consciousness, conscience, dedication—is more important than training in an educator; one who recognizes the obligation to teach will figure out how. The deployment of teachers with minimal formal education was a response both to necessity and to the conviction that, given the opportunity, they would show their ability.

Though always subordinate to military needs, education was pursued for two reasons: to cultivate the skills needed for warfare and to put into practice the ideology that proclaimed that all people are capable of learning and are entitled to the opportunity. These two purposes were not independent, according to the theory of popular education. Learning specific skills must be part of the integral development of human capacities; education forms the whole person.

This interdependence was felt even in training for combat. The FMLN was somewhat haphazardly armed early in the war, so combatants had to be trained to use any weapon. (Later in the conflict, rifles were more uniform.) Octavio, a campesino from Morazán, was a combatant at the beginning of the war. Years later, a refugee, he was at my home in New York. Thumbing through a book of reproductions of murals of the Mexican revolution, he pointed to a rifle and said, "That's a FAL." I cannot recognize rifles but I know that the FAL is a contemporary weapon, so I said I didn't think so, that the Mexican revolution had begun in 1910. He looked again, and corrected himself: "No, it's a Mauser."

He went on: "In the FMLN they taught us all the weapons. That's the difference from the Salvadoran army. They give you one weapon and you learn it. In the FMLN, you learn everything: you know how to take any rifle apart and put it back together." Combatants had to be prepared to use any weapon that might fall into their hands, even of World War I vintage. But in Octavio's telling there was clearly also pride that his superiors recognized him and his compañeros as people who could learn.

Militarily, the FMLN would never be better equipped or armed than the enemy army; to triumph it would have to count on superior use of human resources. Acting on the slogan *"Lograr mucho con poco"* ("Achieve a lot with a little"; López Vigil 1991:359), therefore, required people to learn and to use all of their abilities. But achieving a lot with a little was not only a slogan or a means to military advantage; it was an anticipation of a new society that would recognize the worth of all its members.

The commanders of the guerrilla army, moreover, were convinced that inspiring the fighters to do their best depended on cultivating their morale and commitment. Enhancing combatants' understanding of and belief in the ideology that underlay the struggle, the commanders believed, would inspire them to work to their utmost and to "achieve a lot with a little." To this end the FMLN made politics and ideology an integral part of its educational process. Combatants were called upon to spread the message in their contacts with civilians, moreover. Che Guevara once said to FPL founder Salvador Cayetano Carpio that there could be no guerrilla war in El Salvador because there were no mountains. Carpio countered, "The people are our mountains" (Pearce 1986:126–127)—the guerrilla army depended on them for intelligence, supplies, and recruits.[2] Political and ideological education prepared combatants to arouse civilian support in controlled and contested zones.

Teaching on the Battlefield

As the FMLN's army got organized, it discovered that the high rates of illiteracy meant that combatants could not perform key military tasks: paramedics had to follow written orders to medicate patients; radio operators had to be able to interpret codes; those making explosives had to know arithmetic to mix the chemicals correctly. These tasks required literacy, at a minimum, and sometimes skills ordinarily learned in higher grades. But most of those being trained for these specialties hardly had basic education. Gustavo, a combatant who worked in radio communications, had to teach reading as well as radio operation, encoding, and decoding, "because reading included how to get a message right."

Political education, too, was regarded as essential both to promote morale and for strategic reasons. For one thing, combatants were motivated by their convictions, and those convictions were intensified by discussions of the political situation emphasizing the aims of the war. Because many of the combatants carried out propaganda and organizing among civilians, moreover (increasingly so after 1984, when strategy was revised to strengthen links between the guerrilla army and its civilian base, as discussed below), their education was immediately put to political uses. Political and pedagogical practices were therefore inextricably linked, giving a political content to the training in basic skills.

But if war demanded educated combatants, it also made educating them very difficult. Combatants camped out in the open country. Classes too were taught in the open, without benefit of schoolhouses or desks. Instead of blackboards, Mario told me, "we used old metal roofing sheets. If you carried chalk it crumbled, so we used charcoal." Lessons were interrupted by combat: "Sometimes you could be teaching," Severino remembered, "and the Air Force came.[3] Or troops could attack by land. So you had to have your pencil and paper, and at the same time be ready for combat. It's pretty hard to be doing two things, prepare and then teach class and also be on the alert for whatever might happen."

The stress of combat interfered with learning. But as in most armies, life alternated between overstimulation and tedium. When combat lightened up, more time could be devoted to study. Sometimes, Severino said, "six or eight months would go by and there were no enemy operations. That's when we could teach the most because the kids [*muchachos*] calmed down and learned a lot."

Most combatants were in the equivalent of the infantry—frontline combat troops—but many were in what were called "structures" with special tasks such as medical care, logistics, radio communications, and munitions manufacturing. These structures were based in rear guard areas in more or less permanent camps. Though they were vulnerable to bombing raids, the pace of life was calmer than on the front lines, and the troops' specialties generally required greater academic skills.

For more than two years, Severino taught combatants in three structures located within a two-kilometer radius in Morazán: a logistics unit, an explosives unit, and a clinic. Initially, soldiers from all the structures converged every day to attend his class, and at times he had as many as fifty students. But when security considerations dictated against movement of so many people, he met a smaller group at each location daily.

Like many combatant-teachers, Severino took great pleasure in his students' eagerness to learn. In the clinic where he taught health workers and patients, "there were *compas*[4] who were wounded, and learning always drove [*impulsaba*] them. How could they do it? Even on their crutches they always showed up for class." But his own enthusiasm convinces a listener that, while he drew inspiration from them, he must also have offered it.

Throughout the war, material resources were scarce, combat erupted unpredictably and absorbed everyone's full attention when it came, and the learners had little background. So the basic process of popular education was the same wherever it was carried out. But the details of occasion, personnel, and organization varied from place to place and over the course of the war. Several who participated told me that there was a "system" of education among the troops, but they described rather different systems. Despite efforts to regularize the process, each experience had an element of spontaneity and varied with the particular conditions of the military unit in which it occurred.

The major difference was between the two main periods of the war. From 1981 to 1984, the FMLN controlled approximately one third of the country's territory, and used the tactics of a conventional war, waging large-scale battles from fixed positions. Most combatants were quartered in camps of several hundred people. Slow periods in those camps provided opportunities for relatively well-organized classes meeting for an hour or more a day along with military training.

Then, in a major strategic shift beginning in 1984, the FMLN reorganized its army, abandoned much of the territory it had controlled, and deployed troops in small, mobile squadrons. The reorganization affected education: without large fixed bases, it was more difficult to have teachers available to all the illiterate soldiers. But education continued in the smaller units. According to Mario, who supervised combatant-teachers in the area around Nueva Granada, teaching any illiterate members was one of the duties of the squadron leader ("who necessarily knew how to read"). But others said that a unit normally included a literacy teacher along with a radio operator, someone trained in first aid, and other specialists. The teacher often had very little education, but worked regularly with those who were completely illiterate. The ideal was to hold class for an hour or more a day, but military conditions did not always allow it, units moved more frequently, and the discipline of study was not as strong in the small squadrons as it had been in the camps.

In addition to the combatants in the large camps of the early years of the war and those in the small mobile squadrons of the later years, there was a third group of fighters: the nonpermanent forces, variously known as the militia or the territorial defense forces. Members of the militia spent most of their time at home, but joined the guerrilla army for brief periods to perform special missions, when action heated up near their home villages, or during regional or nationwide offensives that required large numbers of fighters. Almost all the militia members were illiterate, and because they were only present irregularly, their education did not proceed very far. At the war's end, Mario anticipated that the gathering of combatants into camps as part of the peace settlement would finally offer an opportunity to work more intensively with them.

Education for Basic Literacy

Education began with the basics. As Mario, who was a high school graduate, described it, that meant that "you have to start like with a little kid, picking up a pencil: 'You hold the pencil here. Practice! Loosen your fingers, you're squeezing them.'" When possible, combatants were divided into groups according to how much education they had. Oscar, who grew up in a village without a school, and so had no education when he joined up at twenty, was taught in a group of "us dummies [*brutitos*] who couldn't do anything, and some others who knew a little [were taught] separately."

New readers began by reciting and tracing the vowels and then learning generative words. Nacho, who had been a teacher before the war and then organized literacy programs for combatants in the eastern part of the country, condensed campesino life before and during the war into six words. "We proceeded just like in grade school, teaching the words that were most ordinary and common: *papá*, *mamá*, *cuma* [sickle], which is a work tool; *pala* [shovel], which we used for military engineering; *fusil* [rifle], *bala* [bullet]." Or, as Severino put it,

> We always taught class based on the situation we were living in.
> *What aspects of the situation did you pay most attention to?*
> Well, the course of the war, more than anything. For example,
> we could use the word *pala*, and we had a short dialogue about what
> a shovel was for: to dig trenches to fight the enemy.[5]

Few people had heard of Paulo Freire, but they were applying his methods and principles.

Reading material was scarce. Those in charge of education tried to provide each teacher with a dictionary. But books were not just hard to come by; they added a lot of weight to a knapsack, and when combat erupted suddenly, soldiers had to evacuate without warning. The FMLN produced political pamphlets with simple lessons, usually in comic book form. Typically, one or two 8 1/2 × 11" sheets were printed on both sides and folded in quarters to produce an eight- or sixteen-page pamphlet. Duplicated in the field by silk screen, they were light and could be carried conveniently. In Chalatenango a bulletin circulated regularly, carrying news, analysis, and a cultural section including poems and short stories by combatants themselves.[6]

One of the most widely circulated pamphlets was *The Fifteen Principles of the Guerrilla Combatant* (FMLN, Reunión Comandancia 1985). Each page illustrated one of the fifteen principles, which ranged from ideological exhortation (No. 2: "We live to struggle, we struggle to win") through military duties (No. 4: "We will care for our weapons and munitions to the greatest extent possible") to attention to civilians (No. 8: "We must be friends of the people, be deeply aware of their problems, give them guidance, and incorporate them into the struggle everywhere"). The seventh ("We will struggle against ignorance and always dedicate ourselves to advancement") was accompanied by a picture of a group of combatants in an outdoor literacy class, led by a woman writing on a board leaning against a tree.

Combatants carried a notebook, into which a teacher would copy the lesson. Soldiers would sit on the ground hunched over their notebooks, painstakingly practicing letter by letter. Proudly displaying their work, they would tell Severino, "'Look, my handwriting is improving,' [and I would say] 'You're writing better. Do it this way.'"

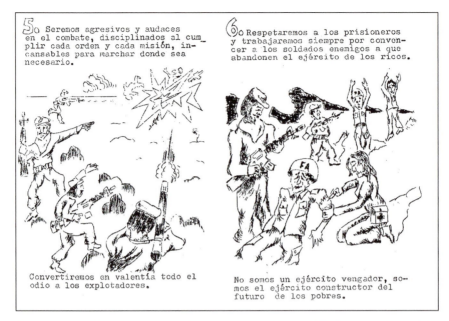

FIGURE 3. *The Fifteen Principles of the Guerrilla Combatant* (FMLN, 1985). "We will be aggressive and bold in combat". "We will respect prisoners and work to convince enemy soldiers to abandon the army of the rich".

Literacy was essential for higher ranks. Although most comandantes came from urban backgrounds and were well educated, some campesinos demonstrated the requisite military and leadership skills; but at a minimum, they had to be able to read and write messages. Severino was assigned to teach a comandante full-time. "There were people who became masters of military strategy, and became comandantes, but didn't know how to read, and to be a comandante and not know how to read is pretty difficult. So I was teaching just one compañero to read, who was a comandante. I worked with him for about four months, and he learned."

Major Fabricio Hernández (only toward the end of the war did the FMLN army, now called the National Army for Democracy, adopt formal ranks) grew up a campesino and only had two years of school. He rose to command troops around Nueva Granada. "You learn from practice. I've been a teacher at times, teaching the vowels to people who never learned them." But even now, "when I pick up a newspaper or read a document or pamphlet I ask people to explain words that I don't understand. That way I've continued improving."

But some resisted. According to Norma, who oversaw education in Chalatenango, "Set a teenager to learn to read and you had to fight with him, because he didn't think it was very important." Some responded to peer pressure, according to Claudio, a combatant-teacher:

You didn't force them. You couldn't force them if they didn't want to study.

But you didn't try to appeal to their consciousness either?

Sometimes you might tell them, "Look, you have a chance to learn." "But I'm old," some said. "Nothing goes into my head anymore." Then you would say to them, "No, man, it's not too late."

Sometimes someone who knew how to write said to someone who couldn't, "Look, man, learn. Then you'll be able to write to your girlfriend." This made him eager to write a letter to his girlfriend, who might be in another camp.

Specialized Training

Beyond basic education, many who had gone to school, or who became literate in the guerrilla army, were trained in special skills, ranging from first aid to explosives to propaganda. Their training was usually brief, and most of their knowledge came from practice. But training was more systematic than literacy education: trainees were often withdrawn from combat to relatively safe rear guard areas for courses lasting several days.

Among the most important specialties was the health worker providing emergency medical care. Among the combatants, health workers were variously called paramedics, *sanitarios*, or *brigadistas* (among civilians they were usually called health promoters). Carmelina, one of the first paramedics, was introduced to her work in a three-day training course taught by two doctors in Chalatenango just before the 1981 offensive. "All they taught us was how to make cotton swabs, to treat wounds, to use direct pressure on a hemorrhage, and to apply a tourniquet if the hemorrhage was serious."

Later the training became more systematic, according to Mauricio, a physician working in Chalatenango (see also Metzi 1988). In a six-day course, trainees learned to do resuscitation, treat fractures, and carry patients. Then they joined a combat unit and treated the emergencies of all the combatants in the unit.

> The lessons have to be presented in the clearest and simplest manner possible, even when the knowledge acquired is complicated. When they learn anatomy, and also when they are going to learn to suture wounds, we try to get an animal and explain where is the heart, the lungs, the intestines etc., and have them practice suturing.

Actually, that's just the way I learned in medical school.

Most of the paramedics were women. Paramedics who took to it well went on to learn more advanced specialties: anesthetist, surgical instrumentist, dentist; some even did minor surgery and amputations. As Mauricio explained, "We started doing advanced training pretty spontaneously [on the job] in each hospital, explaining what to do and how to keep records of what they did. But it soon became clear that we had to give specific courses. So we started giving paramedics advanced training in patient care, nursing, administration, etc."

Those who worked as literacy teachers in their units were also trained, but less systematically. Most of them were ordinary combatants, with perhaps a third- or fourth-grade education. If every combatant was to learn to read and write, people with only a few years of school would have to become educators. They relied on political conviction and camaraderie to equip them for the task. According to Ricardo, a platoon leader who went into the guerrilla army with a third-grade education but became a volunteer schoolteacher in his community after the war, combatants who had been to at least fifth or sixth grade taught because "their consciences[7] moved them." For Claudio, "you educated others as a part of your brotherly affection for your compañero. You didn't want to see him not learn."

So people taught with little education and no formal knowledge of teaching methods, but a strong dose of commitment and affection. They could not be very demanding of their pupils, for several reasons: learning was essentially voluntary; learners lacked confidence in their abilities and were sometimes resistant; besides, classes were constantly interrupted. So the emphasis on commitment and the difficult combat conditions reinforced each other to produce a pedagogy that relied less on academic rigor than on moral incentives in the form of steady encouragement and invocation of the political obligation to learn.

But the teachers' good will had to be fortified with at least some technical knowledge. Combatant-teachers were trained and overseen by middle-level people whose primary task was education, usually people from urban areas who had studied in teacher training school or university. Combatants who had been teachers in civilian life were known as *maestros de ANDES*, teachers who had demonstrated their political commitment before the war by joining the teachers' union. From time to time they held intensive courses of a few days' duration for the combatant-teachers. "We made it simple," said Nacho, a normal school graduate and a public school teacher before the war, "how to hold a pencil, how to develop dexterity with a pencil, then the vowels and then the structure of words and sentences." They also spent time traveling among the camps, observing the combatant-teachers at work and giving them advice.

In this rudimentary training, combatant-teachers were taught to make concientización part of literacy teaching. But at the beginning of the war, according to Nacho, "We didn't connect it to political discussion much. It didn't have what popular education has now [1993], where at the same time as teaching to read, you do consciousness-raising." Though the methods they learned drew on Freire's pedagogy of the oppressed, most combatant-teachers had no firsthand knowledge of it. When Claudio, a combatant-teacher, spoke of "popular education," I asked him what he meant by the phrase. He replied, "We didn't use the term in the war. It was more like, 'I'm going to teach you to read and write.'"

Advanced training was offered in other skills as well. Newly literate campesinos learned to operate microcomputers (with which, astonishingly, the command centers in the mountains were equipped). Others were trained in world geography and global politics so that they could intelligently monitor international short-wave radio transmissions. The FMLN had two clandestine radio stations: Radio Farabundo Martí in FPL-controlled Chalatenango, and Radio Venceremos in ERP-controlled Morazán.[8] Both stations trained announcers, journalists, and technicians. Some foreigners who came to the front to show their solidarity with the FMLN gave special courses; José Ignacio López Vigil, an Ecuadoran, taught a course in radio production to the staff of Radio Venceremos and stayed to write a book about the station (López Vigil 1991) that is a fascinating account of guerrilla life.

Political Education

All combatants took part in political education. In addition to concientización as part of literacy instruction, there were general political discussions. They were conducted not by specialized personnel but by the unit leader, whose role combined political and military leadership. The time and frequency varied, but political discussions occurred more regularly than basic education, normally every day, and the whole unit took part. The leader gathered the troops to discuss political issues—current events, the nature of the new society for which they were fighting, and the need to spread propaganda in civilian communities. The entire unit or camp would discuss the news they heard every day on the two radio stations.

The leaders of the FMLN believed that combatants' recruitment and morale depended mainly on their belief in the cause for which they were fighting, making ideological education essential to the military effort. This conviction was expressed by people from different levels of the guerrilla army. Orlando, a combatant: "The life of the guerrilla combatant was full of enormous sacrifices. You had to have a high level of consciousness and be clear about why all this sacrifice was necessary. Otherwise you wouldn't put up with it."

Norma, who oversaw education in Chalatenango: "Political-ideological education is like the assurance that the militant is going to stick with the process."

Mauricio, a doctor who worked behind FMLN lines: "Ideological strength is what makes someone voluntarily decide to risk life in combat. Life is the most precious thing we have! To say 'OK, I'll go. Give me a rifle. Train me,' and to go fight the government army, one has to have tremendous ideological support."

It is true that some combatants found political education an unnecessary diversion from military tasks. According to Lucía, a combatant from Chalatenango who became a unit leader and then went to Cuba for political and ideological training, "they said, 'We don't want anything to do with politics.' They had a certain consciousness, they knew why they had taken up a rifle to fight injustice, but if you came and talked to them about historical materialism, or dialectical materialism, they would say, 'Don't give us anything about politics. Here we talk about rifles, how many battles we're going to fight, and what matters to us is how many soldiers we're going to kill.'"

Even Father Rogelio Ponceele, a Belgian priest who had gone to El Salvador as a missionary and spent the war years in FMLN-controlled Morazán, was impatient at those who insisted on teaching literacy through concientización: "I insisted that it had to be something quicker, the traditional method, because it was urgent to learn and the compas already had enough political training" (López Vigil 1987:68).

A marching song brought humor to this ambivalence:

Para ser buen guerrillero
solamente necesitas
estar claro por qué luchas
y trotar las mañanitas.

[To be a good fighter
You only need
To be sure of why you're fighting
And jog every morning.] (Henríquez Consalvi 1992:198)

Political education was meant to encourage independent thought, not just the parroting of a line. According to comandante Nidia Díaz, combatants had gut feelings about injustice and oppression from their own experience—"on the coffee plantations they saw that the master's dog had meat and they were dying of starvation. Then there were the massacres and the repression." But their political education led them beyond the raw sense of oppression to consider alternatives: "What kind of new society did you want to create—what do you want to achieve in education, in health, in the economy, in democracy? What do you want to achieve in the country? Ideological and political training was basic to be able to survive the war's most difficult periods." So they discussed political themes: the conflict between rich and poor, the one-crop export economy as the basis of exploitation, and inequality as the main cause of the war.

Through these open discussions and exchanges combatants saw that their talents and contributions were recognized, according to comandante Mariana Chicas: "They develop their capacity for political analysis. They don't just take orders, they have to be able to analyze and develop their thinking." Mauricio argued that, far from "indoctrination or brainwashing," the process had real meaning for combatants: "It's not that someone comes from outside to tell us, or to force us, because these are things that come from the actual needs of people and can't be imported from somewhere else."

Because most combatants were not intellectually sophisticated, some might dismiss their ideological statements as mere rhetoric. But the correspondence between their words and their behavior demonstrates the depth of their convictions. Their ideology had observable effects: they frequently illustrated abstractions by their own experience. This was especially the case when they discussed their relations with civilian communities—and one of the main purposes of ideological education was to train them to communicate their beliefs to civilians, as we will see. Ricardo, a platoon leader, spoke of the obligation to share medicine, if they had it, with sick civilians, to win their sympathy for the guerrilla cause. "But we didn't just do it to make them aware, but because we could see that they were suffering; we were all poor." Alberto, discussing meetings to persuade villagers to support the cause, said, "Anyone can [speak up at a meeting], because everyone who joins the people's struggle knows the ideals he is fighting for."

As noted, many scholars are skeptical of the claim that political education can significantly increase soldiers' morale and commitment. Guerrilla leaders, to the contrary, were convinced that their army traveled less on its stomach than on its hearts and minds. Some of their opponents agreed, including at least one with direct knowledge of guerrilla life. Miguel Castellanos, comandante of the FPL, was captured by the Salvadoran army in 1985, subsequently renounced the FMLN, and supported the government when I interviewed him in 1988.[9] In his view, "It's a life of great sacrifice. What keeps you going is the ideological and political aspect, the struggle for an ideal." He was quick to add that the utility of ideology was running out and that as the war dragged on, many FMLN combatants were deserting. But four former U.S. military advisors to the Salvadoran armed forces, writing in the same year, disagreed and said that the FMLN's "commitment to victory is absolute and unbending" (Bacavich et al. 1988:93).

Apart from political education, lessons in reading, writing, and arithmetic were also promoted in part for their ideological effects: to keep combatants from developing an excessively militarist mentality. People from a variety of social origins believed that education mitigated the psychological effects of a decade of war.

Orlando, a combatant in Chalatenango: "We weren't guerrilla fighters just to fight, but to raise ourselves up and develop ourselves culturally. The purpose wasn't just to spew bullets, but to learn."

Lucía, a squadron leader: "We said we don't want to create an army that just thinks about taking up a rifle and killing, with a militarist attitude."

César, who directed the production of propaganda and educational materials in a clandestine print shop in Chalatenango: the FMLN educated "so that the compañero would not be a war machine, who joins up and his task is to shoot, shoot, and shoot, but would go through a process of growth."

Combatants received political education throughout the war. But it became more important with the change in strategy of 1984–1985. By then it was clear that the FMLN had been overly optimistic about a quick victory, and that a strategy based on large-scale military confrontations could not be sustained over the long haul. Beginning in 1984 an intense Air Force bombing campaign against FMLN-controlled zones forced much of the population to flee. The large camps in which combatants were concentrated were vulnerable to bombing raids and costly to maintain.

The FMLN therefore decided to try to avoid major confrontations with the Salvadoran army and to abandon much of the territory it controlled. Most of its troops were grouped in small, mobile units, usually of seven to ten members, and deployed over a much wider area. Their mission was to carry out lightning attacks on military bases and other strategic targets. Troops were still occasionally massed for major operations, notably the 1989 offensive, but most actions were small in scale. This amounted to a return to the strategy of guerrilla war.

At the same time political work among civilians was stepped up. Until then the strategy had been mainly military. But the Salvadoran army, under the guidance of U.S. advisors, was initiating civic action as part of its counter-insurgency campaign. The dispersion of combatants and the expectation of a longer war left the FMLN more dependent on support from the civilian population. The new small military units therefore had to reach out to the population and attempt to penetrate and organize in areas where the FMLN had until then enjoyed little popular support. In this new phase, known as the War of the Whole People (*Guerra de Todo el Pueblo*), the FMLN placed greater reliance on civilian support and accordingly emphasized local organizing. (The military and political dimensions of the change in strategy are discussed in Byrne 1996:144–145, 158–159; FMLN, Comandancia General 1985; Harnecker 1993:242–274; and Mena Sandoval 1991:333–352.)

The FMLN had expected a quick victory; when it did not occur, combatants' morale weakened. They needed to be fired up. Political work with civilians, moreover, required articulate convictions and skill at organizing. Both circumstances put a premium on ideological work. They also made new demands that many combatants found difficult. This strategic reorientation, Nacho said, "created problems within the fighting forces, because people joined up in hot pursuit of victory. Then when they were told that the victory was far away, and no one knew when, lots of them deserted. So we decided that all the internal education should have a clarity about purposes, and about the causes which produced the struggle, and the need to keep going forward until we achieve the goal."

Combatants had to be able to present the FMLN's political position persuasively. This meant that they had to be sure of the message and be trained in propaganda and organizing techniques. Even if they had a strong gut feeling of oppression from their own experience, they still had to learn to articulate it and communicate it in the communities. Their goal was to bring the population into legal, open organizations such as cooperatives and campesino organizations that would both promote their own interests and support the FMLN's struggle.

Sometimes combatants went into communities the FMLN had attacked, leaving suspicion and resentment which they had to overcome. They asked permission to sleep under the eaves of houses; they bought food rather than taking it (unless it was offered); and they were careful not to insist when people did not even want to sell it. Most important, they had to learn the attitude of the organizer who comes to talk to people in their own language about their problems, and to help find solutions.

Combatants came from communities very much like those in which they now undertook propaganda and organizing campaigns. Still, Norma said, they had to be reminded that "they are not superior to the civilian population; they are equal, and those people are their reason for being there. This fundamental reorientation [*readecuación orgánica*] of the FMLN was really very difficult."

Training combatants to be organizers was a goal of political education courses. The pamphlet *The Fifteen Principles of the Guerrilla Combatant* was adopted by the General Command in 1985 and circulated among the troops to educate them in proper respect toward the civilian communities they were working to organize. Special schools which had trained squadron leaders in advanced military skills now broadened their curriculum to train them as organizers. At the Comandante Clelia school,[10] founded in 1985 in Morazán, soldiers—sometimes as many as five hundred at a time—took courses that combined military training, intensive instruction in specialties, and propaganda work. They also received basic instruction, intended to bring them up to fourth-grade level (Mena Sandoval 1991:333–339). At the Adán Díaz school in San Vicente and the José Dimas Alas school in Chalatenango, squadron leaders were brought together with campesino leaders from civilian communities for political training. Squadron leaders passed their political training on to the combatants in their units, giving them both political education and training in organizing skills.

Instructors in these schools, many of them relatively well educated city people, often commented that the combatants receiving the training were shy about addressing public meetings. As Mario noted, however, "With time they break down the shyness. It's not the same to communicate with your family or your friends at home, as to show up in a community and bring together two or three hundred people you don't know and try to get everyone to understand you. We all did this by practice at first, in the course of the war." Comandante Mariana Chicas similarly noted that many seemed reluctant to participate actively in classes. But popular education pedagogy provided techniques to break down their reserve and stimulate their participation: "We started with *dinámicas*, games to break the ice and get them over their inhibitions to participate more actively."

The shyness, however, was at least in part the misperception of the outsiders, reflecting urban prejudices of campesino inferiority. Shyness may have been due as much to having to perform in front of better educated members of the guerrilla army as to the large size of the community meetings. The reticence of campesinos in front of those they perceive as their superiors is to some extent a measure of self-protection, one not readily abandoned even with superiors with whom they share the rigors of combat and guerrilla life. But many combatants, even new recruits with no special political training, spoke out at meetings. Alberto (who was quoted above) had been to high school, but claimed that addressing a meeting in a community required no special skill. "I admire those campesinos who have an easy-going manner and know how to express themselves. They've broken down the barriers and said, 'I can do it!'" They were often recognized as more effective propagandists than their superiors, because the people of the communities they addressed felt the same distance from more educated combatants as the campesino combatants did, but related more easily to less polished speakers.

Education and Stratification among the Troops

Teaching people was an expression of the FMLN's battle against inherited inequality. Yet inequalities that weigh heavily in Salvadoran society—between people of different social backgrounds and between men and women—made a difference even within the guerrilla army. Those who came from high-status backgrounds and had good educations were more likely to ascend in rank; they also shared some of their society's prejudices against campesinos. Most of the highest command positions went to people from cities with some university education; relatively few campesinos rose to be comandantes. Combatants with relatively high education levels (sixth grade or junior high school, for example) were more likely to receive training in specialties requiring intellectual skills. Some of them were campesinos, but most campesinos were foot soldiers. The FMLN made conscious efforts to overcome these differences, but they continued to tell.

Even the commitment to educating the troops put the well educated in superordinate positions. Despite a shared commitment to the belief that all participants in popular education were equal, in practice the relation of teacher to student reflected their unequal social origins. Nor were the urbanites exempt from the disparaging attitudes toward campesinos that prevailed in their culture, which underlay, for example, their perception of campesinos' "shyness."

Thus the very social inequalities the FMLN aimed to destroy operated within the guerrilla army. Education may even have been a more important mark of social status for combatants than in civilian life because there were few material differences; for guerrilla fighters in the field, command and specialist positions carried few perquisites.

Inequalities in social background were overcome to a significant degree (though they weigh heavily in this discussion because they were particularly relevant to education). Even if they were not overcome completely, however, the FMLN expressed a genuine commitment to educating all combatants, manifest not only abstractly in its egalitarian ideology but concretely in its educational practice. As I have emphasized, the FMLN educated people for both practical and principled reasons: to provide trained personnel capable of performing military functions and to fulfill the revolutionary aspiration to a society of equality that would recognize and promote the full capacities of all people.

The very fact of fighting in the same units gave urbanites the opportunity to appreciate campesinos' ingenuity and ability to live off the land: they were more familiar with the rural terrain, and they were physically tougher. A mystique of combat, which promoted respect for pure military skill and devalued intellectual work, inverted the prevailing hierarchy, honoring the superior skills of those who had grown up in the countryside. This inversion affected people of urban and rural origin alike. Some urban, well-educated combatants felt compelled to prove themselves in combat, like César, who left his position directing a propaganda workshop: "I felt it was a moral duty to go fight. A campesino who had barely learned to read and write had no other choice but to fight. It would be very convenient to hide behind a typewriter when thousands and thousands are dying." Though he justified his decision in moral terms, we can infer that he also felt a desire to prove himself.

Even some campesinos who were no better educated than most combatants also felt inferior for not being on the front lines. Francisca was a young woman refugee who trained the youth in a Honduran refugee camp to return to El Salvador to join the guerrilla army. But because she had never been a combatant, she said, "I didn't feel I had much moral credit to be saying to those guys, 'Look, this is what life is like at the front.'"

At the same time, according to Lucía, "people from the mountains tended to put down those who came from the city, to say that they were queers [*maricones*], that they'd never been sleeping in the mountains or putting up with shit [*verga*]." Many combatants resisted political education because it was usually taught by city boys and seemed abstract and unrelated to the skills they prized. One of the limits to popular education during the conflict was the fact that many uneducated combatants saw no point in mastering intellectual skills when they wanted to excel at combat.

Gender inequality also prevailed among the combatants. Several guerrilla movements of the 1970s (notably Nicaragua's Sandinistas, Peru's Shining Path, and Uruguay's Tupamaros, as well as the FMLN) had relatively high numbers of women combatants—about 30 percent in the FMLN—making them significantly different from earlier Latin American movements (Chinchilla 1983; Mason 1992:64; Reif 1986; Wickham-Crowley 1992:215). But inequality between women and men was confronted even less directly than class inequality. A few women became comandantes, but most performed the traditional tasks of their gender. Many were health workers. Another common women's specialization, as short-wave radio operators, demanded a technical training rare among women civilians, but the *radista's* central position in military communications meant, as Norma observed, that she was essentially the squadron leader's secretary.[11]

Nor was education consciously deployed to combat gender-determined role assignments. Gender differences were discussed in education for women, however.[12] Speaking of health workers' training, Norma said, "Since most of them were women, we introduced the theme of women—without much vision of gender, because we hadn't even heard the word 'gender'—but to make them value their work [and reinforce] their self-esteem." Since "the fundamental thing was the armed struggle," and women doing health work were on the sidelines, a woman in a leadership position was regularly invited to health workers' training sessions to talk about "their participation in the process [and tell them] that we are in a situation of equality with the compañeros. We realized that the women devalued themselves, and so did the men [devalue the women]. The *Frente* [FMLN] has its macho side. So that was one aspect, directed at their self-esteem: 'your participation is just as important as the men's. That one may be a combatant, and you may be a health worker, but you're not worth less.'"

Some problems arose predictably in mixed units. Sessions in gender consciousness addressed them too, Norma said. "The other issue was the dignity of the compañeras. The war—separation from your parents, and from your children, the fact that you might die tomorrow—made you experience relationships between couples very immediately. So you could have a very intense relationship with one man, and then the next day have one with someone else, because you didn't know if you were going to die the day after. This injured the compañeras' dignity and created instability. So we tried to raise their dignity and—without imposing traditional rules, that this is the man for your whole life—encourage stability between couples." Even as Norma tentatively raised gender issues, she revealed the inescapable influence of El Salvador's macho culture, for she took for granted that having more than one partner damages a woman's self-respect—but not a man's—and that women are more likely than men to be the victims in sexual relations.

As with popular education generally, consciousness-raising among women combatants served several purposes combining military necessity and principled struggle: sexual relations caused problems in combat units and also raised issues of equality between men and women. Even though gender education barely addressed the substantial inequalities between men and women, which prevailed among combatants as among civilians, for women incorporation into the guerrilla army was a new experience that undermined prevailing norms, and thereby provided an opening for ideas that had hardly been raised at any level of Salvadoran society previously.

Morale, Combat Capacity, and the Outcome of the War

The FMLN fought the Salvadoran army to a draw despite overwhelming odds against it. The full story of the war's outcome will be told below, but I anticipate it here to examine further the question of the place of morale and combat effectiveness in the FMLN's relative success. As mentioned above, some scholars dismiss the contribution of morale to military success and argue that the outcome of a guerrilla war depends on structural factors to which the combat capacity of the insurgency is irrelevant. But the FMLN held its own even though macropolitical factors—the composition of the insurgency and of the ruling bloc, and limited democratic reforms in the early 1980s—clearly predicted its defeat.

Among scholars who adopt the structural argument, Timothy P. Wickham-Crowley explicitly examines El Salvador and denies that insurgent morale and combat capacity were important in determining the outcome. I therefore take him as an example.[13] He misunderstands the political complexion of the Salvadoran insurgency. He implies repeatedly that members of the urban elite who start guerrilla movements cannot attract campesinos with a program of shared goals but only by offering them material incentives. He regards campesino organizations like those founded in El Salvador during the 1970s as "structures of access" through which an elite guerrilla force recruits combatants, rather than as an integral part of an insurgency. As selective incentives a guerrilla movement provides quasi-governmental services, including literacy education. But to treat education as a "service" ignores what I have shown: that those who taught and learned were not passive recipients but took an active part, thereby ratifying their worth and acting on their ideological commitment to equality.[14] (The same can be said of other "services" like collective self-defense and health care.)

Wickham-Crowley assumes that peasants are rational individualists, and that he can therefore ignore their beliefs and community commitments. He adopts what van Creveld (1991:64) calls the Clausewitzian view of war as a rational extension of a conflict of interests. But as van Creveld says, instrumental rationality cannot explain willingness to enter conflicts as unequal as the guerrilla wars of recent decades. Against such long odds, only commitment to a transcendent ideal justifies the risk, which is why a guerrilla army cultivates the combatants' commitment.

Wickham-Crowley called a 1989 article "Explaining Failed Revolution in El Salvador," and he repeated his assertion that the insurgency had failed in a subsequent book (1992:210). But while it fell short of victory, the peace settlement the FMLN reached with the Salvadoran government in 1992 can hardly be counted as a failure. And though the outcome may have been unknown when he completed the book, Wickham-Crowley's unambiguous prediction of failure calls into question the validity of the theory for the Salvadoran case.

Rejection of one explanation does not prove any particular alternative, but it does cast doubt on that explanation's implications. If the FMLN did better than would otherwise be predicted, its combat capacity may have made a difference. My evidence about the practice of education and combatants' testimonies of its importance show that it contributed to morale, and thereby to combat capacity. Particularly after the strategic reorientation of 1984–1985, the FMLN's military effectiveness depended heavily on combatants' motivation and initiative. Education gave them combat skills and raised their morale by expressing confidence in their ability to be educated.

Nevertheless, the battle against illiteracy, like the war itself, was a mixed success. There is no systematic evidence to tell how many combatants learned or failed to learn. It is likely that success among the guerrilla fighters would compare favorably to that of the Salvadoran public school system, especially if one considers not only the success rate among those who received education but also the scope of access, for many learned in the FMLN who had never been to school.

Education always took second place to fighting the war. And it was most successful when it addressed the practical needs of combat or political organization. Some combatants who had had a year or two of school as children said that it had not taken, and that they had really learned only in the guerrilla army. There they immediately applied their newly acquired skills to practical tasks, and consolidated what they had learned. Claudio taught students who were made radio operators as soon as they had learned the basics: "Compañeros who had studied got their practice there with the radio, writing and decoding messages. The practice of spending twenty-four hours a day working with a pencil, writing messages, made them improve their writing, without having to be doing exercises in a notebook."

Some advanced spectacularly. Said Mariana Chicas: "We start teaching everyone to read, and some stand out—they have a certain vocation, and they get promoted to different specialties. There are compañeros who are radio operators, health workers, or even in charge of a structure who started out from nothing." César, who ran the propaganda workshop, had many opportunities to see newly literate people working at tasks that demanded well-developed skills, "whether in communication, or in health, or in propaganda, or in international work. The result was excellent. Many compañeros learned to read and write there and now they can run computer systems."

Gustavo, the radio operator who explained that teaching others to read was part of teaching them how to get a message right, was himself a product of guerrilla education: he completed first grade when he was twelve years old, in 1980, and immediately joined the guerrilla army because it was safer than staying in his village. There he continued his education: he learned to type, to intercept and translate coded radio transmissions, and he was trained in propaganda; he took an accelerated course for combatants at the end of the war and passed a ninth grade equivalency exam. "I did it little by little," he said. He was almost astonished at the abilities he discovered in himself: "I began to feel confident with the little bit I had managed to learn, because now I could operate all the machines." Of his fellow workers in a communications center, he said, "nobody had been to sixth grade. All of us had only been to first grade or second grade, but as time passed we caught up."

The teachers' stories of their pupils' progress and dedication convey their conviction that the process was effective. But their enthusiasm about their pupils is often modestly veiled delight at proving their own competence. The impact on the combatant-teachers themselves, few of whom had ever thought of themselves as intellectually skilled, must be counted as one of the educational process's important effects. As Claudio put it, "This thing of popular education has been like a discovery that it is possible to do it."

Some comandantes claimed that everyone learned to read, but they exaggerated. At the war's end there were still many, especially militia members and those who had joined recently, who had not even gotten the rudiments of literacy, and others who had only achieved limited ability. But even some of them felt the impact. Oscar, who called himself a dummy, learned a little in the war but admitted that when he wanted to write a letter he had to get someone to help him. But he still felt that the experience of studying had made a difference: "It makes you think more about your family; that you never learned anything, and what if your family didn't either? So you try to see to it that those kids do learn."

Some of the shortfall was due to material obstacles, but not all of it. Some illiterate combatants simply resisted, immune to instrumental persuasion, moral incentives, and peer pressure. Nor were all comandantes and unit leaders fully responsive. According to Norma, "sometimes even the squadron leaders [*jefes*] were lazy. Generally squadron leaders of campesino origin were less interested, because our campesinos, who never had a chance to study, have grown up without education. Leaders who came from the cities were a little more aware of the need for literacy and political education."

Asked what was the greatest difficulty she had encountered in ten years of supervising educational and cultural activities among the troops of Morazán, comandante Mariana Chicas responded, "getting people to take it seriously. Not that they rejected it, but sometimes it was left as something secondary, and people didn't follow up. So we tried to get the person in charge to assure that people would be there on time, and on a regular basis, not do it one day and the next day not."

But most in the command structure did believe that education was necessary and promoted it seriously. The FMLN's commitment was demonstrated, for example, by its use of its own media to promote literacy, as in a "commercial" on Radio Venceremos in 1991, a dialogue between two very hip-sounding young men (my transcription, from memory):

"Did you check out what was in the paper today?"

"How do you know what was in the paper? I thought you couldn't read."

"You're right that I *couldn't*. But now I've learned to read in the National Army for Democracy."

"Don't bullshit me! [*¡No jodás!*]"

"It's true. Besides, I'm there with all my compañeros and we're fighting together for a more just society."

Even prisoners of war were taught. Captured government soldiers were encouraged to remain voluntarily and join the guerrilla army (though they were normally returned in prisoner exchanges), and a school was created in Morazán for prisoners who were regarded as likely prospects. Conversely, Colonel Francisco Adolfo Castillo, undersecretary of defense, taught FMLN combatants to read during his two years as a prisoner of war (Mena Sandoval 1991:21–328; López Vigil 1991:174–181, 288).

Finally, education was important enough that the FMLN negotiated educational benefits for combatants as part of the peace settlement. During a year-long demobilization period when combatants were quartered in camps with no

FIGURE 4. Literacy class for combatants during cease-fire, Chalatenango, 1993. *Photo copyright © Donna DeCesare.*

military activity, full-time instructors conducted classes to enable them to consolidate what they had learned and receive equivalency certificates at the elementary, junior high, and high school levels (though even then some combatants who had not learned to read during the war resisted attending classes). When it ended, every demobilized combatant (and every government soldier) was eligible for either farmland or a scholarship to continue studying.

Because education had several purposes, its success is not reducible to the number who learned to read and write. It was also intended to foster the analytical capacity and breadth of vision that would be needed to run a new society. The FMLN educated to lay the basis for a society in which human abilities would be fully cultivated. According to comandante Héctor Martínez, who fought in Chalatenango, education was an expression of optimism that all those who learned would "participate in the social and economic development of society. With these people it will be possible to raise the social level."

And for comandante Nidia Díaz, "The Frente has always sought the integral development of the human being. And education plays a crucial role, so that people can develop, not only to transform society, but to prepare themselves to run it."

These claims about the purpose of general education are stated in highly general terms. As with the claims about political and ideological education discussed earlier, however, the extent to which they were put into practice demonstrates that they were not mere rhetoric. The influence of these expansive views about human development is visible in the process, scope, and effects of the FMLN's educational practice. Popular education joined the practical and the ideal: to assure military success and to assure that the war would lay the basis for a new and reordered society, education to improve the skills and raise the commitment of the combatants played a central role in military strategy.

CHAPTER 4

Protected Spaces

REFUGEE CAMPS AND PRISONS

---

*T*here were other protected spaces besides the front that were beyond the reach of the Salvadoran government and army; popular education continued in these places after the war began. They included refugee camps in Honduras, and prisons, where political prisoners virtually controlled daily life within the walls. In this chapter I present and compare the process of education in these two sites during the war.

There might appear to be little basis for comparing the two. Refugee camps sheltered people who were driven from their homes against their will; the refugees lived as families, and some of them stayed for as long as nine years. The camps were maintained by the United Nations and other international agencies. Prisons, on the other hand, housed people accused of subversion; they were single-sex institutions (though some children lived with their mothers in the women's prison), and the turnover was high—some people were released and others were captured. Thus in the refugee camps, schools were formed for children, and educators could plan for a relatively long term; they received training, supplies, and equipment from donor agencies; whereas prisoners had to confront their captors' hostility toward their efforts to learn—and indeed, they made education one of the ways in which they challenged their captors' power.

But the two sites were also similar in important ways. Like prisoners, refugees felt they were confined against their will. Refugees and prisoners alike organized to keep themselves busy, to work, to pressure the authorities to improve their conditions, and to teach and learn. They presented themselves as victims to remind the outside world that they had been uprooted or captured unfairly and were unjustly confined, but they refused to submit as victims. Instead they struggled against the restrictions imposed on them. Educating themselves was one more sign of refusal. As they challenged the confinement of the present moreover, they also challenged the submission of the past, which had been enforced in part by their exclusion from education.

Seeking Safe Haven

Popular education was most advanced in the refugee camps in Honduras. There it was not just a part-time, after-hours activity but a major commitment of the whole community; between children and adults, it reached a very high proportion of the people.

The camps were established in 1980 and 1981 when the flood of refugees began, responding to the escalating repression. Targeted killings by death squads gave way to army operations that threatened everyone in some rural areas. Until then women had usually been safe when death squads came hunting for the men; but then army operations began rounding everyone up and burning their houses down. Whole families went to sleep in the mountains, like Rosario from Meanguera in Morazán. "We weren't being left in peace," she said, "because the soldiers were always passing through, burning houses, murdering people. When the army showed up at our houses, we had to flee to someplace else. Some relatives of mine stayed, and they were murdered. They killed an aunt of mine, and her daughter, and the little children. She was pregnant: they killed her, they pulled out the baby, they burned her. So we left. We went and slept in the mountains. At the end we were sleeping in the mountains for three months in a row."

Eventually it became clear to campesinos like Herminio that the only safe course was to cross the border into Honduras:

> There was a repression, and we couldn't live here. They always hated us as campesinos. So we had to leave, because we couldn't work on our own land or go someplace else to earn a salary.
>
> *Who was repressing you?*
>
> The Army. They came and burned houses. They killed children, old people, and young people too. It didn't matter whether you belonged to an organization. There was just a repression, and what they did was kill, burn the houses, and chase you away. They said, "If you don't go, the next time we'll kill you."
>
> *Did the army threaten you personally?*
>
> Yes. They found me working at home. Thanks to God, that time I saved myself. I think it was an injustice that they went around killing us for the hell of it [*de gusto*].
>
> *And when did you go to Honduras?*
>
> I went in '80, with my family, ten people. But they killed my mother and my niece.

Some stuck it out in the areas of conflict for the decade of war, although with difficulty. Others did not do so well. Some, like Rosario's and Herminio's relatives, were murdered when they were taken by surprise in their homes, others in major roundups when whole villages were slaughtered. The worst massacre of the war was in El Mozote, a village of Morazán, where a reported one thousand people—men, women, and children—were slaughtered in three days in December 1981 (Binford 1996; Danner 1994).

Many who made it across the border reported that Honduran villagers gave them food. Others, not so lucky, encountered the hostile Honduran army, which drove many of them back into El Salvador. Some refugees were caught in hammer-and-anvil operations between the two countries' armies, such as the one in May 1980 on the Sumpul River, the border between Honduras and El Salvador's Chalatenango department; as the refugees tried to swim across, Honduran troops drove them back into the river where Salvadoran soldiers could fire on them. More than six hundred people were killed.

The refugee crisis was an intended consequence of U.S. counterinsurgency policy in the 1980s, which called for low-intensity conflict and required driving the civilian population out of an area of insurgency (Gordenker 1987; Miles 1986; Neier 1989; Zolberg, Suhrke, and Aguayo 1989). According to Mao Zedong, the people are the sea in which the fish—the guerrilla army—swim. The response of counterinsurgency, then, is to drain the sea by killing the people or driving them out. Honduras cooperated by keeping the refugees under military guard. (In exchange for military assistance, the Honduran government let its territory become the beachhead for U.S. intervention in Central America, and governed its policy toward Nicaraguan and Salvadoran refugees to support the U.S. policies toward their countries of origin. Nicaraguans in refugee camps in the southern part of the country, who were generally hostile to the Sandinista government, came and went with fewer restrictions, and the contras recruited freely in their camps.)

As the flow of refugees turned into a flood, the United Nations High Commission for Refugees (UNHCR) and Caritas, the international Catholic relief agency, began to provide food and construction materials to build houses. The refugees in Honduras were concentrated in three border villages: Colomoncagua near the department of Morazán; San Antonio, opposite Cabañas department; and La Virtud, facing Chalatenango (the refugees at La Virtud were later moved to Mesa Grande, fifty kilometers from the border). In 1988 there were more than 15,000 refugees in these camps: 8,000 in Colomoncagua, 6,000 in Mesa Grande (where the number had been over 11,000), and 1,200 in San Antonio. The number fluctuated as some refugees chose to repatriate. A few families at a time left to go to peaceful areas of El Salvador, especially San Salvador; beginning in 1987, groups numbering in the thousands repatriated to rebuild depopulated villages in the war zones.

In the camps, refugees were highly organized. They governed themselves and kept order among thousands of people crowded into a small space. Many of them were veterans of the base communities, peasant organizations, and emerging political-military organizations of the 1970s. They applied their organizing experience in the camps. In the political movement they had acquired a vision of a good society, in which all would work together for their mutual benefit, and the refugee camps offered an opportunity to put that vision into practice. The more experienced among them assumed leadership positions and promoted a communitarian ethos that encouraged all the refugees to join in learning and working.

In camps around the world, international agencies provide refugees with the goods they need for subsistence, under the leadership of UNHCR. By 1980, however, relief agencies began to recognize that their assistance often made refugees dependent; during the cold war's last decade, moreover, millions of people fled from conflicts on several continents, increasing the demands on the agencies' scarce resources and forcing them to cut costs. They therefore sought "durable solutions" that would permit refugees to be self-sufficient (Loescher and Monahan 1989; Stein 1986).

Living conditions in the Honduran camps were difficult. Housing was crowded—in Colomoncagua, most families lived doubled up, with as many as twenty people to a two- or three-room house—and rations were short. But even though they had just suffered the traumas of war and flight and had come together in a strange setting, the discipline with which the refugees ran the camps made the relief agencies regard them as among the best organized refugees in the world. They organized committees to run schools, health campaigns, work, and the distribution of relief supplies; to attend to the needs of children and elderly people; and to conduct worship and catechism.

Though the relief agencies provided food and other goods, the refugees wanted to work to meet their own needs as much as possible. Some worked the land and tended animals, and their produce was divided among the whole community. But within the perimeter of the camps where they were confined by the Honduran army, there was not much land to farm. So they persuaded the agencies to set up workshops where they learned new trades. They made shoes, hats, furniture, hammocks, pottery, tin pots and pans, musical instruments, handicrafts, toys, and other goods. (In Colomoncagua there was even an auto repair shop—the refugees had no cars, of course, but they maintained the cars and trucks of the relief agencies.) In these surprisingly well-equipped workshops, refugees learned skills that were unknown in their villages. Most able-bodied adults worked. Children, too, who went to school half of each day, spent the other half in a training workshop. The agencies supplied the materials, but the camps were self-sufficient in most of the goods produced.

Communal tortilla kitchens had a dramatic impact on the daily life of women. Instead of having rations distributed in the form of cornmeal, some women worked making tortillas that were then distributed to the households. This freed women from one of their most time-consuming tasks so that they could participate in other kinds of work.

Highly organized camps could be a mixed blessing to the agencies, for the refugees also organized to press their demands for better living conditions—an extension of activities in which they had participated in El Salvador. For example, refugees in all three camps in Honduras went on a fast in June 1988 to protest their poor physical conditions and Honduran army harassment. The fast was well organized and clandestinely coordinated among the three camps; the number of participants escalated daily for several weeks. Refugees sometimes portrayed UNHCR as an enemy that deliberately withheld benefits to which they were justly entitled, and they enlisted international support.

But the real enemy was outside. The camps in Colomoncagua and San Antonio were close enough to the border for refugees to hear the sounds of battles in El Salvador, and they claimed that Salvadoran soldiers sometimes raided. Nevertheless they were nearly always safe from the Salvadoran army. But the Honduran high command accused them of providing logistical support to the guerrilla army in El Salvador. Honduran troops patrolled and frequently harassed them, capturing and torturing refugees they accused of being guerrilla soldiers. They even captured children and tried to get information from them. A few refugees were killed in these raids. The refugees did give support to the FMLN, though publicly they denied it. Young people were recruited into the guerrilla army. Combatants who were wounded or pregnant often left the front to spend several months in a camp. (If their mothers returned to combat, babies stayed in the care of grandmothers or other relatives.)

Refugees Learn and Teach

Education became a central activity in the refugee camps for young and old alike. These camps became a model of popular education for communities in El Salvador and throughout the western hemisphere. With few alternatives to idleness, the large populations of the camps constituted a captive (albeit willing) audience for schooling. Campesinos who had grown up living in isolation and farming the land individually learned a new way of life. Now they worked collectively, they learned industrial and administrative skills, and they went to school.

Idleness is the biggest problem of many refugees worldwide. Salvadoran refugees kept themselves busy working and learning. They emphasized education for the same reason they had promoted it at home before the war: literacy was an essential skill, a necessary step to liberation, and a means to larger political goals. For all these reasons it was seen as a political duty. Many campesinos who had never before felt much need to learn were persuaded to take up the task on political grounds.

Education began in the camps almost by accident, as a way to keep children out of trouble. According to Julia, eighteen years old when she fled to Colomoncagua, "We took that horde of little kids to play. Those of us who were a little bigger played with the little ones. We tried to make little soccer balls out of pieces of paper or nylon and tied them up with string."

More was needed, however: they should be in school. But there were no teachers. So the task fell to the refugees who had been to school, if only for a few years. Gabriela had a third-grade education.

They said we should find people who knew how to read and write, so that they could teach those children, so they wouldn't just be idling, because they weren't free to go anywhere and had no place to play. The place was very small. They came to me and asked if I was willing to teach. I said yes, I would share what I knew.

There was nothing to write with: no pencils, no chalk. We used pieces of coal, or even stones. We started teaching the children their letters. But then some foreigners started arriving. Some Nicaraguan nuns came and saw that we were interested in having education, so they sent us some paper and pencils. We would break these pencils in half to give a piece to each child. We were out in the open air, sitting on rocks. And when we started in the open air, we carried boards that we could use as blackboards. To save paper, if they didn't get it right, they erased it until they got it right.

Bad as the physical conditions were, the newly recruited teachers were even more sensitive about their own shortcomings. "When they met with me to ask me to work in education," Rosario worried, "I felt pretty inadequate, because I hadn't done it before. I had been to third grade. And I felt that maybe I couldn't handle it."

Many of the recruited teachers doubted their ability but acquiesced only because they wanted to share "the little bit I know." There was no false modesty in the phrase. Even if they had been to school, it had only been for a few years, and a long time ago. But they agreed to take on the task out of conciencia— commitment and responsibility to the community. On arriving in Colomoncagua, Rosario first helped in the distribution of food because, knowing how to read and write, she could keep the records. Then she was sent to work in a health center. Then she was asked to teach. In each case she complied willingly; when I asked what she would have done if she hadn't wanted to change jobs, she replied simply, "But one saw what was needed there."

Putting their heads together and remembering their own schooling from long ago, new teachers invented activities for the children, "singing with them, playing, making circles with them," Luisa said. "Some people remembered one song, others another of the ones we had learned before. So we started singing and teaching them to the children. But it's true, we never dreamed that one day we would be teachers, because we had never been before."

At first they did not even have cartillas, so people teaching the same class in different parts of the camp met to work out their lesson plans, Ramón said, "to teach just one thing in every subcamp. What you're teaching here, I'm teaching in another subcamp, and someone else in the other one." Gabriela remembered: "we prepared, we talked everything out. So what one person taught, the other one taught too. We always met to see how to do it. We thought up what to do: we would do the vowels, we would start with a few letters. For children who already knew a little, we gave simple words, like mama and papa."

Ramón and Gabriela explained their meetings as if they were for quality control. But they had other purposes as well: first of all, everyone got an idea of what to do next. Because they had no training as teachers, they concentrated on rote learning methods: write a simple "generative" word and a family of syllables on the board (or on a box recovered from the garbage) and have all the kids copy it, as the teacher walks among them and checks their work. But teachers also met because they were committed to collaboration as a governing principle of community life. "Everything was communal" in Mesa Grande, said Alfonso, who taught there. "For example, pupils had duties to fulfill. Second and third graders would water the vegetable gardens, or prepare hot milk for the old people. The teacher gave classes in the morning, and then in the afternoon got together with everyone: if there were four teachers of first grade, they got together, and no one moved on to the next topic without a decision by all four of them."

Education went on outside the classroom as well. In the workshops people learned both craft skills and organizational techniques. Some refugees became health workers. Besides learning basic diagnosis and treatment, they ran health campaigns in which they taught all the refugees sanitation and preventive measures.

Plant and equipment were gradually improved. After a few years the war was less intense and the flow of refugees slowed considerably. Yet the war was clearly going to go on, and the refugees and the relief agencies alike recognized that they would be there for a long time. They built more permanent buildings, including schools. "Now," said Gabriela, "we didn't have to endure the rain. Now we didn't have to endure the sun. Now the children sat on benches. Now we could make drawings and put them up on the walls." Conditions were still far from ideal: in some school buildings, several classes met in a single large room divided at best by canvas, so there was no way to shut out the noise. But they had lights—lanterns at first, then electric light from a power plant—making night school possible.

The long stay created an opportunity. Most adult refugees had never been to school, and now they had the chance. Adult classes were offered at night for those who worked during the day. Others worked only half a day and studied the other half, especially some of the younger adults (anyone over thirteen was considered an adult and expected to work), who went to the higher grade classes offered in the afternoons.

There were also classes in the afternoon for elderly people (who were not expected to work), to take advantage of daylight, because many complained that their poor eyesight made it hard for them to read by lantern light. Refugee camps received donations of eyeglasses. Learning to read and write was a major new experience for many old people. Remembering her first adult classes, Rosario said, "Some of them held a pencil like this," making a fist. Some older people thought it was too much trouble to learn when they had so little time left in life to take advantage of it, but they were urged and entreated. Alfredo, a teacher in

FIGURE 5. Refugee, Colomoncagua. *Photograph by Steve Cagan.*

Mesa Grande, was one who argued to persuade them. "As the Cuban poet José Martí said, education begins in the cradle and ends in the grave. That means there's no age for education; one can do it at any age."

The basic method for teaching reading was the same as elsewhere. Students discussed and reflected on a generative word and then learned to write it. Ramón gave the example of "the word 'soldier.' What do soldiers do? What do they do to us? And we start motivating people. 'Why? Who? Why did they drive us here?'"

Concientización was incorporated into classes for children and adults. Children were invited to deal with the trauma of war by drawing pictures of the bombing they had lived through. A common motif was a triptych, with a picture of a village at war, the refugee camp, and a village at peace to represent the past, the present, and the future. In Mesa Grande, according to Alfredo, "we started raising their consciousness, asking why they were bombing us, when we were in our own homes. The children understood because they had lived through it themselves."

I asked Ramón how children could understand such topics.

> With first graders you can explain it some. But many first graders there were already older children, since practically nobody knew how to read. They understood why they had gone there.
> *So you might have a seven-year-old kid and someone who was fifteen in the same class?*
> Back then, yes.

Discussions went deeper among adults, and nearly any word brought up associations to the war they had fled. Rosario told how a generative word might lead to reflection: "With the word 'house,' we could put 'Maria's house.' Then we could say 'the burned-down house.' Then it said, 'Maria's house was burned down.'" This story has a poignancy which the translation does not capture, because the words in Spanish have the simplicity of a first-grade text: instead of "see Spot run," *la ca-sa de Ma-rí-a e-ra que-ma-da.*

The war could not help but be a topic for reflection. Political interpretations—in whatever depth the understanding of the children or adult students permitted—infused the classes, not because a line was being laid down but in response to the refugees' real lives. The Freirean premise of starting with people's own experience determined the political content.

International attention to the Salvadoran war brought help to the refugee camp from abroad. Caritas sent supplies and equipment. The agency also recruited volunteers from Europe and the United States. Young people wanting to do a year or more of international service went to Honduras to work in the camps. Some with teaching degrees worked with the education program and trained the popular teachers. Informal meetings among teachers to discuss what they would teach were replaced by formal training sessions led by the internationals. Teachers now spent half of each day with their own classes and half the day in training.

When the system was fully in place, there was an advisor for each grade. Second-grade teachers, for example, taught their classes every morning and met in a group with the second-grade advisor all afternoon.

Often these training sessions simply concentrated on the material they were to present in class the next day. The training also emphasized improving teachers' general academic skills: they studied arithmetic, reading, and science at a higher level than the grade they were teaching. Formal training was important because education in the refugee camps, unlike most popular education before the war, went beyond the basics. Both children and adults advanced to the upper primary grades, and many teachers taught material they had never formally studied.

They also learned teaching methods. Teachers conducted practice classes in front of the advisor and the other teachers. The advisors taught pedagogy as well—"not abstractly," according to Anita, an advisor from Belgium, "but—what is the goal? What do we want to achieve with this topic, and how are we going to achieve it? For example, teaching language, we worked with generative words, so I had them prepare different words in small groups. And we always ended with a little story using that word. They did some nice things."

Children who showed academic talent were recruited as teachers after they had completed third grade or so. As the years in exile wore on and larger numbers of refugees completed the available offerings in the camps, new grades were added, and many refugee teachers were "promoted" almost every year to fill the new slots. This created a problem: if the most able and experienced teachers were moved up to the higher grades, those who gave children their all-important first experience of school might be the less able or the youngest, newest teachers. As with so many issues, scarcity inevitably forced choices and those conducting the schools simply had to do the best they could with the available means even as they recognized that those means were less than adequate.

In their classes, teachers regularly had students copy from the blackboard, not just lessons in writing but in all subjects—just as they do in Salvadoran public schools. A teacher learned a canned text (called a *guión*, or script) in a training session, then took it to class and wrote it up on the board. The pupils copied it into their notebooks and read it aloud in chorus and individually. With no books, these notebooks were the only material pupils had to read outside of class. But a pupil copying could easily make mistakes. Copying was also a prop for teachers who had not always fully mastered the lesson themselves.

Drawings were used widely. To illustrate a lesson, especially in science and social studies, teachers would copy a complicated drawing (such as a map or an anatomical diagram) from a book into their own notebooks, then put it on the blackboard, and students would copy it into their notebooks. Gabriela found this very difficult: "I never learned to draw. [A laugh.] It was the one thing I never learned. Everything else, all the other classes, I learned, but not drawing. I always looked for someone to make drawings for me so I could give them to the children, or to the adults." Others rose to the challenge, like Rufino: "I was interested in learning to draw. I had to draw on the blackboard until the drawing came out the way I wanted. I would use chalk, chalk, and more chalk until it was right."

While they often relied on canned lessons, popular educators also showed a delightful creativity. Games, skits, and songs were part of their tool kit. Teachers at Mesa Grande made up a song to help children learn the vowels (freely translated to preserve the rhymes):

> A, A, the parrot flew away;
> E, E, the parrot came to me;
> I, I, the parrot flew so high;
> O, O, the parrot flew so low;
> U, U, the parrot is you!

Teachers sometimes complained about the children's misbehavior, but advisors taught them how to get and hold their attention, Ramón said. "They taught how to motivate the group. Sometimes a child is very distracted. They arrive very excited, and if you tell them a little story they pay attention. They pay more attention when you say to them, 'Do you want me to tell you a riddle?'"

Several teachers, when asked what they had learned from the advisors, mentioned classroom games (*dinámicas*). Ramón used them to win the children's confidence, Rufino to calm them down when they were disruptive. Some games have a specific learning objective, while others serve mainly to release pent-up energy or are just for fun. (Those with a specific purpose are also fun.)

Games and recreation sometimes taught political lessons. Alfredo described singing with a class of children in Mesa Grande. "We went outside and joined hands in a circle, which meant unity, and we explained to the children that that's how we had to be: always united. This wasn't hard for children [to understand] because they were growing up in that environment."

In Colomoncagua, one training session a week was recreational. Advisors taught music, art, folk dancing, aerobics, sports, theater—some offering their own specialties, others their hobbies. Each teacher chose an area to concentrate on. They were discouraged from shopping around from week to week; they made a commitment to stay in a class for several months to learn the material in some depth. The theater group created its own plays and performed them throughout the camp. One play was about reading. Some people played letters of the alphabet which others struggled to understand.

Pupils who failed at the end of the year were held back. Requiring students to repeat was a common practice in official Salvadoran schools too. Teachers and parents regarded it as a measure of the schools' seriousness. It bore no particular stigma, but foreign advisors like Anita counseled greater flexibility. "I insisted on promoting them, because they repeat the grade, they think they know it, they don't pay attention, they play and waste time. Better to tell next year's teacher that that child has to shape up."

Despite draconian promotion practices, in general the attitude of advisors and teachers toward their students was one of warmth and encouragement. They believed that performance depended as much on good will and commitment as on native ability or training. Students would learn, it was assumed, with sufficient effort and attention. A student who was having difficulty had to try a little harder and the teacher had to offer more encouragement. After Rosario discussed exams and holding children back, she explained how she worked with adult students who were having trouble. "I had some elderly people who could read but had problems with writing—pretty serious problems. Some of them could move on to second grade, but you had to get closer to them to help them more."

Organizing to Combat Illiteracy

Some resisted learning, but others kept after them, like Alfredo. "'My father didn't know how to read and write. Why should I learn?' You have to teach them to discover new things. If they read the Bible, they can see that what is happening now is part of what went on two thousand years ago. It's part of Christian theology. Jesus wanted to spread it, and that's why he was killed. And now something is coming up just like Jesus said, and just as Jesus was killed, that's why our people are being killed."

To reinforce the reading ability of the newly literate, organizers of work areas presented the written word wherever possible. Health education posters were made for the health centers. Nutrition centers (where children, pregnant women, and old people got a snack every day, in addition to the food rations their families received) posted menus. Small libraries were established with donated books. Pamphlets about hygiene and bulletins on the political situation in El Salvador were reproduced and distributed.

In each camp, refugees formed an education committee to coordinate schooling. Their major task was to promote enrollment and attendance by persuading adults to go to school and urging parents to be sure their children attended. The entire camp leadership was committed to getting everyone educated, but it was up to the committee to see to it in practice, by calling public meetings and making house-to-house visits with those who had not signed up or were not attending. Elsa was one who responded:

> They told us it was important to know how to read. I liked the meetings a lot because they explained things.
> *Like what?*
> They said we had to educate the children, and we had to learn something too, to encourage the children so that they wouldn't grow up like we had, not knowing anything. My teacher, Lorenzo, explained that he was going to teach the little bit that he knew, but that we had to make an effort too, because he didn't know so much and he needed our help if he was going to teach us. We couldn't just sit there with our hands folded.

Although she had gone to school for a year as a girl, Elsa said, she had not really learned anything before her adult class in Colomoncagua.

Learning was made a political duty, and nearly everyone came through. In Colomoncagua, 85 percent of the refugees were illiterate when they arrived; when they returned home in 1989 and 1990, 85 percent knew how to read and only 15 percent were illiterate. At the end, about two-thirds of the camp's population was enrolled in school. Classes were offered up to sixth grade for children and to fifth grade for adults. Advanced students learned vocational skills such as typing, auto mechanics, and mechanical drawing in the small technical school. Occasional visitors offered short-term courses in more exotic skills such as administration, grant writing, and photography.

The education committee also had to deal with the danger the Honduran army posed to the children, Luisa said.

> They could go outside the camp to gather fruit, you know? So we had to make the teachers aware, and the teachers had to make the parents aware to avoid these captures. Because at one time they were capturing all the time, five children in a row.
>
> *And what could you do about it?*
>
> The people responsible for children had to tell them to keep inside the lines: "You can go this far, but no farther." And they had to stand and watch, and if they saw a child go beyond the line, they had to get him back. But the teachers also had to tell the kids in the classes not to go outside. Life was hard in Colomoncagua; it was practically a prison for us.

The committee also handled administrative matters, such as distribution of supplies. Setting policies regarding curriculum and pedagogy was not its main task; these decisions fell mostly to the advisors. They did consult the committee on some issues, and it generally welcomed their suggestions, Anita said. "You suggested any initiative to the education committee. They said, 'We'll think about it.' A week later they came back with the answer and they almost always accepted it. You said, 'Look, I need this, and this, and this many people,' and they gave it to you."

The refugees fought with the Honduran authorities over their right to run their own education. In 1987, Honduras demanded that UNHCR transfer administration of the camps from the voluntary agencies to its government refugee agency. This would have meant, among other things, that the education and training projects would be run by Honduran personnel, using the Honduran school curriculum (as was done in the camps for Nicaraguan refugees), and the refugees would lose both the support of the international volunteers and the right to provide for their own education. At the same time the government harassed the international volunteers by restricting their access to the camps. The refugees successfully resisted the change, although the government periodically raised the issue with UNHCR until the refugees began to prepare for their return to El Salvador.

Education profoundly affected all the refugees who took part in it. Adults who had never gone to school or had attended only briefly and learned little now had the chance to learn for the first time. Rito said that in Mesa Grande "I started out in grade school, except that I didn't go to kindergarten. I started with first grade and learned the vowels and all the letters."

As they acquired basic skills, refugees also chipped away at the sense of inferiority that they had in large measure internalized. Severino, who took refuge in Colomoncagua after teaching for several years in the guerrilla army, observed that "it was one of the most terrible things that the people who learned were the people who had money. That's who could be a teacher, that's who could become a lawyer, that's who could become a doctor. But campesinos never learned anything. I heard people say that whoever was born to be a doctor had to be a doctor, and whoever was born to be a campesino had to be a campesino. But in practice we see it isn't true. If people don't learn it's because of lack of opportunity or poverty."

When asked how he might encourage another adult to study, the newly literate Herminio said, "I would have to tell him my story. Because I started as an adult, and I learned, so it's not so hard." Campesinos are reluctant to draw attention to themselves, but Herminio could venture a little bragging to get others to follow his example.

It was the teachers on whom popular education had the greatest effect, for reasons discussed in more detail in chapter 6. Like many others who worked as popular teachers, Gabriela overcame her feelings of inadequacy:

> I felt very nervous about facing a whole group, whether children or adults, because I was very shy. Where I came from, I had never participated like that. If I went to a fair where there were a lot of people, I was shy just walking in the middle of so many people.
>
> *And how did you get over this shyness so you could teach classes?*
>
> The advisors had us get up in front, introduce ourselves, say our name, where we were from, in front of the other advisors and the other teachers. So I started getting over it. Lots of us were shy like that. We were ignorant, we didn't know much. How were we going to stand up in front of a group of people? But by now we've forgotten all that.

She proved to herself and the world that she could do it.

Teachers were proud to see their students advance. Alfredo described how his pupils felt when they put up their drawings: "The child is so happy to get up in front of the class, stick up a drawing, and it's left there." His broad smile as he remembered made clear that he had been as pleased as the child. Other teachers proudly reported that their students had gone on to learn more than they themselves had ever learned.

The sense of accomplishment made the burdens they shouldered worthwhile. Luisa "got up early to do my household chores, because I was happy to have that group of children. I felt happy playing games and teaching them to read and write, using the little bit I knew." Some of them worked a double shift in the classroom, teaching children in the morning and adults at night while spending the afternoon in training.

The teachers felt privileged to learn from the advisors, just as the advisors relished working with them. Gabriela said that "the foreign teachers who came gave us an opportunity to learn. They could open our minds that were blind, so to speak: we didn't know how to prepare something. These experiences helped us, and are helping us still today [in 1991, back in El Salvador], and they are things we'll never forget."

The teachers claimed little individual credit. Reluctant to draw attention to themselves, they were much more likely to applaud the accomplishments of their pupils or give credit to their advisors. Their own role was actually greater than they recognized. There had been no advisors at the beginning, after all; they had had to figure out how to start teaching on their own. Even when the advisors came it was still the teachers who put their counsel into practice. When they returned to El Salvador, many who had been teachers in the refugee camps became leaders in their communities because they were recognized as some of the most capable and well-trained people.

They repaid the debt they owed by their service to the community. Doing so, they were rewarded further when they saw the results. The desire to share "the little bit I know," while on the surface a confession of shortcomings, was also a statement of their commitment.

So the new learners gained from teachers, the teachers gained from their pupils and their advisors, the advisors in turn got something from the teachers they taught. But they did not see the process mainly as an exchange between Salvadorans and foreigners, or between professionals and popular teachers, or between any of them and new learners, as if each group's gains were distinct. Even though they were aware of differences, they felt like equal partners who all shared in any benefits that accrued to the community.

This enthusiasm and sense of reward could not quite overcome refugees' resentment at confinement and their desire to return home. Refugees struggled against their confinement and called it what it was. Alfredo explained why he chose to be both a teacher and a health worker in Mesa Grande: "It was a lot of work, but you learned a lot; and besides, being in a camp like that was like being in prison." (He had reason to know. After repatriating to El Salvador, he was detained in Mariona prison in 1986.) Luisa saw the chance to learn in Colomoncagua as an ambiguous blessing. "The refugee camp was a school for us. Of course it was a prison, but still it was a school." As we shall see when we examine popular education in prisons, the comparison is more apt than it might appear.

Internal Refugees

The camps in Honduras held only a small fraction of the hundreds of thousands who fled El Salvador during the war. Most refugees found other places to live: some settled in the towns and cities of the countries of Central America, or further afield in Mexico; at least half a million (10 percent of the country's population) emigrated to the United States. Those who lived in refugee communities in Nicaragua and Costa Rica taught and learned, although not on the same scale as in the Honduran camps.

Others fled, not across borders, but to the cities and towns of El Salvador. Technically, people who flee but remain within their own country's borders are considered "displaced persons" rather than "refugees," although they are often referred to as refugees as well. Many displaced people lived in shantytowns and earned a precarious living peddling on street corners or in other irregular work. Others found refuge in camps for displaced people created in the main cities and towns outside the war zones, especially in San Salvador where the archdiocese encouraged parishes to shelter them.

The church promoted education in these camps. Parish youth groups often took part, and the archdiocese had a paid staff that administered the camps. Adelinda joined the staff of the archdiocese after she left Aguilares, where she had been a catechist. She and a group of literacy workers went to Nicaragua to study the techniques of the literacy campaign there and bring them back to San Salvador.

Elena, a high school student and Christian base community member in the parish of Soyapango, near San Salvador, taught third and fourth grade to elderly people sheltered in the parish and learned about life from them. "Imagine a refugee center," she said, "where you don't do anything except mainly wait for mealtime to arrive. In the countryside what they do is go work in the field, or take care of animals, and they didn't do any of that."

Teachers in the displaced people's camps were often relatively well-educated, paid staff or volunteers, unlike those in the camps in Honduras, who were all refugees. These outsiders got a lot out of the contact. Elena said that she "wound up learning from them too, about life, apart from what people learned in the city, and about sufferings that I had never experienced. And I learned more about the Christian spirit." When they returned to a rural community, she went to live with them.

Refugees taught too. The archdiocese brought together refugee teachers from several camps to be trained and to collaborate in creating a cartilla. They chose a list of generative words and held a contest, asking refugees to submit drawings and selecting the best to be reproduced in the cartilla, entitled *Caminemos* (Let's walk or Let's go forward). Humberto, a popular teacher in the camp in Zaragoza, helped to write the cartilla and was proud that his drawing of a guitar had been included.

Education did not achieve the scope or success among the displaced that

FIGURE 6. *Cosecha* (harvest). *Caminenos: Cartilla de Alfabetización.* Archdiocesan Social
Secretariat, San Salvador, 1986.

it did in the Honduran refugee camps. Life was less stable. People could leave
more freely, and the camps had less international financial assistance. Moreover, the displaced people directed most of their energy toward getting out of
the camps and back to the countryside. When this became a realistic possibility, it took priority over education. The church looked for farms in relatively
peaceful areas where displaced people could move in a group and form cooperatives. The displaced people themselves pressured the government for permission
to return as civilians to the zones of conflict. Beginning with the repopulation
of San José las Flores in Chalatenango in 1986, they succeeded.

Refugee communities in Nicaragua, Costa Rica, and the United States also
organized education. But nowhere did it reach the level seen in the Honduran
camps. Other refugees shared the political commitment to education, but the
UNHCR camps had more international assistance for supplies, equipment, and
foreign advisors. Refugees elsewhere lived in open communities or were considerably less restricted than the refugees living close to the Salvadoran border.

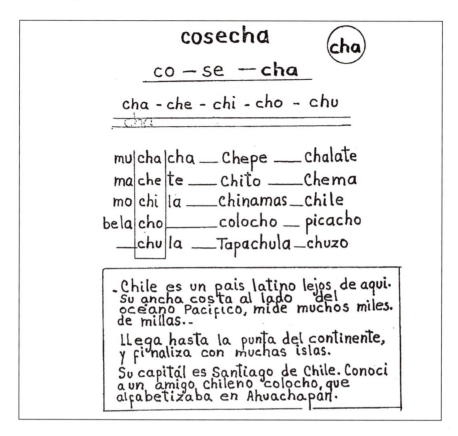

In Honduras, confinement and the lack of alternative activity gave them both the freedom to concentrate on education and the incentive to avoid boredom, while the large concentration of people and assistance from outside made it possible to acquire both supplies and experience.

Mutual Self-Education in the Political Prisons

Before and during the war, many regime opponents were held as political prisoners. Though not the worst victims of government repression—that distinction goes to the tens of thousands murdered and "disappeared"—they were routinely tortured to extract confessions or information; they were held in overcrowded prisons with inadequate facilities; and the great majority were never brought to trial (only a handful were ever actually convicted).

But by organizing in prison, political prisoners managed to win significant say over their daily lives. They also took advantage of their captivity to learn.

Many illiterate prisoners mastered basic education; all the prisoners participated in political study. They turned prisons into virtual controlled zones. Prison officials of course retained the ultimate authority to keep them locked in. But the prisoners won some surprising partial victories.[1]

Political prisoners have often organized in jail: in India under the Raj (Gordon 1990:117–150), Peru in the 1930s (José María Arguedas offers a fictional account [1974]) and 1980s (Poole and Renique 1992:10–13, 97–100; Rénique 1991); U.S. conscientious objectors during World War II (Sykes 1958:80); and Northern Ireland (Sands 1985). They have used captivity for education, both basic and political, as in Chile under Pinochet (Truscello 1979), Palestine (Peretz 1990; Abed-Rabbo and Safie 1990:233–247), South Africa (Bam 1989; Mandela 1994)—where Robben Island was known as "Mandela University"—and among black prisoners in the United States (Cummins 1994). Prisons might seem an unpropitious site for internal education. Regimentation and control would appear to rule it out; prison authorities had every reason to try to prevent political detainees from learning skills or imbibing subversive ideologies. But they studied and learned nonetheless. In doing so they demonstrated their determination to resist the deprivations and humiliations to which prison subjected them.

The Salvadoran government imprisoned its opponents and perceived opponents even before the war broke out. Co-Madres, the first committee of relatives of prisoners and disappeared, was founded in 1977. During the war, political prisoners numbered in the hundreds. Responding to international pressure, the Salvadoran government declared partial amnesties in 1983 and 1987. In 1987 some 400 political prisoners were released, leaving only 16 in jail (Americas Watch 1987:247; Amnesty International 1984:150–151; 1988:111). Then the number crept up again, especially after the 1989 offensive, to 370 in 1990 (Americas Watch 1990:138; 1991:77; Amnesty International 1989:122). Many were released before the end of the war, and the remaining few were amnestied following the 1992 peace settlement (El Rescate Human Rights Department Report from El Salvador, June 8–15, 1992).[2]

Between 1982 and 1987, all male political prisoners were held in the country's main penitentiary in Mariona. After the 1987 amnesty and a brief hiatus, the number of political prisoners began to rise again. At that time, most of the men were dispersed to prisons in the departmental capitals, especially Santa Ana, San Miguel, and San Vicente. The great majority of political prisoners were men. Women prisoners were held in the women's prison in Ilopango (which, like Mariona, was near San Salvador).

Many were captured who had only taken part in peaceful political activities, or been active in trade unions or cooperatives, or worked for humanitarian agencies. Some were falsely accused, sometimes by other prisoners who had been tortured (International Human Rights Law Group 1987:32–40). Some of the prisoners had in fact been involved in clandestine military activity, but for all detainees, judicial treatment was rife with abuses. The judiciary was deeply compromised, so much so that the promise of judicial reform became an important element of the peace settlement, and the UN-sponsored Truth Commission created in that settlement called on the entire Supreme Court to resign because of its "enormous responsibility" for its failure to hold perpetrators accountable for state terror (*Acuerdos* 1992:22–26; Comisión de la Verdad 1993:189).

Members of the military and security forces, usually in civilian clothes, initially detained suspected subversives in those forces' clandestine cells without acknowledging that they held them. There prisoners were routinely tortured, and many women were raped. Five imprisoned members of the nongovernmental Human Rights Commission of El Salvador (CDHES) surveyed the prisoners in Mariona in 1986. Of the 434 prisoners who entered in the first eight months of the year, 430 said that they had been tortured physically and 431 psychologically. Preferred methods of torture were those that left no physical marks: immersion in filthy water and the *capucha*, a hood filled with lime placed over the prisoner's head until it induced choking (Americas Watch 1986:56; Comisión de Derechos Humanos 1986:69; Neier 1993:259; Tula 1994:161).

Many detainees were released within a few days or weeks, but some were formally charged and held without trial for lengthy periods, occasionally as long as five years. According to the International Human Rights Law Group, "*few political prisoners are serving sentences and most are unaware of the status of their cases*" (1987:18, italics in original). But they were unlikely to be tortured again. (The effects, physical and psychological, nevertheless remained with them.)

Daily Life in Prison

For political prisoners and other ("common") prisoners alike, imprisonment is an ongoing contest. Jailers do all they can to dominate and dehumanize prisoners, and prisoners grasp at every opportunity to resist. Resistance by common prisoners is likely to be covert and sporadic (Goffman 1961:14, 58–60; Sykes 1958:80; Toch 1982:39). Political prisoners have resources that enable them to wage more sustained struggles. Shared political beliefs (provided the prisoners all come from the same political movement) give them a solidarity that encourages joint action. They surely all believe, moreover, that they are imprisoned unjustly, and regard prison as but a new arena for the same struggle in which they were engaged on the outside. Armed with strong convictions and schooled in organization and internal discipline, they may persuade their custodians, in the interest of maintaining order, to grant them considerably more leeway than a less organized group could win.

Political prisoners in El Salvador created a community that organized collective protest and imposed the prisoners' will whenever possible, despite the harsh response of prison authorities. Prisoners refused to follow orders, made demands of their jailers, barred entry to their cell blocks, went on hunger strikes, issued manifestos to the press, and enlisted international solidary support. Their shared ideology was the basis of their organization and struggle in prison, just as it was on the outside. They displayed FMLN propaganda and listened to the clandestine radio stations (actions that, if done openly on the outside, could have led to imprisonment).

In the prisons they formed collectives that established their own regimens and rules and made a point of challenging restrictions. Male prisoners in Santa Tecla created the Committee of Political Prisoners of El Salvador (COPPES) in 1980 (Alegría and Flakoll 1984:47–49). Women formed a chapter of COPPES in Ilopango in 1981. The organization flourished there and in Mariona, where the Santa Tecla prisoners were moved in 1982.

After the 1987 amnesty, COPPES declined among the remaining handful of political prisoners, but when the number grew again over the next few years, COPPES reemerged and spread to the other prisons where political prisoners were held. In April 1989, more than sixty people were rounded up in simultaneous raids on the offices of several popular organizations. Many were tortured and then consigned to prison. One of them, Victoria, interviewed in Ilopango three months later, said that she and her fellow inmates refounded the COPPES chapter as soon as they were all in the jail.

COPPES led the prisoners' struggle against the rules of confinement. Azucena, jailed at the same time as Victoria in 1989, said that the political prisoners immediately demanded to be kept together:

> The day after we arrived, we couldn't walk, because we had all been beaten and tortured. They practically had to carry us downstairs. But we met and everyone proposed ideas for the list of demands of the political prisoners in Ilopango, because the next day was Sunday, visitors' day, and we were going to send the list out [with a visitor] to be published as an advertisement. So we demanded that they give us a separate room for the political prisoners, a place to cook just for ourselves, access to the field every day to do exercises, to let national and international delegations visit us without restrictions, to let us have medicine brought to us. Many of us were very sick and they didn't let medicines in.

Edmundo was a member of the executive board of COPPES in San Vicente, where he was imprisoned from 1989 to 1991. He described the prisoners' struggle to gain freedoms, one by one. "We got an agreement with the director of the prison for a separate dormitory. We struggled fiercely to change the food system, which was so depressing—a little bit of beans, with rice which was totally spoiled, fermented, decomposed. We got a lot of things with the help of the International Committee of the Red Cross and Doctors Without Borders. . . . It was a hard struggle, a tremendous and difficult struggle against the guards and the administration of the prison. At the beginning the director didn't even let us listen to Radio Venceremos."

They could only achieve concessions if they were united. According to

Rafael, a prisoner in Mariona in 1991, "we had lockup at four o'clock and we got them to lock us in at six. We had meetings and protests and everything until they had no other choice but to meet our demand because the whole prison was active. Through the political work, the whole prison got active."

At first prison authorities responded with repression. But with time they gave in on many demands, finally allowing the prisoners de facto autonomy to run their section of the prisons. The authorities apparently recognized that the prisoners could keep order better than they could. According to María Teresa Tula, imprisoned in Ilopango in 1986, "We didn't have any security guards inside the political prisoners' section because they knew that we were responsible" (Tula 1994:163).

Part of the role of COPPES was to maintain unity by handling any discipline problems that arose.[3] As Edmundo acknowledged, "We know in fact that none of us human beings is so easy to control." But the prisoners I interviewed insisted that such problems were rare. Some prisoners acquired and used drugs (which COPPES forbade), and others refused to participate fully in the prisoners' collective life. A prisoner occasionally refused to attend classes or meetings, Azucena said, complaining, "'What am I preparing myself for if I'm going to die in prison?' And the compañeras who were closest to her talked to her in a friendly way and tried to get her out of whatever had come over her."

Men handled disciplinary problems differently, according to Edmundo. Violators were made to do calisthenics and cleanup duty, or not allowed to share the food brought by the political prisoners' relatives. "One compañero, only one, was expelled from the political prisoners and had to go stay with the common prisoners. After six months he asked us to forgive him and let him come back."

Maintaining internal discipline could be a way of doing the authorities' job for them. But it won improvements in the conditions of daily life that made confinement significantly more tolerable than it would otherwise have been. Discipline also enabled prisoners to make the best of the conditions they could control. As Iván, who was imprisoned in Mariona from 1985 to 1987, explained, "In prison we had to act collectively. With eighteen men sleeping piled up in a cell for eight people, we had to be a collective and not have problems. And the beds were given to older people, to people who had health problems, to the war-disabled, to those of us who had been tortured, and to the new arrivals."

According to Raquel, a university student and civil servant who was in Ilopango from 1980 to 1983, collective discipline was "a way to create our own therapy." Rafael elaborated the same point. "People fall into despair because they are shut in and can't always control themselves. We tried to control them as much as possible. . . . Sonofabitch, your nerves have to explode."

COPPES chapters worked closely with prisoner support committees. These groups were initially formed by wives and mothers who had met while hunting for missing relatives. As the security forces acknowledged holding more and more prisoners, the committees provided material and legal support for them and their families. They became an integral part of the popular movement

(Schirmer 1993; Tula 1994). COPPES also dealt with organizations that monitored the treatment of political prisoners, such as the CDHES, the International Committee of the Red Cross, and Doctors Without Borders, and maintained contact clandestinely with COPPES chapters in other prisons.

Prisoners also organized for work. They made handicrafts—key chains, wooden boxes, wall hangings—all painted with pictures of campesino life in the La Palma folk art style, and sold them on visitors' days. They set up workshops with donated equipment and materials; in Mariona (until 1987) they had shops for carpentry, tailoring, mechanics, and electricity. They organized clinics—sometimes there was a doctor among the prisoners who attended the patients; if not, prisoners who had been trained as paramedics in the guerrilla army ran the clinic. They cooked and cleaned. A legal section collected prisoners' testimonies of mistreatment and conveyed them to outside organizations; it also maintained contact with lawyers and kept track of prisoners' cases.

Among the many virtues of work was that it filled empty time productively. It thereby contributed to maintaining discipline:

> We spent four hours doing manual work—everyone—and four hours in school and that's how we spent the whole day, in a very special dynamic. (Edmundo)

> As the main psychosocial therapy, we had work, and lots of it. The day's activities began at six in the morning and ended at eleven or twelve at night, daily. Everyone knew what he had to do and where he had to be. The time was programmed, including relaxation and some collective recreation. (Iván)

Rafael, when asked what prison life was like, summarized:

> As far as being locked in, bad; but the truth is we were always busy with political tasks, studying, and everything. You can say that we didn't find it so bad.

Prison Education

Many political prisoners were illiterate or had very limited education. According to the CDHES torture study, slightly over two-thirds of those in Mariona were small farmers or farmworkers (Comisión de Derechos Humanos 1986:21). Some of them, and most of the inmates with urban occupations, presumably knew how to read, but a substantial number did not. Edmundo estimated that one-third of his fellow inmates in San Vicente after 1989 were illiterate.

When COPPES first proposed to organize classes, prison officials refused permission. Some prisons already offered classes officially. According to Edmundo, the director of the San Vicente prison did not want to allow political prisoners to hold any meetings. But "we struggled, we organized, we fought, we demonstrated to claim that inside we had that freedom of expression and communication, and that prisons were [for prisoners] to learn, and to change them, or, as they say, to rehabilitate the human being. . . . We got the support of lots of people outside; we got the people from the [prisoner support] committees to go to the national prison director with our demands to have a school inside the prison."

Prison officials especially objected to political education, according to Manuel, a prisoner in Santa Ana. "We had conflicts when they saw we were offering that kind of education: conflicts with the guards, and with the higher-ups: the inspectors, the commanders. They even called us in to see what we were teaching." Raquel recounted that when Ilopango administrators discovered in 1981 that prisoners were writing poems in class condemning their imprisonment, they confiscated blackboard, chalk, and teaching materials, but the prisoners nevertheless continued, writing on the walls in charcoal.

For prisoners, studying both improved their skills and affirmed their ideological commitment. Like work, studying filled time that would otherwise weigh heavily on them. The opposition of the prison authorities, moreover, made studying another form of resistance to oppression.

Life in the prisons and the refugee camps was similar in many ways; so was the practice of popular education. Involuntary confinement was the central fact of daily life, and much of education was related to it. Material resources were few; teachers were recruited for conciencia and good will as much as for academic level; work was made an educational experience; political education and concientización were integral parts of the process. People took enormous pride in their educational enterprise. For campesinos who had never been to school, demonstrating that they could learn was an affirmation of their worth as human beings.

The prison setting where education was best organized was Mariona before the 1987 amnesty. The population of political prisoners was greatest there, and all the male prisoners in the country were together. They lived in extremely crowded conditions (a prison designed for 1,600 inmates had 4,000, including common prisoners). In later years prisoners also educated themselves, but less intensively, thanks to shorter detention periods and the dispersion of the men to departmental prisons.

Classes were held for three hours a day (four hours in San Vicente, according to Edmundo). The first step was to teach illiterates to read. Learning was not easy for adult campesinos. Not only had they never been to school; many of them were used to thinking of themselves as incapable of learning. Writing, moreover, involved unaccustomed muscular activity. According to Iván, "the anatomical movement for an agricultural tool goes from the arm down. So they are going to have less manual dexterity than a shoemaker, for example, whose physical strength goes from the wrist down. . . . So we made special notebooks, bigger ones, and gave the campesino compañero more time than a shoemaker to work on writing."

Some political prisoners, members of ANDES, were teachers on the outside.

In some cases they took the lead in offering basic education. But prisoners with far less formal education also taught. Some of them knew about popular education pedagogy from previous political activities, like Iván.

> We always tried to make our education as close as possible to real situations. We weren't going to talk about Disneyland in a prison for political prisoners.
>   So we connected the word *libertad* [freedom] with the alphabet—what letters it contains. Everyone in the class explained his idea of what freedom was, and then later we wrote the word. No one was ever going to forget how to write that word—because we didn't have freedom in prison.[4]

For those who successfully learned (or already knew) how to read, classes were offered at higher levels. The second level gave the fundamentals of elementary education, arithmetic, and more advanced reading. Here too problems were posed that were related to concrete experience, Iván said: "How much fertilizer a field of six hectares needed, if we needed two ounces of fertilizer per plant, and we were going to sow x plants. So the people connected arithmetic to their experience. A campesino is interested in how much fertilizer to use so he doesn't waste it."

The third level was political education. Political content pervaded basic education, but there were also organized political discussions in which all members of the political prisoners' collective participated. They discussed current events and topics in foreign policy such as U.S. intervention, and read a few political texts that had been smuggled in.

The purpose of political education was to reinforce the prisoners' ideological commitment, so as to help them withstand the difficulties of prison life and not give in to their jailers. "From the news we received from here [outside of prison]," Manuel commented, "we chose themes to bolster their commitment and keep their morale high." According to comandante Nidia Díaz, a prominent prisoner of war in 1985, "In prison, if you don't hold on to your convictions, to your ideology, you're lost. . . . I lived minute by minute in prison, putting up with it, resisting" (Díaz 1988:8). Díaz's situation was different from that of the civilian prisoners, because she was held in solitary confinement. In the prisoners' collectives, ideological discussions assured social support for resistance.

An important topic of political discussions was their legal situation. As Iván said, "Practically all of us got very familiar with the penal code of our country." "Above all, our political studies focused on the unanimous struggle to get us out of prison, to win a general amnesty or piecemeal liberation for all of us," Edmundo explained. The discussions, Edmundo said, "went quite well, since I, as the instructor, just had the role of throwing out a topic for everyone to develop."

The prisoners had little by way of school supplies. Education began in Mariona without chairs or desks. People sat on the floor. (Later the prisoners' carpentry shop made benches for the classes.) Books were few; notebooks and pencils had to be begged from relatives or the support committees. Iván "tried to give assignments to be done in groups, not individually. Since we didn't have much paper, either, it was easier for a whole group to use just one piece of paper."

Classes were informal, following the popular education principle of equality between those leading the classes and those learning how to read.

> The education promoter—we didn't call him professor, or teacher, but promoter of education—didn't stand at the front of the room, but was in [the middle of] the group. Sitting in the circle was more efficient and more pleasant. The teacher only stood up to write on the blackboard. [One of the reasons for the teachers' success was that] since we lived with our community, we were perfectly familiar with it, and we were part of that problematic situation because we were prisoners too. We didn't leave the prison, we were prisoners. This made us feel the same way the compañeros did. (Iván)

Prisoners also learned as they worked. Training in vocational skills was made an integral part of the prison education program—Iván called it the fourth level. People learned woodworking and painting to make handicrafts—"We all did it. You haven't been a political prisoner in my country if you haven't made handicrafts." Men who knew skills like carpentry and electrical wiring taught them to others. In San Vicente prisoners formed what Edmundo called a technical training school, with instruction in mechanics, carpentry, woodcarving, and silk screening. Edmundo, who was a trained draftsman, learned silk screening in prison and started a commercial silk screen workshop after his release. Paramedics in the clinics trained other prisoners. Some newly literate prisoners became education promoters and went on to teach others to read.

Because the men who had worked as craftsmen were not the ones with the most formal education, training in skilled trades meant that teachers and students switched roles. The principle that everyone has something to contribute and is thus a potential teacher as well as a learner was put fully into practice. Iván and other prisoners who taught reading and arithmetic learned manual skills from others, reinforcing the sense of equality engendered by their common fate as prisoners. "The fact that I had been to the university, and had taught in a nursing school, made a difference between a shoemaker and my position as someone who had had access to education. But the fact that I would go to this compañero—me, a teacher, with university training—to ask him to teach me how to make handicrafts, wiped that difference out." They learned from their own activity as teachers as well. As Edmundo put it, "Prison is the best university."

Teachers were enormously proud both of their own work and of the accomplishments of their pupils. Speaking of the success of education in Mariona, Iván exclaimed, "it was incredible that compañeros who had not known how to read or write were at the third level a year later, discussing sociology, etc. . . . It filled us with pride to see that we had twenty-five trained health promoters; approximately forty compañeros who had learned a trade or a handicraft pretty well, and twenty-three education promoters, who had originally been among the compañeros who had just begun to read and write. We were surprised by what we had been able to accomplish."

From basic literacy to technical training, education was inseparable from the prisoners' political struggle, in the prisons and in the country as a whole. This was true in several respects: the pervasiveness of political content, the motivation derived from the conviction that education is a right, the fact that education became a focus of conflict with prison authorities, and the goal of giving people skills they could apply to later political work. As in other settings, integration with community life and political struggle is an important characteristic of popular education, one to which formal discussions of popular education have not paid sufficient attention.

Education was consciously oriented to the future, the vision of a new society prisoners expected to create with their compañeros after the revolutionary triumph. Universal literacy and political education would prepare the whole population to participate in running a new society democratically. Iván, reflecting not only on his two years in Mariona but on a decade of educational work in several settings, concluded enthusiastically, "We believe that what we've done in the middle of a war proves the capacity and willingness of our people. You can imagine what we could do in peace!"

The Perspective of Victims and the Perspective of Protagonists

The practice of education in refugee camps and prisons differed in ways that derived directly from the nature of their respective communities. The presence of families in refugee camps made children the most important focus of education (though the success rate of adult learners was dramatic). The refugees were from very similar backgrounds, while the prisons housed campesinos without education together with well-educated people from towns and cities. Many refugees therefore had the experience, rarer for prisoners, of teaching material they had barely mastered in their own formal education, expanding their own educational horizons and deriving a sense of mastery as they did.

Education nevertheless took on a similar meaning in the two sites because people defined it politically—not only by giving political content to the lessons, but by understanding teaching and learning as a political act, one that expressed their rejection of the confinement to which they were subjected. Many who sympathize with the plight of refugees and political prisoners, including the international human rights movement and the political solidarity movement, present them as innocent victims of mistreatment by abusive authorities. To do so is to overlook their equally significant refusal to be consumed by their victimization.

By educating themselves and by organizing to assert their will against a hostile confinement, refugees and prisoners showed that they would not be ground down by repression. They acted not as victims but as protagonists. Mary McCarthy's distinction between exiles and refugees captures the difference: "If a group of Greek writers draws up a manifesto, they are writers-in-exile, but if we are trying to raise money to help them, they are refugees" (1985:71).

Salvadoran prisoners did not wait for handouts; they issued manifestos. Nor were refugees passive in the face of the regimentation and humiliations inflicted on them. Both groups resisted and struggled to overcome the limits set by the authorities. They were also often frank about their political beliefs and goals. Some prisoners (after their release) were even frank about the activities, sometimes clandestine and illegal, that had led to their arrest.

Accounts of the treatment of campesinos and prisoners published during the war depicted them as innocent victims in order to arouse sympathy for them. Many books published in El Salvador portrayed the campesino population as devout, humble Christians organizing base communities and asserting their dignity as human beings (e.g., *La fe de un pueblo* 1983; López Vigil 1987), or as refugees driven from their homes by bombing raids and military ground operations that targeted civilians and guerrilla forces indiscriminately (e.g., Montes Mozo et al. 1985; Montes 1989). These sources portrayed people as victims rather than protagonists in order to condemn the Salvadoran government's conduct of the war on theological or moral grounds without openly siding with the insurgents, and to plead for sympathy and improved treatment. They therefore omitted from their depiction the refugees' initiative and their ability to take care of themselves, both in flight and in the sites of refuge. They presented the refugees as innocent bystanders rather than as people capable of taking a political position.

Nor do accounts of imprisonment highlight prisoners' resistance. Human rights reports usually take a legalistic approach, exposing judicial and penal authorities' violations of internationally sanctified guarantees of due process and humane treatment. The validity of these denunciations notwithstanding, the language of the accounts often suggests something further: an effort to construct the victim as an object of pity and an innocent—not only innocent of criminal guilt but ingenuously simple and, like a child, incapable of responsible action. If prisoners are guilty, such accounts seem to imply, imprisonment might not be unjust. If they can resist, prison conditions might not be cruel or inhumane. Depicting prisoners as victims of unjust treatment seems to require implying that they did nothing to cause that treatment and have no recourse against it.

Many reports on prison conditions and judicial treatment of prisoners in El Salvador during the 1980s created this impression by citing the numerous cases of prisoners for whom there was quite strong prima facie evidence that they had not committed any crime. Nowhere did these reports claim that all prisoners were innocent of any offense, but neither did they suggest that some were not. The *Amnesty International Report* for 1990 contains an account of "the imposition of the state of siege in November [1989 in El Salvador]," the imprisonment of five hundred people, and the murder of six Jesuit priests, professors at the Central American University, by the government army (1990:87–88), but fails to mention that the FMLN was conducting an offensive at the time!

Human rights reports are written not to analyze a political situation or describe the experience of incarceration but to denounce the mistreatment of prisoners according to standards of international law, the laws of the country itself, and common decency. Though much of their information comes from prisoners themselves, the authors solicit accounts of mistreatment. It is clearly not essential—nor even appropriate, one might argue—that they detail the political activism of their subjects or their active resistance in confinement.

Prisoners and refugees find the mantle of victimhood convenient. Refugees cannot assert a right to international assistance unless they can credibly claim neutrality. Prisoners, for their own protection, encourage the human rights organizations to cloak them in an aura of innocence.

When they are on safer ground, however, prisoners and refugees make clear that they acted as protagonists. I conducted most of my interviews after the refugees had returned and the prisoners had been released, when they could talk about their political activity without undue fear. They often presented the prison experience as exhilarating, despite its rigors: as Edmundo said, "Prison is the best university." Armando of the Human Rights Commission (CDHES), who spent his working life confronting the abuses others had suffered, said that "without [having been captured] I would never have known firsthand what it was like to be tortured." Paradoxically, they frequently find it liberating. As Luisa said of the Colomoncagua refugee camp, "Of course it was a prison, but still it was a school." Octavio described life there, with its opportunities for work and learning, as "one of the greatest experiences of my life." (Even a U.S. Embassy officer was reported to have called Mariona prison "the freest place in El Salvador"—International Human Rights Law Group 1987, 86.)

These claims sometimes find a more moderate expression: "You can say that we didn't find it so bad." (Rafael) But in whatever form, they cannot be dismissed as mere rationalizations of cognitive dissonance following a bad experience one would prefer to have avoided. They are similar to the view many soldiers have of combat: an ordeal, but one shared with compañeros and from which one can take pride in having acquitted oneself with honor.

Salvadoran prisoners and refugees are not alone in continuing in confinement the struggle they waged outside. I have already referred to prisoners' activism in Chile, Northern Ireland, Palestine, South Africa, and elsewhere. Refugee communities around the world have continued to play an active role in the political struggles that drove them into exile (Jean 1993:112–115; Zolberg, Suhrke, and Aguayo 1989:275–278).

Advocates create an image of innocence in response to the convergence of political factors and the interests of the "victims" themselves. The pressures are somewhat different for domestic and international human rights organizations. Domestic organizations, often tacitly allied with the political opposition, refrain from acknowledging opposition activities for fear of appearing to acknowledge—and even condone—military or clandestine activity, because to do so would jeopardize their own legitimacy or that of the opposition as a whole.

International organizations, to get attention, want to produce, in Rony Braumann's phrase, a "100 percent victim" for the news media (1993:154). Braumann offers some trenchant comments (implicitly critical of the organization that published his essay) on the collusion to arouse international attention between the mass media and international NGOs providing humanitarian aid to refugees. The NGOs supply "victims" because the media are more likely to publicize violations committed against the "innocent" than against active political opponents. By doing so, the organizations not only misrepresent the people they are defending as victims pure and simple; they also concede to the media the power to decide who shall be considered victims of human rights violations, and therefore which violations shall be denounced. The strategy serves the interests of the prisoners and refugees themselves in keeping international attention on their plight. Nevertheless, the omission of their response is striking.

It is common that dominants presume to speak for subalterns, thus depriving them of their voices. Gayatri Spivak accuses colonialists of that offense, referring disparagingly to the prohibition by British authorities of *sati* (widow immolation) under the Raj as "white men . . . saving brown women from brown men" (1988:296). Situating herself firmly in anticolonial discourse, Spivak does not consider whether those who thus took up the white man's burden can be regarded as having benefited the brown women. Though the title of her essay is "Can the Subaltern Speak?" her question is equally, "Can the colonialist hear?" and she answers with a resounding "No."

I do not believe that the defense of human rights by the international human rights movement, in which I myself have been active, represents covert imperialism. That movement has saved lives and secured due process and release for political prisoners in El Salvador and many other countries. Without constant attention and pressure from governments and voluntary organizations, the war on Salvadoran "subversives" might have left few survivors to tell about their resistance. Furthermore, human rights rhetoric is not necessarily due to narrowness of vision; it serves a strategy intended to arouse the maximum international repudiation of violations.

But that strategy presents a dilemma: the most effective means of defending rights may indeed silence the voice of those it is intended to protect. Without going so far as Spivak, one can recognize that accounts of atrocities are often divorced from the experiences of the victims. Resistance is an important condition, reminder, and assertion of their integrity as human beings. Their political convictions and their determination to act on those convictions make internal organization, education, and protest inseparable. Self-improvement, membership in the collectivity, and resistance to injustice are all part of prisoners' and refugees' collective assertion of self. To present them only as victims is to negate the resourcefulness with which they confront imprisonment and exile. Their political activism and their resistance to inhuman treatment do not in any way justify repression against them. But to ignore their action is to fail to understand the causes of their plight, their response to it, and what it means to them.

CHAPTER 5

School and Community

Communities in the war zones did not offer a protected space for popular education, but they eventually became its most important sites. Some communities in contested and FMLN-controlled zones remained inhabited throughout the war; others were repopulated as combat let up somewhat in the mid-1980s. Cut off from the national society, these communities had to provide public services on their own, most importantly education (along with health care). Popular education became part of everyday life and the normal means of organizing schools. Some popularly run schools predated this period; with the advent of war they became more organized.

This chapter will examine education during the war years in several community settings in the two main FMLN-controlled territories: eastern Chalatenango and northern Morazán. Early in the war, groups of civilians wandered through the mountains for months or even years, moving to avoid the army; later, communities returned to the depopulated areas of Chalatenango, first displaced people who had fled to San Salvador and then the refugees from Mesa Grande. In villages of Morazán that were never completely depopulated, community life had to be recreated after several years of stagnation; the largest repatriation community in El Salvador, Segundo Montes City, was founded in 1989 by refugees returning from Colomoncagua. (We will also look briefly at communities and cooperative organizations in the more peaceful government-controlled areas of the country.)

Villages in the FMLN-controlled zones were not ordinary communities. Beset by war, they could act collectively only if their residents' energies were mobilized by political appeals. And those energies had to compensate for scarcity of resources and lack of professional personnel. Keeping community schools running thus depended on the integration between politics and pedagogy, and between learning and community organization, on which popular education was premised. Like the guerrilla army, these communities put a high priority on education for both technical and political purposes: the technical to foster the skills needed in the struggle; the political both to reinforce learners' ideological commitment for political engagement and to transform and liberate learners. And they appealed to community spirit and political commitment to mobilize people's efforts as teachers, as learners, and as parents of school children.

Popular education therefore evolved in close association with community life. Those who stayed in the FMLN-controlled zones shared political goals. They had to meet all needs simultaneously, collectively, and, at least at first, in an improvised fashion. They had to provide themselves with food and protect themselves from military incursions at the same time they were creating schools. Education, like defense and subsistence, was an act of the whole community. It was a need widely recognized by people who in their early lives had had to struggle to get even minimal education, or had been deprived of it entirely. They did not take it for granted; they worked hard to make it happen. In turn, the new schools offered an education designed to serve the larger community.

This close integration of education with community life depended on a high level of community solidarity and the sense that everyone contributed to, and stood to benefit from, collective activity. Before the war, people had helped each other out with farming tasks, and few had ever had either opportunity or reward for individual acquisitive effort. Communities had shared the consciousness-raising and organizing experiences of the 1970s. In the war zones, moreover, communities probably had greater political cohesion than before the war. Many who were most opposed to the insurgency had fled and did not return to repopulate. Most of those who remained or returned sympathized with the insurgency, either because they were already politically conscious or in reaction to the army's repression, and all the people in the zones had to work together to resolve the emergencies imposed by the war. Though working collectively was always difficult, they were likely to look to the community as a whole as a source of betterment and were correspondingly willing to contribute to it.

The sense of community was evident in the organization of education. Whole communities put a great deal of effort into building and supporting schools. Teachers worked voluntarily out of a desire to contribute to the community. Community leaders insisted to parents that educating themselves and their children was a duty to the community as a whole. Educators did not have higher status than learners in the eyes of either, both because they came from the same background and because popular education's principles insisted on the equality of learners and teachers. Lessons included overtly political content. Schools strove both to meet political needs and to contribute to the reconstructed society to which the communities looked forward at the end of the war. On the other hand, the integration of school and community also meant that the schools suffered severe material shortages and were vulnerable to harassment by the Salvadoran army.

The relation between school and community is one of the defining features of popular education. Their integration—the refusal to treat education as a distinct function separate from other community practices—was one of the sources of its strength. The story of popular education in the war zones is a story of a close symbiosis in which education and organizing often appear as different aspects of the same act. This identification, I believe, is the most distinctive feature of the Salvadoran experience of popular education.

Schooling on the Run

The state of war arrived gradually. Over time, however, community life was completely disrupted. At the very beginning, schools and other government services simply closed up shop, as teachers fled the areas of conflict in fear for their lives—whether as bystanders to combat or as direct targets of repression. The withdrawal of government services began even before the outbreak of full-scale war, in the disorder of the late 1970s. Some schools closed as early as 1977 (Guzmán et al. 1993:33–34). Just as the descent into war was gradual, likewise those who were under attack took steadily increasing precautions: from not coming home at night, to spending longer periods in the mountains near one's home, to constant movement through the mountains to avoid encounters with the troops. Many fled the country; many who did not were massacred.

Those who wandered in the mountains for lengthy periods sought temporarily safe places and moved whenever they sensed danger. On these pilgrimages, known as *guindas*, groups of people stayed together—as few as a few dozen or as many as two or three hundred. Not daring to remain in villages, they slept in caves or under makeshift nylon tents. They hid during the day and moved at night, hoping to avoid both bombing raids and direct confrontations with troops. "They're a human radar, practical and self-taught," according to teachers' union leader Julio Portillo. "Who knows how they do it, but they know that there's going to be a military operation." According to Carmela, who wandered the hills of Chalatenango from 1980 to 1986, they sometimes had to move every day for as long as three weeks, with hardly a chance to hunt for food.

During the periods of calm, they attempted to create a semblance of community life. They improvised to find food: some stayed within a small enough radius that they were able to plant crops and see them through to harvest. Elba, who spent five years in the mountains of Morazán, said that she and others gathered wild mezcal and took it to sell in village markets when military operations let up.

Though constantly on the move in guindas, these groups nevertheless became the nucleus of future communities. Even though they had to spend most of their time foraging and seeking shelter, Elba said, they attempted to hold classes for the children.

> There was a teacher who taught us classes, like a school, except that it was under an *ujuste* tree. And since there had been a school in La Joya before the war, we went there to get the blackboard and a chair.

Had he been a teacher in the school?
No, it was just that he knew a little bit and was sharing it with us. That's what he said.

Isabel taught in Chalatenango. "It was an effort to hold class," she said, "for the teacher as well as for the student. And with a minimum of resources. There was no paper. We wrote on the ground or with charcoal on doors. But we kept at it."

Of all the conditions for popular education during the war, these were undoubtedly the most difficult. There were many other places where people had no supplies, books, or furniture. But they might hope someday to acquire them and to get a building with a roof, and in the long run those who taught might get outside help and improve their skills. Even the guerrilla army, where conditions were most similar to the guindas, had a structure of support and some connection to an outside supply line.

Though communities in flight might appear inherently unstable, they had to organize to survive. In Chalatenango and nearby departments they created formal structures known as local popular powers (PPLs). PPLs emerged under the political direction of the FPL. Of the FMLN's five political-military organizations, the FPL was strongest in Chalatenango, and it was the one that promoted civilian organization most assiduously in conjunction with its military effort. As a result, civilian organization was consistently strongest in Chalatenango. Nothing comparable to the PPLs emerged in Morazán, which was controlled by the ERP.

The PPLs openly declared themselves the guerrilla movement's civilian support base. The structures existed within individual communities, known as "bases"; PPLs also formed links between communities. They attempted to supervise agricultural production and defense and to provide for health care and education. Close coordination with military structures allowed the PPLs to learn from the example of education in the guerrilla army. Through the higher-level PPLs, the bases linked up with military units to take advantage of the presence among the combatants of professional teachers, veterans of the struggles of ANDES, the teachers' union (de la Cruz 1983:92).

The teachers felt the same doubts about their abilities as volunteer teachers elsewhere. They needed technical training and texts to guide their own work. Some professional teachers who had joined the guerrilla army and supervised its education campaign designed a cartilla for popular classes in the civilian bases. It had a much more overt political content than many that were used later (a page is reproduced by Pearce [1986:260]; I examine the political and didactic content of these cartillas in chapter 6). Teachers in more stable civilian communities in the later period felt the need to justify themselves as neutral civilians, whereas those who were part of the PPLs expected nothing but hostile confrontation in any encounter with the army and did not think that neutrality could protect them.

Because the bases were geographically dispersed, according to Isabel, the professional teachers worked alone to produce the cartilla, so the experience was "not very participatory." But once it was written and duplicated, its authors held two week-long training sessions in 1984. In each, they presented the cartilla to a few dozen civilian and combatant popular teachers and taught them how to use it in their classes. The teachers appreciated the cartilla because it told in an entertaining way about the experience of war and flight in which they were living: "like stories, but you knew it was true. The people in the stories were people we knew," said Carmela.

"Maintaining that effort, writing the cartilla and then holding the first training session was one of the greatest successes of that period, in wartime conditions," according to Isabel. The success demonstrated both the strength of organization that made it possible and the priority given to education despite the exigencies of war.

PPLs were strongest in Chalatenango between 1982 and 1984, though they also existed in other FPL-controlled areas during the same period. As civilian structures, they had considerable autonomy from the FMLN. Asked what role the FMLN played in education, Isabel replied that it "always had its priority. During the war, it was the war itself. But we can't say that it ignored education and training for the people who were within its structures. That's why so many people were teaching campesinos to read in the first stage of agitation [the 1970s]." Some civilian informants undoubtedly overemphasized their separateness from the FMLN to maintain a cover of independence, but Isabel's claim of autonomy has a ring of genuineness because she appears to be responding to the implication that the FMLN should have been *more* involved: "I feel that it wasn't against the effort of education in the communities. It had no reason to be. And I think that it always stimulated an effort within its own structures. . . . The communities had a lot of autonomy to decide how they were going to do it. The Frente had its own role, which was well defined, and the community had its space too."

Open identification with the FMLN made the PPLs vulnerable to government attack, and they grew weaker as the war stabilized in 1983 and 1984. Both sides adopted a new military strategy: the government turned to "low-intensity conflict," Vietnam-style: intense bombing coupled with civic action, intended to drain the "sea" in which the guerrilla "fish" swam. For its part, the FMLN adopted the new strategy described in chapter 3, the War of the Whole People, dispersing its forces and emphasizing local work to promote community activities.

This strategy was implemented gradually as stable communities reemerged in the FMLN-controlled zones. In 1987 the FMLN called for "popular power of the double face [*doble cara*]." In this two-pronged strategy, civilians were to form open and clandestine organizations simultaneously (FMLN 1987). The open organizations sought to maintain legality and claimed to be independent of the FMLN. They pursued two goals: meeting local needs and building the FMLN's military strength. Even earlier, displaced people in and around San Salvador and refugees in camps in Honduras prepared to repopulate the mountain villages of Chalatenango, while civilians who had remained in Morazán emerged from hiding to remake community life. They worked hard to create schools for their emerging communities.

The Revival of Organization in Morazán

In Morazán the new stage began with a renewal of Christian base communities. The department of Morazán is divided in half by the Torola River, which separated the FMLN- and government-controlled zones. The FMLN retained control of northern Morazán and adjacent areas of San Miguel department after it withdrew from much of the territory it controlled elsewhere in the country in 1984. The majority of the population was displaced, and many villages were destroyed. But some were never completely emptied. The few people who remained ventured outdoors as little as possible out of fear of bombings, mortar attacks, and military confrontations. Some left home only to tend their crops. They still fled into the mountains periodically and stayed for extended periods. Even when in their home villages, they were unwilling to take on community activities for fear: fear that anyone who strayed into the path of the army could get hurt, fear that those who tried to organize would be singled out as targets.

Former catechists who had joined the guerrilla army returned to these communities and attempted to break through this atmosphere of fear to promote base communities again. With the war going on, however, pastoral organizing had to adopt new goals. According to Héctor, who had been a catechist since the early 1970s and joined as a combatant at the beginning of the war, "We couldn't concentrate so much on preparing people because that would be wasting time. We had to go straight to the point [*al grano*]: 'Look, we have to join the struggle.' We gave them texts from the Bible, like when Jesus goes to the temple and finds it full of merchants. 'Look where the rich have got us, and Jesus took steps against those who were abusing the temple of God.'"

Morazán was part of the diocese of San Miguel, where Bishop Alvarez was no friend of the base communities, even before the war. Base communities had stopped functioning when combat broke out and so many of their members had fled. They reorganized in 1985 when the Archdiocese of San Salvador (crossing jurisdictional lines) offered to send food supplies to Morazán. Because the army frequently confiscated large loads of food being brought into a controlled zone, churchpeople decided that an organization under their auspices might be safer—even more if it was a women's organization. According to Héctor, "We wanted a name that wouldn't give us away. In San Salvador there was the Mothers' Committee, but to talk about a 'committee' here was a red flag. So we baptized it the Congregation of Christian Mothers for Peace."

As catechists attempted to establish an autonomous civilian presence, some tension arose between them and the FMLN. Christian base communities had been a fertile recruiting ground for the guerrilla army, and there was a considerable overlap; but a reassertion of the base communities' autonomy required a new division of authority and at least a working agreement on their respective roles. According to Father Miguel Ventura (who lived abroad during part of this period), the Christians were convinced that base communities should not be subordinate to immediate political goals. They should preach the gospel and welcome believers into the Christian life before demanding any political commitment. To that end, they felt, pastoral agents should act independently of the Front. FMLN leaders agreed that local community organizing should be autonomous, but thought that it should contribute directly to the war effort.

This division was far from an overt split, because base communities and FMLN agreed that the war was necessary and required tremendous effort, and because there was considerable overlap in affiliation. The difference was one of emphasis rather than of outright opposition. From the success of the Congregation of Christian Mothers, according to Ventura, the FMLN learned that "if they didn't grant autonomy to the civilian population, the process would be poorer." Mobilizing women had been effective not only because it provided political cover but because it drew in some women whose main concern was to feed their families.

Building on that lesson, the FMLN began to encourage the creation of community councils (*directivas*) in individual villages and hamlets. They started slowly; people met in fear. Marta, who became a popular teacher, said that when a group met in her village, Laguna Seca, at the end of 1984, they were "afraid and trembling. No one would go outside. When they heard the airplanes, they stayed huddled indoors; when they heard the mortars, or realized that the army was coming, they just hunkered down, because there was nothing else to do." But Marta and a few neighbors nevertheless thought the time was ripe, and they organized a community council.

In 1985 a few more communities organized councils. Formally independent of the FMLN, these councils primarily responded to immediate community needs: agricultural production, health care, education, and security from military attack. Since there was no formally constituted authority in the controlled zones, they came to act as governments. For example, they enforced rules against the use and sale of alcohol.

One of their main purposes was to create schools. Felipe of Perquín said that councils were formed because "the children were growing up and could be nine years old without having had any education. So the councils decided, 'We have to get popular teachers to build up education in every community.' The schools reopened in 1985."

Councils had to start schools on their own. They had to recruit teachers, find a place to hold classes, and acquire basic school supplies. In some villages there was an abandoned school; but some of these had deteriorated for lack of upkeep or been destroyed by combat, and in other villages there had never been one. In those places, the council had to find an empty home to use. In La Laguna, a hamlet in the north of the department of San Miguel adjacent to Morazán, a school was started, but without a building—children sat outdoors on rocks. But the council raised money to buy a lot and build a school. One man who had been a construction worker did most of the work, and other men in the village took turns tending his cornfield while he worked on the school.

Recruiting teachers was even more problematic, for few in the communities had more than a rudimentary education. Marta and another woman in Laguna Seca agreed to start a school and offer first and second grade. Marta had a fourth-grade education; her compañera, sixth grade. Abilio, of La Laguna, had grown up in Honduras before the soccer war and completed sixth grade before his family was forced to return to El Salvador. He was the main initiator of the school in his village, and he volunteered to teach.

The Repopulation of Chalatenango

The face of eastern Chalatenango began to change dramatically in 1986 when groups of people asserted their right to live as civilians in permanent communities. Gradually they moved back to the villages that had been emptied at the beginning of the war—first a few families at a time, and then larger numbers from the camps for displaced people around San Salvador and from the Mesa Grande refugee camp.

The PPLs had been broken up by the government army's bombing campaign in 1984. Bombing was stepped up in 1986. Nevertheless, some political factors favored the drive to repopulate. When José Napoleón Duarte was elected president in 1984, his administration felt pressure from Washington to maintain a democratic image. Repression of the urban population let up considerably, and the political opposition found some freedom to organize. At the same time the FMLN, following its new strategy, encouraged its civilian sympathizers to operate legally. New organizations emphasized specific economic and community demands to distinguish themselves from the broader political demands of the FMLN (Byrne 1996:133; Harnecker 1993:254–255).

While union members and shantytown dwellers organized in the cities, refugees and displaced people chafed at the enforced idleness and isolation of the camps. Even though they recognized that the war would not end nor peace return to their villages anytime soon, displaced people in San Salvador founded the Christian Committee for the Displaced (CRIPDES) in 1984 and began planning to return to the depopulated areas. As the FMLN won support internationally, foreign governments and international organizations could be enlisted to call on the Salvadoran government to respect the noncombatant status of people living in war-torn areas. And when a severe earthquake hit San Salvador on October 10, 1986, tens of thousands of people who had created the shantytowns that had proliferated in the capital saw their shacks crumble like matchsticks. Many of them were eager to return to the countryside they had fled.

The heart of the FMLN-controlled zone of eastern Chalatenango was a string of communities east of the town of Chalatenango: San Antonio los

Ranchos, Guarjila, Corral de Piedra (later renamed Ignacio Ellacuría for the Rector of the Central American University, one of the Jesuit priests murdered during the 1989 offensive), and San José las Flores, and further east across the Sumpul River, Nueva Trinidad and Arcatao. (Small villages and hamlets radiated out from each of these larger towns.) The bridge crossing the river had been destroyed early in the war and the road had deteriorated, so that when the first resettlers came, access to these communities was extremely difficult.

Arcatao, high in the hills at the far end of the road, was the first community to be resettled. During the mid-1980s families returned a few at a time. San José las Flores was the first organized repopulation. (Communities formed by displaced people were called repopulations. Those formed by refugees returning from abroad were called repatriations.) Especially heavy bombing campaigns coordinated with ground operations in 1986 drove many families into the mountains again. When a group sought refuge in the church in Dulce Nombre de María in April 1986, after a guinda, soldiers broke into the church, captured them, and took them to the Calle Real camp for displaced people north of San Salvador. Their capture coincided with CRIPDES's campaign for the right to repopulate. They became the first group to return to a mountain village under CRIPDES's auspices, going to San José las Flores on June 20, 1986.

The repopulation of Las Flores set the pattern for later repopulations in several respects, notably the organization of the community and the hostility of the government. Right-wing politicians and the army waged a major propaganda campaign against the repopulators, accusing them of representing the FMLN and accusing the Diaconía, the ecumenical agency assisting them, of being collaborators. Nevertheless, other groups from camps for the displaced in the capital soon followed the example of the Las Flores repopulators and organized to go to other communities.

Refugees in Mesa Grande also seized the chance to return home. A large group prepared to repatriate to Copapayo (Cuzcatlán department), Guarjila and Las Vueltas (Chalatenango), and Santa Marta (Cabañas) in October 1987. The Salvadoran government opposed their return, demanding that they go only to places under government control, but the refugees insisted on choosing the sites. They prepared a massive logistical and political operation financed by the international agencies that maintained the refugee camps. They dismantled houses and workshops, filling 127 trucks with everything they could move to begin building the new communities. More than four thousand refugees, in 150 buses, moved to the Salvadoran border, planning to enter on October 10. The government still refused permission, and finally on October 9 the refugees announced that they would cross the border on foot if necessary. Only an intervention from UNHCR headquarters in Geneva persuaded the Salvadoran government to authorize their entry the next day (Edwards and Siebentritt 1991:107–115; Weiss, Fagen, and Eldridge 1991).

Refugees returned from Mesa Grande to Chalatenango and other north central departments in further mass repatriations between 1988 and 1991. (A handful of refugees remained in Mesa Grande until the camp was finally closed in 1992.) Refugees and displaced people from the capital settled other communities. All these communities drew on their past experience in base communities, campesino organizations, and the FPL in Chalatenango in the 1970s to establish a solid base of community organization. Communities were created (recreated) intentionally by people who chose to leave refugee camps fully aware that they would face the heavy burden of economic survival, community organization, and the hostile army.

Repatriates from Honduras had an influence that spread to the repopulated communities, according to several informants in Chalatenango. The refugees brought home with them the lessons of collective life in Mesa Grande and their extensive training in teaching, health, and production skills. On the other hand, some implied that the refugees, who had escaped the worst of the war by going to Honduras, had had it easy. Norma, a combatant and education supervisor, observed that "Las Vueltas [a repatriation] had a much stronger form of organization and production than Las Flores, but the political level and combativeness of Las Flores was always higher than in Las Vueltas. So we said that Las Flores was the political capital and Las Vueltas was the industrial capital."

Each community had a community council with representatives overseeing production, education, health, and other tasks. Their first priority was always meeting material and security needs: they had to secure food, create a system of defense, and provide at least rudimentary health care. But they moved forward rapidly. Five years after repopulating, San José las Flores had installed piped water in houses and built latrines; the community owned 105 head of cattle, worked communally to grow food for old people and orphans, and had a clothing factory, a bakery, a medical clinic, a dental clinic, and an artisans' cooperative producing hemp bags and hammocks. Neighboring communities had a furniture factory and a shoe factory. Arcatao had a bakery and a disabled veterans' handicraft cooperative.

Members of these communities cultivated individual plots on farmland whose owners had abandoned it years before, but they were also expected to give one day a week to community work on ongoing projects like a communal farm or special projects like maintaining the road. Some worked full-time on community production projects and were paid a salary or shared the receipts.

Though production came first, education was not far behind. Unlike many communities in Morazán, where schools were started by the efforts of only a few individuals, the community organizations that undertook the repopulations and repatriations in Chalatenango embraced education as a major purpose from the start, and continued the schools conducted on the guindas and in the refugee camps. In Arcatao, three teachers started offering first and second grade in 1986: Carmela, Alfonso, and Eugenio. Carmela had taught during her years in guinda and Alfonso briefly in Mesa Grande. The school built up slowly: in 1988 it offered three grades; later fourth grade was added; and at the end of the war fifth grade was planned for the 1992 school year.

At the same time, schools opened in neighboring hamlets. The first was Teosinte, where during the first year Alfonso and Eugenio walked forty-five minutes each way every day to hold class after teaching in Arcatao—"because there was no one there to do it," according to Alfonso. "But we were young then." He was twenty-two at the time he said this, describing himself some five years earlier.

Community councils took responsibility for recruiting teachers. Some were tapped because they had achieved unusually high levels of education before the war—two who were teaching in Arcatao in 1992 had completed eighth grade. More often, however, organizers recruited teachers for their *conciencia* rather than their intellectual achievements. Because they had hardly more education than the people in their classes, they wanted training to improve their teaching skills. In 1986 the three teachers in Arcatao joined a training session the FMLN offered to its own literacy teachers in the guerrilla army. Even at the end of the war, Alfonso was circumspect in justifying his participation. "There was no one who could give us guidance. The fact is, we went to those meetings to get a broader vision of the work of education. If there had been other, more appropriate means, maybe we would have broken away from them, but since there weren't, we had to work with them."

Soon there were others to give guidance. The church was the first. Chalatenango was part of the Archdiocese of San Salvador until 1987, when Chalatenango was made a separate diocese. Priests went to live in the repopulated areas and serve the communities, sometimes teaching. The diocese set up a training program for popular teachers, paid them a small monthly stipend, and sent nuns and lay volunteers to train them. The Archdiocese, and then the new diocese, supported the repopulated communities in other ways. The church was the most important institution supporting their demand for recognition as civilians and freedom from military harassment.

CRIPDES formed the Coordinating Committee of Communities and Repopulations of Chalatenango (CCR) in 1987 to promote development projects. All the resettled communities were represented. The CCR coordinated community activities, especially health, education, and agricultural production. It provided training for popular teachers and raised and administered funds from foreign development agencies for the schools. Eastern Chalatenango was divided into four regions: one centered on Arcatao, another on Guarjila, and two more further north. As schools increased both in number—from two in 1986 to fifteen in 1988, twenty in 1989 and twenty-eight in 1992 (Guzmán et al. 1993:33–34)—and size, a CCR representative oversaw education in each of the regions, and more teachers were recruited and trained.

Community organization evolved more gradually in Morazán. Even though many of the communities in the northeast were never completely depopulated, the army kept people intimidated. The first community councils were formed slowly and independently of each other. Then some of them joined forces to found a regionwide organization, the Community Development Council of

Northern Morazán and San Miguel (PADECOMSM). Seventeen community councils began meeting jointly in 1987, and formally created PADECOMSM the following year. The number of member communities grew to sixty-seven by 1991. (The development of organization in Morazán over the course of the war is discussed by Leigh Binford [1997].)

PADECOMSM had its headquarters in Perquín, the largest town in northern Morazán. It had several goals; the most important was stimulating agricultural production. According to Felipe of the executive council, they wanted to make the region economically self-sufficient rather than dependent on outside assistance. "We no longer expect any humanitarian agency to come like they did at the beginning of the war and say, 'Perquín is at war; we have to bring them clothes, we have to bring them toys for the children, we have to bring some food,' because the people didn't go out to work the fields." To promote agricultural production, PADECOMSM bought large quantities of fertilizer each year and distributed it to campesinos on credit at the beginning of the growing season.

Narciso was president of the community council of the tiny hamlet of El Zancudo in the mountains near Perquín, part of the area ceded to Honduras by the World Court's 1992 resolution of a longstanding border dispute. When I met him in 1991 at the PADECOMSM office, he was returning from San Francisco Gotera, the departmental capital, where he had bought the fertilizer for the community council to give out. (Meeting Narciso made me realize that I unconsciously judged people's social background from the condition of their teeth. Most people who grow up poor and in the countryside have visible gold or silver, or a noticeably missing tooth. Narciso had a very friendly smile and one of the handsomest sets of teeth I have ever seen, but he was unquestionably a campesino.) Narciso echoed Felipe's theme when he explained, "Lots of people say PADECOMSM should give them the fertilizer; they got used to it when the Red Cross gave them fertilizer. We say no, we're not a welfare program [*asistencialistas*]. We want development." While people generally tilled their cornfields individually, PADECOMSM and local councils organized them to log and grow coffee on privately owned lands whose owners had abandoned the zone at the beginning of the war.

PADECOMSM charged truckers a "tax" of ten colones per truckload on wood shipped from northern Morazán; the money went into a fund to pay the popular teachers what they called an "allotment" or "assistance." At first the teachers received 100 colones a month; gradually this was increased to 250 colones, still so little that several people said, "It can't be called a salary." Teachers worked not for pay but out of commitment to the development of the community.

PADECOMSM also trained the popular teachers. In June 1990, it sponsored a three-day conference in Perquín for more than sixty popular teachers, inviting representatives from the National University branch in San Miguel and nongovernmental organizations that supported popular education. An officer of the FMLN addressed the closing session. Beginning in the following year,

PADECOMSM hired professional teachers to travel regularly to the communities, train the popular teachers, and oversee their work.

Despite the goal of self-sufficiency, PADECOMSM did not disdain the funds of outside agencies. A grant provided zinc sheets for new roofs on abandoned schools and materials to build new schools in ten communities that had never had government schools, but had started them with popular teachers. Men from the communities provided the labor. A Spanish church agency financed the Bread and Milk program, paying for a daily snack for children in all the schools of the region. Volunteers from the Christian Mothers for Peace baked the bread and prepared the powdered milk.

In areas controlled by the FMLN, community councils were coordinated by regional organizations like CCR and PADECOMSM, each close to one of the five parties that made up the FMLN (in the case of CCR and PADECOMSM, the FPL and the ERP respectively). Salvadoran nongovernmental organizations, staffed by (mostly Salvadoran) professionals and usually funded by foreign sources, provided the organizations with technical assistance. Each of these NGOs was also close to one of the five parties.

After the 1989 offensive foreign governments put pressure on the Salvadoran government to negotiate with the FMLN. To heighten the pressure, international donor organizations (governmental, intergovernmental, and nongovernmental, mainly church-related) increasingly bypassed the government and gave development assistance to popular organizations and NGOs close to the FMLN (Alvarez Solís and Martin 1992; Spence et al. 1994:26). International agencies often tacitly accepted that part of the aid they provided for allegedly nonpolitical development projects was diverted to supporting guerrilla forces, according to François Jean (1993:112–115), though he does not refer specifically to El Salvador.

Outside the Controlled Zones

Communities and popular organizations educated their children and adults throughout El Salvador. In government-controlled zones, they were subject to direct surveillance and had to be cautious, so their efforts were limited and sporadic and did not usually have the same political content as in the controlled zones. A few examples will indicate the variety.

In the mid-1980s, some displaced people living in camps in the capital, seeking permanent resettlement outside guerrilla-controlled territory, took over idle farms in government-controlled zones and formed cooperatives. Some farms were available through the agrarian reform program initiated by the military government in 1980; others were bought by development NGOs, usually with money donated by international agencies. The NGOs assisted the displaced in relocating and starting agricultural cooperatives. These communities—often referred to as relocations (*reubicaciones*) to distinguish them from repopulations in the war zones—also faced problems, but generally not as severe as those of the repopulations. Relocations close to combat were occasionally engulfed by military operations, but most were relatively peaceful. Nevertheless, the new arrivals, who had fled the war zones, were often regarded with suspicion and harassed by the military.

One relocated community created a cooperative on the coast in La Libertad department in 1984. Children from the cooperative could attend a public school, but it was two and a half kilometers away and they had to walk along the heavily traveled Coastal Highway to get there. The cooperative decided to start its own school to save the children the dangerous walk. They did not recruit teachers from among themselves; instead they hired unemployed teachers, who were paid a very small stipend by the Foundation for the Promotion of Cooperatives (FUNPROCOOP).

The cooperative had not had very good relations with the adjoining village, according to Gabriel, the president. "Since we come from outside, they see us as subversives or guerrilla fighters." (He and the other members of the community council, as it happened, formed a band that played and sang political folk music at popular movement demonstrations.) But when they started the school they invited families of the village to send their children. "Now they aren't afraid of us anymore; now we're not the subversives. We have four grades, with sixty children from the cooperative and sixty from outside."

Most of the agrarian reform cooperatives were settled not by displaced people but by the campesinos who had formerly worked there for wages. A very large cooperative near Zacatecoluca, created by the agrarian reform of 1980, had 2,000 manzanas of land (about 3,400 acres) and nearly three hundred families, who lived in two separate settlements on the grounds of the farm. Each of the two settlements had its own education committee. They built two schools, one in each settlement, according to Adolfo, a member. Families contributed the labor and the cooperative hired teachers until the ministry sent official ones.

Heriberto, a young Christian base community activist in the parish of Teotepeque, argued that it was good for communities to have to pay their own teachers so that they did not fall into the habit of relying on handouts from the government: "We shouldn't wait until somebody gives; we should just do what we have to do on our own." But agrarian reform cooperatives had other resources: they could use government credit for operating expenses, and they did not always repay it (Thiesenhusen 1995:152–153).

Some communities tried to get the Ministry of Education to recognize their popular schools officially. They hoped that pupils would get official certificates of grade completion and that the ministry would provide (and pay) professional teachers. These did not necessarily go together. As discussed in the next chapter, local ministry officials exercised some discretion over the giving of certificates, and a supervisor or a principal of a nearby official school sometimes certified children at the end of a school year as if they had attended the official school. Ministry teachers were assigned to some communities, but very few. In a few schools (even in FMLN-controlled Morazán) professionals hired by the ministry taught alongside popular teachers.

Other cooperatives promoted adult education to train their own members. In conjunction with the agrarian reform, the Ministry of Education founded the National Literacy Program (PNA) to teach campesinos on the newly formed cooperatives. From 1980 to 1982 the PNA hired young literacy promoters—some with formal teacher training, others with secondary education—to organize literacy classes on the agrarian reform cooperatives and to recruit and train volunteer literacy teachers. Many of these organizers went on to careers in national-level organizations that promoted literacy in the later years of the war.

The new Christian Democratic government elected in 1984 came to power with a declared commitment to formal democracy and allowed opposition groups to organize more freely. Restraints on the repressive apparatus opened up a space in which popular organizations regrouped and new ones formed. Many of them took advantage of the opening to organize literacy campaigns, and others extended popular education to other topics besides basic literacy, such as cooperativism, agricultural methods, and health (including natural medicine).

Cooperatives encouraged all members to learn about cooperative organization and management so that all could take an active part in their operation. But members who were illiterate or had limited schooling could not hold office or perform administrative tasks. Cooperative federations encouraged cooperatives to organize literacy classes, and some even provided materials and training for volunteer teachers as well. Jorge Rivera taught literacy to the members of his cooperative in San Agustín from 1985 to 1987, never losing sight of the relation of literacy to larger goals. "The teaching had a result in the level of organization and literacy, and it aroused people's initiatives. As a result, eight buses were mobilized [to demonstrations in San Salvador]."

Rivera suffered for his involvement.

> We three compañeros who were teaching cooperativism and literacy were captured by the chief of the [Sixth] Brigade in 1987.
> *For how long?*
> We were held for five days.

Undaunted, he went on to become national president of FENACOA in 1990.

The Association of Salvadoran Women (AMS) promoted a literacy campaign as an adjunct to supporting small production projects for women such as raising chickens and making clothes. Every community with a project had to have literate women to run it, and especially to keep the books. Maribel, who ran the AMS's literacy campaign, said that illiteracy was one means of keeping women down even in their own families. More men were literate, and men and women alike were more willing to sacrifice for their sons' education than for their daughters'. She acknowledged, however, that few women identified this different treatment as discrimination or oppression.

In the late 1980s many popular organizations received foreign funding in government-controlled areas as well as in FMLN territory. In 1988 several organizations—among them PADECOMSM, but also some working primarily outside of the war zones, including the AMS, FENACOA, and the Lutheran Church—came together to form CIAZO, the Inter-Association (*Intergremial*) Literacy Committee of the Eastern Zone. Though CIAZO was formed by people close to the ERP, it worked with popular organizations allied with other political-military organizations of the FMLN as well.

CIAZO hired professional teachers to assist the literacy campaigns of the individual organizations. The teachers developed educational materials, including *Alfabetizando para la paz*, the cartilla in which Chebo and his literacy circle found the picture of the campesinos (see chapter 1). CIAZO trained the popular teachers of the participating organizations and gave them multiple copies of the cartilla, a parallel math text, and a workbook to practice writing so that everyone who enrolled could have a copy. CIAZO (and other professionally staffed development organizations) did not replace the grassroots organizations or move into communities on its own, however. It was up to the local organizations to organize the classes and recruit the students and volunteer teachers.

The Biggest Repatriation

The refugees in Colomoncagua and San Antonio did not immediately follow the example of the Mesa Grande repatriation, which began in 1987, but by 1989 they were planning to return too. The largest repatriation was from Colomoncagua, where 8,400 refugees planned to return as a single group to near Meanguera, just north of the Torola River. The Salvadoran government opposed their return, because it did not want to allow such a large concentration in Morazán, but the refugee community laid plans to come home beginning on November 18.

On November 11 the FMLN began the biggest offensive of the war, attacking the heart of San Salvador and holding its own for eleven days despite massive bombing of the working-class residential neighborhoods it had occupied. In one of the war's most shocking incidents, army troops invaded the campus of the Central American University before dawn on November 16, rousted six Jesuit faculty members, including the rector, Ignacio Ellacuría, and their housekeeper and her daughter from their beds and murdered them all. The offensive was defeated, but it made clear that the FMLN's fighting power was much greater than the Salvadoran government and the United States had assumed and that it could continue the war for many years. Recognizing that the war was unwinnable, the government began the serious negotiations that produced a peace treaty little more than two years later.

Even as the offensive raged, the first contingent of refugees from Colomoncagua decided to return on November 18, without permission and on foot. Seven hundred men, women, and children walked the twenty-five miles in one day, set up temporary shelter, and immediately began the task of clearing land and building temporary structures to house the remaining refugees as they arrived. A second group came in December, but it was only on January 14 that the Salvadoran government finally authorized the return. Even more than the returns from Mesa Grande, this move was a major logistical operation. From mid-January until the end of February, a caravan of one hundred trucks made two round trips every week, carrying people, their few belongings, and the dismantled remains of the refugee camp.

The returnees were overjoyed to leave the refugee camp behind and to come back to their homeland. Many of the children had spent their whole lives within a two-kilometer radius, closely watched by their parents lest they come too close to the Honduran soldiers. "You should have seen them," said one father shortly after returning. "They had never been anywhere else. Now they can run, climb the hills, swim in the river. When we arrived there were still fresh mangos, and the kids loved to climb the trees for them." They named their new community Segundo Montes City. Montes, one of the slain Jesuits, was a sociologist who had been to Colomoncagua and written about the refugees.

They had great ambitions for the new city: not to return to farming, but to make Segundo Montes City the industrial center of northern Morazán. They planned to establish small factories, practice the artisans' skills—cabinetry, tailoring, shoemaking—that they had learned in the refugee camp, and supply the surrounding rural communities. They also foresaw the settlement as a model of egalitarian community organization, following the patterns of community developed in the refugee camp (Cagan and Cagan 1991).

The return of eight thousand people to a war-torn and depopulated area had an immediate effect on the entire zone, heightening the anticipation of a return to normal life with the expected peace settlement. The UNHCR built a bridge across the Torola River. Previously inaccessible to vehicles during the rainy season, northern Morazán was now linked to the government-controlled zone to the south and began to receive significantly more commercial traffic. Foreign journalists and agency personnel became regular visitors.

The new community had a political effect in the zone as well. Fifteen repatriates, trained as teachers in the refugee camps, taught in the popular schools of northern Morazán in 1990. Some of the original residents, who had fled to other parts of El Salvador in the early years of the war, began to return to the surrounding villages, in part because publicity about the repatriation encouraged them to think that the zone was livable again. Two small abandoned villages north of Segundo Montes, Arambala and La Joya, were repopulated the year after the refugees returned.

Returnees to Segundo Montes immediately resumed the education that had been universal through sixth grade in the refugee camp and had turned an adult illiteracy rate of 85 percent into its exact opposite, an 85 percent literacy rate. Elementary classes through fourth grade began again almost immediately; school opened for the earliest arrivals among the younger children even before the rest

FIGURE 7. Outdoor class, Segundo Montes City. *Photograph by Steve Cagan.*

of the community had returned. The scope of schooling was reduced, however. No adult classes were offered. Because there were no buildings and the community had to construct homes, schools, and other infrastructure from scratch, classes at first met in the open air. Many teachers complained that the children had no desks to write on and were easily distracted by other classes meeting nearby or the chance to get up and run around.

Segundo Montes City had by far the largest single program of popular education in the country, with 2,600 pupils and 111 teachers in 1990. A committee of five people who had been among the most active in education in Colomoncagua ran it. They oversaw schools and promoted enrollment in each of the five settlements into which the community was divided. During the first year after the return, they conducted daily training sessions for the teachers (the following year the community hired professional teachers as trainers). They administered what was by the standards of popular education a very large budget, including stipends for the teachers (and for some other personnel, including those who worked in the kitchens that provided a snack for all school children every day) and money for supplies.

In Segundo Montes City, as elsewhere, school events became an occasion for community activities: public festivities were held in each of the five settlements to celebrate Teachers' Day (June 22, a school holiday throughout El Salvador). In 1991, Teachers' Day featured public ceremonies honoring the teachers, music, a play about school performed in each settlement by the community theater group, and the traditional soccer games.

But the division of labor in such a large community meant that the education committee took most responsibility and the community as a whole was not as involved as elsewhere. This made education more like an interest group competing with other activities for community resources. Construction of infrastructure was one of the community's major needs, and school buildings had to compete with the demand for homes, medical posts, administrative offices, and production sites. Teachers who held classes five days a week gave time on Saturdays and during school vacations to construction projects. But most of the construction was done by a bureaucratically separate work team with priorities decided by the community's governing council.

As a consequence, the schools took on precisely some of the bureaucratic features that popular education in general claimed to eschew: segmentation as a specialized institution, responsibility in the hands of a few specialists, and distance between the school system and the community as a whole. With such a large population, it was difficult to maintain the level of community involvement found elsewhere, and not only in education. Similar problems of bottlenecks, competition, and lack of funds were felt in Segundo Montes City in other areas of community responsibility—especially health, housing, and the production of goods for market. The community's plans proved overly ambitious, demanding more financial support than donors were willing to give. Having to generate income in a market economy and facing internal conflicts over development policies and allocation of resources, the community cut back on services, and many returned to farming for survival (Cagan 1994).

Meeting Community Needs

For the community councils in the controlled zones, education was an essential community function because their work—and development in general—required trained people. Jorge was president of the community council of El Carasque, a tiny hamlet reached by a footpath from Nueva Trinidad, the site of one of the first schools to reopen in Chalatenango. He explained that for the council, education was a practical necessity: "Sometimes you have to read a paper or a book for something important, not just for yourself but for the community. And we don't do it because we can't." Jorge had had two years of school as a child.

Activists also recognized that many parents were eager for their children to be educated, so starting a school got them committed to the community. But some parents resisted sending their children to school. Giving up a child's field labor could be a hardship. School itself was free, but to send children well dressed, shod, and equipped with a notebook and pencil meant a significant expense for a poor family most of whose livelihood was outside the cash economy (even more so in wartime when the controlled zones were cut off from the rest of the country). According to Carmela of Arcatao, "Some fathers or mothers want to send their kids to school, but since they're very poor they don't have clothes—they may have just one set of clothes to wear. Shoes? Forget it! They can go to school without shoes."

Some disdained education for their children, or feigned disdain to hide the fact that they could not afford it. According to Daniel of La Laguna, many parents believed their children had no more need for education than they did, saying, "I was born that way [illiterate], I've always been that way, I don't live from book learning, I support myself completely with my machete in my hand, working, and that's how I earn my daily bread." But Celina of Arcatao assured, "Most people do want our children to be able to study." Community councils tried to raise money to buy every child a pencil and a notebook (literally the full complement of school supplies for most children). The councils, moreover, "have tried to raise the parents' consciousness so they send their children," according to Felipe of PADECOMSM. "Maybe not in fancy clothes, but let them get the education."

Teachers, community councils, and the regional organizations, CCR and PADECOMSM, called meetings to urge parents to send their children to school. They insisted that it was an obligation. "Ladies and gentlemen," said Felipe, imitating his own best speechmaking style, "what good does it do us if there are two thousand people in this community, and there's no one here who can write a simple letter or sign something when we need it?"

Some even thought that the community organizations should make attendance compulsory. According to Pedro, a teacher and member of the community council of San Diego (in the department of San Miguel adjoining Morazán), "We have to impose a little repression [*represioncita*]. We'll charge [parents] a fine of twenty-five pesos a month." Asked if the council would actually do it, he replied ambiguously, "We'll announce it." Felipe, showing more generosity, nevertheless also thought parents owed it to the community and quoted his exhortation to resistant parents:

> "PADECOMSM is going to give you school supplies, at least a pencil." What we've done is raise the parents' consciousness, and appeal to them: "Don't leave your children illiterate. We don't want things to stay the same and have this society grow up without knowing anything."

And he was not above invoking social pressure:

> In a meeting of a hundred adults, seventy-five percent say, "We'll manage to send our children one way or another," and the rest sit there silently. They are embarrassed to say they won't. So maybe they resent it, but they send the children.

Felipe also led by example. Having finished sixth grade in 1965 when he was fifteen, he was one of six adults who enrolled in the junior high school in Perquín when it reopened under community auspices. He graduated in 1989.

According to Sonia, a Spanish church volunteer who trained teachers in the area around Arcatao, persuasion by people from the community counted for a lot: "It would be very different for you or me to go and say 'Someday you're going to study like I did.' It's much more important that it be someone from the community who is now in the community council or a project and has *benefited* from having learned—or, actually, the whole community has benefited because they have learned. They're working in health, or the teachers, or someone working in the community store, who has to know how to read and keep books."

CCR and PADECOMSM sought assistance from international agencies. They also created bonds of solidarity with sister cities in the United States and Europe whose donations financed new school buildings and special projects. Parents paid nothing. "The share that they pay," according to Alfonso of Arcatao, "is their good will: the good will of the children, and the good will of the parents."

The community councils and the regional organizations did call on the parents for support: to raise money through community activities, prepare snacks, build and maintain the schools and keep them clean, and provide some subsistence help to the teachers. In some places teachers received a small stipend—from the lumber tax in Morazán, provided by the church in Chalatenango—and some received part of the corn harvest. But with only a pittance for the teacher and no money for other staff, keeping the schools running put a premium on volunteers. The school in Nuevo Gualcho, where the refugees from the San Antonio camp in Honduras repatriated, had a separately organized parents'

FIGURE 8. Community construction project, Nuevo Gualcho. *Photo by Dody Riggs.*

committee. But in most cases volunteer effort was mobilized on a community-wide basis.

Community organizations sponsored activities that would normally have been provided as government services. By doing so, in effect, they claimed sovereignty. They exercised that sovereignty under the tutelage (usually indirect) of the FMLN. They ran the schools (and provided health care and credit for agricultural production); they used the power of persuasion to get parents to send their children to school; they taxed commerce and banned alcohol. In the first half of the decade, the PPLs of Chalatenango claimed dual power overtly; now the community councils only made that claim implicitly. The strategy of the *doble cara* required that organizations maintain the appearance of independence and try to get the government to acknowledge their legality (FMLN 1987:26).

The organizations' sovereignty was in any case partial and contested. The boundary between areas controlled by the government and by the FMLN was permeable. There was some contact across the lines of demarcation. Commercial traffic circulated. Residents who traveled from the controlled zones to the larger towns to buy and sell had to pass through military checkpoints where their goods might be confiscated.

Some government services, like mail, continued to function in some places, though erratically. The Ministry of Health mounted an annual vaccination campaign with which the FMLN and communities in the controlled zones cooperated. Even as they claimed sovereignty, people condemned the government for withdrawing services, demanding, for example, that it support their schools. The Ministry of Education paid the salaries of a few teachers working in the controlled zones. Official school authorities in neighboring government-controlled areas occasionally helped the popular schools out—with leftover pieces of chalk and a few textbooks—because they supported the education effort, and perhaps the politics. The popular schools themselves cultivated legitimacy by claiming to offer the same education as state-run schools elsewhere in the country. They hoped that following the Ministry of Education program would not only guarantee the validity of the certificates they issued at the end of each school year, but would prove that they were offering legitimate education, not communist indoctrination.

The most important limit to sovereignty was the presence of the army. Military operations were a frequent reminder that the areas were not truly liberated. When an army unit marched through, people had to stay out of its way. The war affected the functioning of the schools along with the rest of life. Traumatized children had trouble concentrating. During one big bombing raid, Marta said, "The children trembled; you thought some of them were going to faint. Another time we were giving out certificates at the end of the 1986 school year, and we were going to dance and break open some piñatas, and the mortars fell nearby. And that was just when we were encouraging them, and they were beginning to lose their fear."

Interference with classes was not just an accidental byproduct of the war,

FIGURE 9. Bullet-pocked classroom, Valle Verde. *Photo by Dennis Dunleavy.*

because the schools were accused of being centers of subversion, and those who ran them, along with community council members, were targeted. Soldiers harassed children on their way to school. At roadblocks, Felipe said, "They took their notebooks, child by child, to check them because they suspected that the popular teacher was giving them a class of communist doctrine." According to Alfonso of Arcatao, "Sometimes the soldiers ask about the teachers: who put them there, who's paying them." Teachers were accused of indoctrinating children. But they insisted, somewhat disingenuously, that their activities were not political. The army accused Abilio "of giving an hour of class and then another half hour of political talk. It reached the point that they showed up and pulled me out of school, and they were interrogating me for an hour, when I was in the middle of teaching. But they only questioned me."

The communities did everything they could to keep the schools open. The teachers at Nueva Trinidad started teaching in August 1991, only a few months after they had returned from Mesa Grande. Shortly thereafter they faced a major army operation. As Virgilio put it, "We don't suspend classes, because if we stop, we're giving in to the situation. But the point is not to be passive; we have to show that we have the spirit and the will and the interest to keep going, working and learning."

The army confiscated school materials.

> We had a donation of books from the Central American University, and we bought some others, a fourteen-volume encyclopedia. We want to open a cultural center. I was bringing them when I was detained at a checkpoint and they took me to the base. I was interrogated for six hours. Lieutenant Bonilla, one of the most repressive lieutenants of the unit, said to me, "Who's going to read this in Perquín when there are only ignorant people there? You couldn't have a cultural center there. This must be for the comandantes of the FMLN to read!" (Arturo)

The army captured teachers and community council members, like Daniel of La Laguna in 1988: "They held me seventy-two hours. They tortured me for practically two days; I was blindfolded."

Alfonso was captured when troops occupied Arcatao in a massive military operation in March 1987.

> I wasn't supposed to be giving classes at that hour, but some compañeras asked me for support. They felt very nervous so I went to back them up.

They had a large store of school supplies in a storeroom.

> In 1987, through the church, we had requested supplies—notebooks, pencils, erasers, rulers, paper—and in December, 1986, we had gotten some help from our sister city, Madison. A delegation brought

the material and got the necessary permission to bring it here. That material was legal.

When the soldiers started removing it, Alfonso went to the commanding officer to protest; in response, he was detained and taken in a helicopter—along with the school supplies—to the Fourth Brigade Headquarters at El Paraíso and then to the National Police in the town of Chalatenango.

> In the police headquarters they stuck me with something—I don't know if it was wires or needles, but they pricked me to make me give information. And they pulled you out blindfolded in the middle of the night to get information.

The International Committee of the Red Cross, the church, and the teachers' union ANDES all intervened to get him out. Knowing that they were working on his case cheered him up, because

> in those days your family couldn't speak up for you. Your dad or your mom were afraid, and they couldn't stick their necks out.

After twenty-three days of detention, he was released, and most of the confiscated material was returned.

> Back then there was no road; vehicles couldn't get up here. They take it in a helicopter and in fifteen minutes it's in El Paraíso, and then it takes us practically two days to get it back here.
>
> I was seventeen years old. It was an experience. I didn't know much about my rights.

Later that same year, his compañero, popular teacher Francisco Rivera, was murdered. He was presumably not singled out as a teacher; he just happened to be walking home—to the edge of Arcatao—alone after dark when the village was occupied by a military operation.

The School and the Sense of Community

Popular education embodies community spirit. In their work and in their attitudes, teachers, learners, and organizers all stressed the intimate relation of education to the whole of community life. It is impossible to understand popular education without placing this relation to the community at the center of the analysis. The formal literature on popular education usually emphasizes its participatory pedagogy and its ideological content. These are both central to the intellectual design of popular education. The community, however, provides the material context. The social setting in which education is practiced imposes material constraints—in the case of El Salvador, poverty and war were constants. But the social setting also creates opportunities. Schools depended on the support of the communities that established them, and they owed much of their effectiveness to the fact that the educators were rooted in the community and conscientiously molded education to meet community needs. (In chapter 8 I will address the need to modify theoretical accounts of popular education by emphasizing the community context more strongly.)

The schools' names express their connection with their communities. A name is formally bestowed when a new school building is inaugurated, an event that celebrates the community's effort to erect it. The names are usually those of the fallen martyrs of the struggle, from the immediate community or belonging to the country as a whole. Some schools were named for teachers: in Arcatao, Francisco Rivera; in San José las Flores, Buenaventura Chinchilla, martyred in the struggles before the war. Others were named for Archbishop Romero, the murdered Jesuits, or the heroes of the FMLN (Guzmán et al. 1993:44). By placing these names on their schools, communities honored the ideals of the martyrs and pledged that the school would carry those ideals forward.

Community festivals were often held to celebrate such events in the life of the school as the inauguration of a new school building and graduation, which was one of the biggest events of the year in many communities. These daylong celebrations included a ceremony with speeches, athletic events (generally soccer for the men, volleyball for the women), sometimes a play prepared by a theater group, food, and a night of dancing in the center of the village, perhaps even with a band hired from outside the community. People from the surrounding communities were invited and fed. It took weeks of planning, a good deal of cash from the community council, and the work of many people to make them a success.

Communities depended on education and believed in it. They put their collective energy into it because they believed it was the key to improving their lives. In turn they counted on the schools to support the communities' development. Some people had a generalized faith in the efficacy of education to bring change; it was on that basis that they urged those parents who resisted to educate their children. Felipe of PADECOMSM encouraged parents to send their children to school because "we don't want everything to stay the same." Life in Segundo Montes City, argued Luisa, the education coordinator, was going to be different because of everything the returnees had learned in the refugee camp: it was unthinkable "that the child should just sharpen his machete and have us go back to the life we had before." Luisa was very soft-spoken, but she became palpably angry at the thought that parents might consign their children to the same ignorance they had grown up in.

Some had a more specific vision that the schools could train people from the community itself in the technical skills needed to achieve social change—so that they did not have to rely on outsiders, Luisa said. Comandante Nidia Díaz expressed much the same thought: "For us [the FMLN], it's basic to overcome ignorance—and I don't just mean literacy, but in general—because for us freedom is based precisely on the domination of man over nature and society, and to the extent that you learn to understand it, you're capable of transforming it; you're not a slave."

The relation between school and community was not perfectly harmonious—they could come into conflict at many points. The war had to take priority: during the guindas, a military operation could require a whole community to relocate and suspend classes until everyone had settled down. In Morazán, the adult literacy circles were suspended in 1991 when an army operation kept militia members occupied for several months.

Even in peaceful times there were competing priorities, Alfonso said. "There have been times when we've gotten into different activities with the pupils, and sometimes without the pupils, and we've had to suspend classes, though not for long periods: peace demonstrations, marches to support workers in San Salvador, rebuilding the bridge, reopening the road, festivals, conferences."

In Segundo Montes, much larger than any other of these communities and with an elaborate bureaucratic organization, schools had to compete with other community facilities for priority in construction and assignment of budget.

Schools sometimes lost teachers because they were reassigned to other tasks. Being a teacher was often a proving ground for someone who would then be promoted to a more responsible community position. (But at least they were replaced, according to Antonio, who supervised education for the FMLN in Chalatenango during the war. "With the government, when a teacher leaves, that's that. But not there [in communities with popular education]. They choose someone from the population itself.") In Segundo Montes City, those who had been trained as teachers in Colomoncagua were generally the most skilled at tasks requiring literacy. Since the community's elaborate organization required a large office staff, many teachers were reassigned to work in the offices where their skills were needed, leaving the schools to recruit new, inexperienced teachers.

Young teachers also left to join the guerrilla army. (As Orlinda of San José las Flores pointed out, however, they did so for self-protection as well as duty: "They might as well, if they're going to be stopped at a roadblock all the time.")

Placing a high value on education could demand the surrender of deeply held values and traditions, as with Luisa's insistence that people could not just sharpen their machetes. Or Orlinda of San José las Flores: "In assemblies we tell them that it is important for their children to study, because they are not always going to be campesinos like their parents." Guatemalan Nobel Peace Prize winner Rigoberta Menchú reports in her autobiography that although her father was a campesino activist, he did not want her to learn to read, because he was afraid she would reject her Indian heritage and abandon the community (1984:89).

Conflicts could arise between people at different levels in the community structure. Some traded on their superior preparation or political position. In the mid-1980s a combatant who was a university-educated math teacher, conducting a training session for popular teachers in Chalatenango, criticized Francisco

Rivera, the popular teacher later murdered by the army in Arcatao, for not learning fast enough and wanted to expel him. The other popular teachers protested. According to Antonio, another university-educated combatant, the math teacher "acknowledged his mistake, criticized himself, and offered to resign. We teachers who were doing the training said he should stay, because we weren't against him. And it was worked out."

Political cadres sometimes made imperious demands. At a teacher training session in Torola in 1991, Soledad complained that community council members were sometimes rude and overbearing. Pedro, who was both a popular teacher and a member of the executive council of PADECOMSM, countered that "it's worse when the people treat the council members badly. Sometimes we have to get a little tough [*radicales*] to get people to work." (Pedro also called for "a little repression" to compel parents to send their children to school.)

They were bantering. But there were real differences between those in political office and others (just as there were between well-educated outsiders and community members) that could lead to conflicts. FMLN cadres and community leaders demanded discipline and dedication and complained when others slacked off. I asked Gilberto, who coordinated farm work in the repopulation of Panchimilama, near Lake Ilopango, how he got the men in the community to work together. "It's not easy [*¡Cuesta!*]," he replied. Civilians, on the other hand, guarded their freedom of action, as in the case of the reemerging Christian base communities in Morazán that had struggled to assert their autonomy from the FMLN.

Most of the time, however, mutual learning overcame the hierarchical distance between teacher and pupil or leader and follower. Political cadre and professional educators frequently proclaimed that they learned more from the communities than they taught them. This claim may seem exaggerated, particularly since it was often repeated like a slogan. Because I approach education as a professional, I myself was sometimes skeptical. But I was persuaded that the sentiment was genuine by some spontaneous expressions that emerged in interviews. To the fieldworker, the most surprising responses are often the most revealing. An unexpected reply can expose one's faulty assumptions. When I spoke to people in leadership roles, I sometimes asked questions that presumed that they acted as teachers, not learners, but they replied by putting themselves in the same category as learners. When Antonio told me the story of the math teacher who wanted to expel Francisco Rivera, I asked whether the math teacher had learned his lesson. "Yes," he replied. "The thing is, we learn [*es que aprendemos*]." With his "we," he spontaneously identified himself with those who were learning.

When I met Narciso, the president of the El Zancudo community council who had gone to San Francisco Gotera to buy fertilizer, we both had a day to kill in the PADECOMSM office in Perquín. He was waiting over for a PADECOMSM meeting the next day, and I was laid up, having pulled a muscle during recreation at a teacher training session. During a long afternoon's conversation, I asked whether his council sponsored educational work in the community. To my surprise he began by talking not about reading and writing, but about how hard it was to get people to join in collective production, because everyone wanted to farm his own piece of land. But people had reached the point that they now harvested collectively, even though they then sold the crop individually. "That's how we go about teaching each other [*así nos vamos educando*]," he concluded.

Narciso clearly assumed, first, that education is manifest in community participation, not just in knowing how to read. It embraces everything people do together to improve themselves. Even more important, "We [*all*] teach each other." The form in Spanish, "*Así nos vamos educando*," like many Spanish reflexive constructions, cannot be translated into English satisfactorily because it combines two meanings: "that's how we go about teaching ourselves" and "that's how we go about teaching each other." But either way it emphasizes that everyone learns and teaches at the same time. Education is not a one-way street.

My questions to Narciso and Antonio presumed that they were educators, not people to be educated. But both answered by placing themselves among the learners. Spontaneously expressing their sense of mutuality, of everyone learning together, they showed that mutuality is a felt reality. Education is supported by the whole community because everyone wants to learn, and can learn. Those whom an outsider might see as conducting the process view themselves as participants along with everyone else.

Despite occasional contradictions, most saw no fundamental conflict between education and their strong sense of membership in, and commitment to, their communities because they genuinely believed that the schools' existence was a fulfillment of their rights as community members. They made this clear in statements about the meaning of popular education. In chapter 1 I summarized participants' vision of popular education, and in chapter 8 I will elaborate on that summary by analyzing the ways they used the term. I anticipate that more detailed discussion here with two points that illustrate the close relation they perceived between the community and popular education. First, many informants defined popular education by universal access; second, they identified educating for community participation as a major purpose.

Popular education is for everyone. The right to education is enormously important to people who grew up in a society where education was a class privilege, even though it was nominally free and universal. The fact that popular education makes that right a reality informs their understanding of education itself, of their communities, and of themselves as individuals.

They also believe that the goal of education is to make people contribute to the community. This belief sometimes takes a rather conformist form: schools should teach their children to behave. (In fact, one meaning of *educado* in Spanish is "well-behaved.") But more importantly, popular education is education for cooperation: it teaches people how to cooperate, it teaches them to value cooperation, and it provides the skills that enable them to make a contribution to their communities. Popular education imparts specific skills and values at the same time.

Universal entitlement and education for community participation go hand in hand. That both were presented as intrinsic to the meaning of popular education illustrates once again its integration into the whole of community life. People who get education receive a clear benefit, but they are obligated in return. The community both provides education and gives it its purpose.

CHAPTER 6

The Classroom

————

*T*he immediate objective of popular education is to teach basic academic skills. Its scope is broad, embracing consciousness-raising, organizing, and human liberation, but teachers and learners nevertheless devote most of their attention to reading, writing, and sometimes arithmetic. And although they espouse an open-ended and dialogical pedagogy to engage the learners' attention and stir them to action, classroom practices often resemble the conventional pedagogy they claim to eschew. In this chapter I will examine the process of popular education in the classroom.

The story of the popular classroom is primarily the teachers' story, because its greatest impact was on them, not the students. While popular education rhetorically proclaimed the equality of teacher and student (and realized it to a significant degree, more than in most schools), the teachers nevertheless played the larger role. They took responsibility for what went on in a class. If their practice often fell short of the ideal, it was in part due to their lack of training and experience—often they had just barely mastered the grade level they were teaching. Most of them doubted their legitimacy as teachers; some feared being exposed as frauds. They faced other problems as well: lack of adequate resources and the constant disruptions of the war. But they discovered that they could do it. For all their limitations, many of them turned out to be far more competent than they had allowed themselves to believe.

Collaboration and voluntarism were hallmarks of popular teachers' work. Collaboration among themselves, and sometimes with advisors, helped them gain confidence. Their willingness to work was rooted in ideological commitment and group solidarity, reinforced by the belief that their effectiveness as teachers depended more on their community spirit and their desire to educate children than on their training or technical skill. This perspective had costs as well as benefits. Skill was not always rewarded, and poor performance was often not acknowledged. But mobilizing people's commitment allowed the schools to operate at very low cost; it would have been impossible to run them if they had required more resources.

In this chapter I will look most closely at refugee camps and repopulated communities rather than the more ephemeral processes in communities in flight and in the guerrilla army. Classes held on the run were an important proving ground for popular education, but they did not allow teachers to adopt a defined curriculum or practice a consistent methodology. The more stable communities could routinize their schools (to a degree). A teacher and a group of students could expect to work together for a significant period, and their work could be part of a long-term program.

Becoming a Popular Teacher

Becoming a popular teacher was an adventure. As with other adventures, people anticipated it with excitement, but also with trepidation and fear of inadequacy. It tested them, and passing the test earned them well-deserved pride. But at the start they expressed their self-doubt poignantly. When Rosario was asked to teach in Colomoncagua, she "felt pretty inadequate." Chebo, the fisherman who taught adults near San Salvador, said that the hardest thing about being a teacher was overcoming his fear. Gabriela said that she "felt very nervous about facing a whole group, because I was very shy."

Teachers felt these fears even though they had managed to get educated against heavy odds when they were growing up. Further, they had managed to maintain their skills, an achievement not to be taken for granted. Where they grew up, there was little need for literacy: no newspapers, few books, no street signs, none of the everyday occasions that make knowing how to read a necessity in a literate culture. So even for someone who had learned, finding opportunities took an effort. Many people who went to school for a few years let their skills atrophy.

The fact that those who later became teachers maintained their skills, therefore, may mean that they were especially motivated. I asked them what they had done to keep them up.

> I've always remembered. When I was a girl I liked to read books. Sometimes I saw a book and asked to borrow it, and I studied it. (Marta)

> My grandfather had a lot of books. I had a book about Christopher Columbus and the discovery of America. And there were some books in the *Mantilla* series. (Gabriela)

Gerardo remembered his early reading material:

> I tried to keep on reading and writing, so I wouldn't forget.
>   *And what did you find to read?*
>   I had a book—I think it was called *Colección Sembrador* [Sower collection]. It was a book of stories. I got a geography book. And then I had bought a book called *Spanish Grammar*.

Where did you buy these books?
In San Miguel.
Did you go to San Miguel pretty often?
Once in a while. Not so often.

Others took on special tasks that required them to read. Pedro trained as a health promoter. "People gave me some books. They came from the Red Cross, and gave away a book that said, *Where There Is No Doctor*." Several people, including Pedro, mentioned *La escuela para todos* (School for everyone), an annual almanac for all of Central America that includes a broad range of articles: practical advice about crops and livestock, short stories, and descriptions of distant places for cultural enrichment.

Writing was even less a necessity of everyday life than was reading. Some made a point to practice, like Gerardo.

I just wrote a few little things, sometimes a letter, or [hesitation] other little things, notes. And what I did sometimes work on a little bit was numbers. For example, reviewing the matter of adding, multiplying, dividing.
And you did that just for fun [gusto], *additions and multiplications?*
Yes.[1]

Rufino never went to school.

My parents were poor. And we were a big family, nine children, and we older ones had to help our father to support the littler ones.

But he learned to read when he went into the army at seventeen.

When I left the barracks, I had gotten interested in learning to read and write. So I wrote on hemp leaves, I wrote on the ground, in the dirt, on stones, on trees.
You didn't have any paper?
No, I didn't have any paper.
And what did you write?
I wrote things that I saw in a book where I read the word of God. It was a book of the gospel, and I wrote what I saw there.
Copying?
Yes. In that way I got more and more skilled in writing and reading.

Some people used their skills in their political activity. Pedro, who had read *Where There Is No Doctor*, was a member of the PADECOMSM executive council as well as a volunteer teacher. To invite people to a meeting or publicize a vaccination campaign, he had to write messages. But he also clearly had a strong desire. When he mentioned that he had read a book about raising cattle even though he had none, I asked him why. "Because I'm curious to know all these things. Because it's useful. If somebody has a problem with a cow, you can help solve it."

Teachers described their recruitment as somewhat random. Others may have spotted them as having special interest and aptitude, but the teachers themselves generally did not think they had been singled out. Someone asked them and they were willing. Teachers were chosen for their *conciencia*: they had good will and a desire to contribute to the community, but not necessarily more education or technical skill. They emphasized their willingness to share "the little bit that I know," helping others to the extent of (what they saw as) their limited abilities.

> I said yes, that I would share what I knew. (Gabriela)

> In the canton where I live, the government doesn't send teachers. And since there are so many children who are going without learning to read, it moved me. I was on the community council, and we were promoting it, and the community chose me to work. (Gerardo)

> They met with me to talk about the need, because there were lots of people who did not know how to read and write. And they wanted me to become a teacher. You could see how great the need was. (Rosario)

> As the saying goes, the one who knows a little has to teach it to the one who doesn't know anything. (René)

Volunteers who were uncertain that they were good enough to handle a class were reassured that all they needed was to try hard and want to do a good job; their political consciousness and community spirit were more important than their education. Education organizers emphasized that technical skill was not the most important qualification: literacy teachers "are not necessarily the people with the most education. They need to know how to read and write, and to have a certain understanding of the situation. Some have only been to first or second grade, but we train them," said Angelina, who worked in FENACOA's adult literacy campaign for its cooperatives.

Once a community had operated its own schools for several years, recruitment became more routine. Experienced teachers continued, and new ones were recruited from among the star pupils of the popular schools themselves. Arcatao had had a junior high school before the war, so its volunteers were somewhat better educated.

Teaching was a commitment. Teachers worked for free, or at best for a minimal stipend. There were some whose good will ran short. Leonardo, who had completed seventh grade in Arcatao before the war, was a disabled veteran of the guerrilla army; he had lost his left hand (his writing hand) when a grenade he was carrying exploded. After the accident he took refuge in Mesa Grande and then joined the repatriation to San Antonio los Ranchos. He taught during the 1992 academic year but declined to continue: "I thought the subsidy that they gave was pretty low. It's not a salary, you can only call it a subsidy. It didn't support my family."

Those who did teach did so on top of their normal day's work in the field or the home: men had to go to the fields every day to work, since they had to feed their families; and women worked a double day (something women do nearly everywhere, but in most places they get paid for at least one of their workdays). Some in the popular schools taught two shifts (the normal school day was three hours, in the morning for younger children and in the afternoon for older ones), and some taught three. When the refugees in Colomoncagua returned to El Salvador, Ramón was one of the teachers sent by Segundo Montes City to work in neighboring villages. In La Joya, he was expected to teach morning and afternoon classes. But he also taught a class of adults from five to seven in the afternoon—"that was of my own free will." Fernando from the mountains of northeastern Morazán also taught three shifts every day after getting up and leaving home at five to work in his cornfield for three hours.

But they were less concerned about the workload than about their abilities. Some described becoming a teacher as a risk, but they did not mean the risk of capture, imprisonment, disappearance, or death at the hands of the security forces, although all these were real dangers to popular teachers. What they worried about was being exposed as frauds. Ramón was afraid that his pupils' parents, refugees in Colomoncagua, would find mistakes in their children's notebooks and blame him. "I was afraid of making a mistake. Because there are parents who may know how to read, and would check what the child did. And if there was a mistake, the parent could say, 'Look, he made a mistake.'"

When Alfonso said that a popular teacher needed "courage"—even though he had been captured in Arcatao and imprisoned for three weeks—he meant the courage to attempt to teach. "We've been developing our classes to the best of each one's ability. What has counted most is each person's initiative and courage, but you always have problems—for example, how to develop this topic or that area. Sometimes pupils ask questions that leave you—you can't find a way to help them understand." The teachers, he added, "helped each other by giving each other more courage. We raised each other's spirits."

At the beginning of the 1992 school year, Leonel of San Antonio los Ranchos was asked to teach third grade. He declared his reluctance at a meeting of all his fellow teachers: "I want you to evaluate my ability." Justino, education representative for the community council (in effect, the school principal), responded, "I think we all have deficiencies." Leonel insisted: "I don't feel like I can. I've never gone to class"—his four years of adult education in Mesa Grande apparently did not count. He was persuaded by Justino's reassurances, however, and the following year he became education representative himself.

One can ask whether these expressions of modesty might in part have been reactions to a tall, light-skinned, bearded, inquisitive gringo. Leonel, however, was talking not to me but to his fellow teachers. Even in interviews, I believe such remarks were unguarded. When Ramón feared that his pupils's parents might find mistakes in their children's notebooks and blame him for them, he was talking about people whose level of literacy was surely lower than his own. This lack of self-confidence appears too ingrained to be attributed to my presence.

There were many who found themselves at sea in the classroom at first. They had to figure out what to do in front of a group of restless children or tired adults. They drew on memories of school from childhood:

> I remembered that when I was in school, the first thing they taught me were the vowels. So that's where we started. But sometimes when you don't know what to do, you teach a whole bunch of things really fast, but the kids don't learn them. (Gerardo)

> [We thought of] the little bit we had learned when we were children. We started out with no book. So we set out a little group of words. For example, the word "house," the word "shovel," the word "ruler," "top." And we took apart the syllables to put together more words. And that's how we taught: the same as we had learned. (Marta)

> I studied spelling books to be sure of how to write. I also practiced spelling, on the blackboard. And I studied social studies books, because in social studies the knowledge is vaguer. (Rufino)

Mateo, who was one of the first teachers in San José las Flores after the repopulation, found that "you wound up crazy because sometimes you didn't even understand what you were teaching." Once, while addressing an academic conference, I said that popular teachers are often only one step ahead of their pupils. Getting an unexpected laugh, I added that this was of course unknown among full-time professors with Ph.D.s. In fact, all of us who teach know that that is the best way to master a subject; no matter how much we know when we start, we discover that we still have a lot to learn.

Popular teachers brought to the classroom a spontaneous warmth, fortified by the conviction that all the children were capable of learning and had a right to an education. Men and women alike, without evident self-consciousness, used the word "love" when talking about their relations with their pupils. According to Rosalina of Arcatao, teachers work "out of conciencia and love for the people, out of love for having these children learn a little." Abilio joined the pupils' games during recess "so that they would gain confidence and love for me."

Popular teachers were determined not to reproduce one trait many remembered from their own education in official schools before the war, said Rosalina. "We don't use force or mistreat the children the way teachers used to: pulling your ears, or your hair." Justino said that love was precisely what those teachers had lacked. "They didn't have that fraternal love between teacher and pupil. Whenever the pupil made a mistake, crack! with the ruler."

Most teachers professed that every student, no matter how slow, was capable of learning. A pupil who had a hard time in class simply needed extra attention. (There were exceptions, however. Mateo thought that some children were just too backward and couldn't learn. Moreover, as already mentioned, it was not uncommon for children to be held back, although it was not particularly stigmatized.)

Classroom Pedagogy

Popular educators endorsed participatory, liberating teaching and criticized the authoritarian, rote-learning classes of traditional education, and some dynamic teachers threw themselves into the material with enthusiasm. Many, however, presented lessons by rote; group recitation and copying were their most common activities.

In 1991 in a second-grade classroom in El Carrizal, a young woman was teaching multiplication by 3 and 4 to six children. (A couple of other children were there, but spent their time running around making mischief rather than attending to the multiplication tables. I never determined if they were supposed to be part of the class, or if they were perhaps younger siblings a member of the class had had to bring along.)

The teacher wrote the threes on the board ("$3 \times 1 = 3$, $3 \times 2 = 6$," etc.) and waited while the children copied them down. They then recited them in chorus. The first time through, she guided them by pointing to each entry. Then they tried it a second time without her pointing, but the group very quickly fell into a confused babble, as some recited more quickly than others. She called on a few pupils to recite them to the whole class. Then she listened as each child, individually and very quietly, recited from the notebook. Some appeared to have gotten the point, others not.

Recitation in chorus meant that children who had not grasped the material or were inattentive simply sat in silence. When a teacher called on pupils to read individually, some read with assurance; some sounded out the words on the page but conveyed no understanding; and some could not read at all. But most of the time they could get away with not being called on to know.

Teachers also relied on copying from the board—even the teachers in Segundo Montes City, who were better prepared than most. Those who had taught in Honduras had had the benefit of working with international volunteers in daily training sessions, and school had had no competition from the demand to work in the cornfield. Even those who only began teaching after they returned to El Salvador had gotten an intensive elementary education in the refugee camp. But they, too, had their limitations. Eighteen-year-old Tobías, who had spent half his life in Colomoncagua, taught a third-grade class outdoors in Segundo Montes City. As he wrote on a small blackboard propped up on a makeshift easel, fourteen children sat on rocks hunched over the notebooks on their laps and copied from the board. Twenty yards away in each direction was another similar group of children.

Tobías wrote out the "script" he had learned in a training session the day before:

The Bones

The joint is the union of two or more bones. Example: the elbow, the knee, the fingers. The joint allow [*sic*] us to move the arms, the legs, the neck, walk and make all movements.

He read the text aloud, and all the children then read it in chorus. He offered no further explanation and did not prompt any discussion. Next he drew diagrams showing the body parts in cross section and labeled them "joint of the knee," "idem of the elbow," and "idem of the hand." The diagrams were complicated, but he made them clear and fairly well-proportioned. As the children copied them he walked among them and checked their copying. He picked up one child's notebook and redrew something. Like the script, the drawings were something he himself had learned in training only that day or the day before: he had copied them from the blackboard into his notebook (although he may also have had a chance to look at the textbook from which they were taken), and their accuracy depended on his ability to copy (twice—from the blackboard to his notebook, and from his notebook to the blackboard in his own "classroom").

There were twenty-five children in the class, but nearly half were absent. It was July, the height of the growing season, and Tobías explained to me that parents often expected children to skip class to go help out in the fields.

After a while he announced a recess. But the children sat on their rocks, did not get up or even talk very much. Then, though the class was scheduled to continue until 4:00, its appointed time for afternoon snack was 3:15, so all went off for a snack. Snacks were provided in the school kitchen, a covered building where each class had an appointed time and all the children in the class came and lined up. The kitchen was full all morning and all afternoon, as each class marched through. Since it was close to quitting time, Tobías picked up the blackboard and moved it to under the eave of a building where he hoped it would not get too wet overnight.

Some teachers were only on the borderline of literacy when they started. (If they taught for several years, they invariably improved, though the students they taught in the first years doubtless suffered.) Others were more advanced, but had poor handwriting and spelling, which they passed on to their pupils. Some who had fully mastered the material of the early grades nevertheless had little confidence or originality, and relied heavily on group recitation or prepared scripts because they felt incapable of presenting the material spontaneously; they had to have a crutch to rely on.

By following a script, teachers had something concrete to offer to their pupils that conformed to a formal curriculum, but it provided little more. Advisors discouraged copying because it dulled the children's creativity. When she trained first-grade teachers in Colomoncagua, Anita said,

I always insisted that they had to arouse the children's interest. My struggle was against copying. Of course, you can understand why if you have no resources and all the children are there together and you have a headache, you set them to copying and you calm down. I understand.

What did you want them to do?

Not put the lesson on the board for the children to copy, but begin with "Let me tell you what happened to me today!" Something to get their attention.

There was another reason for the reliance on copying: the children had no textbooks. The only written material they saw was what they copied from the blackboard into a notebook. In this, too, popular schools hardly differed from many official schools, especially in poor communities, which likewise lacked textbooks. Copying was part of the school culture, and neither the children nor their parents expected anything different.

This limited the amount of material students could receive in a day's class, and what they got was likely to contain errors. Teachers sometimes wrote their scripts on the blackboard with errors, and the children were even more likely to make mistakes in copying. So even if they studied the material in their notebooks, they would perpetuate errors made at any stage in transmission.

If some teachers were short of both academic preparation and creativity, all the schools were short of equipment and supplies. When a community first tried to organize a school the scarcity was at its most extreme. Marta "went around from one place to another looking for benches. We had no blackboard, we had no chalk. There was a teacher working in Loma de Osicala [south of the Torola River, in the government-controlled zone] and I asked him with all my heart, begging, to give me a few sticks of chalk. He sent me a handful of tiny pieces. I could hardly hold them. And the blackboard was a piece of plywood. In fact it's still there. We still haven't solved that problem."

Many communities had no school building at first, forcing classes to be held outdoors. During the rainy season, classes had to be suspended when the rain fell every afternoon. Sitting on a rock hunched over a notebook on their laps did not encourage children's good posture, good handwriting, or concentration. Other classes meeting nearby, children running around (who might be cutting school, or might attend the morning session but hang around during the afternoon), and in general all outdoors competed for their attention. When teachers in Segundo Montes City complained about having to teach outdoors, they showed how quickly the relatively luxurious plant and equipment in the refugee camp had made them forget their early experiences.

In El Carasque adult classes met only from 5:00 to 6:30 p.m. because they could not afford to light a lantern every night. If learners were lucky, each had a notebook and a pencil; some only had a torn sheet of paper. To save paper in Colomoncagua, Gabriela said, teachers correcting pupils' work had them erase it and do it over.

FIGURE 10. Popular school, El Sitio del Lago, Cuscatlán. *Photo by Lois Kleffman.*

Teachers often scolded children for wasting supplies and equipment and complained that they made paper airplanes out of pages torn from their notebooks or did not return the notebook they had been given if they dropped out of school. These complaints sometimes sounded petty to an outsider, but in most respects teachers were warm and generous to the schoolchildren. If they complained about waste, it was because they really could not afford supplies—besides, their lives of poverty had schooled them in frugality. Most popular schools provided children with free supplies. The issue of costs was so important that this became an argument to persuade parents to send their children to school: they should seize the opportunity because they would not have to pay for notebooks or pencils.

Popular educators developed their own teaching materials. The basic item, for children or adults, was the cartilla, the first reader, intended to teach all the letters of the alphabet through a few simple words. In it, teachers who had developed an ordering of the material in practice put it in writing. The first word taught was a long word containing all five vowels: in Colomoncagua, *refugiado* (refugee). Jaime, a member of ANDES who helped popular educators to develop curriculum materials, showed me the cartilla produced by ANDES, which began with the word *educación*. "Originally we used *revolucionario*, but it was too dangerous." (The choice depended on the setting. A cartilla used by the PRTC among its own combatants did begin with the word *revolucionario*.)

Though a word that uses all five vowels is necessarily long, a cartilla uses a small vocabulary of simple words (typically fewer than twenty) that includes all the letters. A page is devoted to each word; the word is broken into syllables, and the "syllabic family" (e.g., ma-me-mi-mo-mu) of each syllable is presented. As already mentioned, this is the usual method of teaching beginning readers in Spanish-speaking countries. Some teachers supplemented the cartilla with a *tarjetero*, a set of flash cards with two-letter syllables that can be combined into words. The cards are easy to make and provide an activity for children.

Traditional cartillas began with the word *papá* and the syllabic family of the letter p. According to Cristina, a teacher who worked with CIAZO training volunteer teachers and developing materials, "We think that it should begin with the letter m [for *mamá*], because the majority of Salvadoran families are headed by women; [the children] don't have papas."

But the cartillas of popular education included words chosen for reflection and presented illustrations to stimulate discussion. Elena, who taught in the camp for displaced people in Soyapango and then joined them in their repopulated community, wrote a cartilla. "Some people asked me if we used that method—what's it called?—concientización, like r for repression. I said no, but later on I realized that it was true, because the only thing I wanted to do was gather ideas for the cartilla that were things people live with to identify the letter better and remember it."

Teachers were an important resource for each other. They worked together to solve their problems and find more effective ways to present the material.

FIGURE 11. Popular teacher with *tarjetero* (flash cards), Segundo Montes City. *Photograph by Steve Cagan.*

Teachers offering the same grade met and planned lessons together. This was possible only in the refugee camps and the larger repopulated communities, because only there, and only for the lower grades, was there likely to be more than one person teaching the same grade. Teachers in San Antonio los Ranchos had a three-room house, separate from the school building, which they used as their headquarters. They met there every night to prepare the next day's classes.

Planning meetings filled a gap for those who did not even have a book to tell them what the next lesson should be—Gabriela and Ramón said that in Colomoncagua the main purpose of meetings was to assure quality control and prevent them, in their ignorance, from teaching the wrong thing. But teachers also met to develop cartillas and other texts together. They practiced new methods. Most of all, they reinforced the cooperative spirit that had brought them to volunteer.

Often teachers did not fully understand why the methods they had discovered experimentally or learned from advisors were effective. It appears that they tested their innovations empirically and figured out which ones worked, but without understanding exactly why. Sometimes they offered justifications that seemed extraneous, secondary, or even self-deprecating (such as meeting to assure uniformity in the classes). Some justifications were consistent with a view of education as punitive and tied to a rigid curriculum. Gonzalo, who began teaching in Colomoncagua at thirteen, explained why he asked pupils to go to the front of the room and write answers to questions on the blackboard. "Sometimes I checked their notebooks, but you didn't know if they had copied from someone else. Getting someone to go the board, you could see how smart he was, and whether he could do it or not." Even though Gonzalo thought that he should march students to the board to test whether they had learned, the exercise could serve other, more positive purposes. Many popular education techniques will stimulate an active response even if the person conducting the session does not contemplate all their effects.

Adult Literacy Circles

Adult education was conducted more informally, even though teaching adults to read is often regarded as the most important goal of popular education. (In many countries, in fact, the term "popular education" refers only to adult education. In El Salvador, though, it included the community-run elementary schools; education of adults and children was seen as a single effort and based on the same set of methodological and organizational principles.) Theories of popular education gave adult learning higher priority. However "popular" the educational process in elementary schools, children attended mainly because their parents sent them, and they accepted what they were offered. If adults studied, presumably they chose to be there. They knew what—and why—they wanted to learn, and, more than children, they could shape the process to their needs. Most of what theorists present as specific to popular pedagogy is designed for adults and intended to arouse their motivation, on the assumption that they would not take the trouble to learn for the sake of literacy in the abstract. Concientización is therefore necessary because dialogue about everyday life will motivate adults to participate and make what they are learning relevant. Raising their consciousness, moreover, will make the literacy circle an organizing tool.

In practice, however, adult education was generally not the first priority in communities. People were determined to give their children the opportunity to learn, but many doubted their own ability and resisted. And those who joined a circle as teachers or learners frequently found themselves called away by the demands of making a living or by political duties.

On an agricultural cooperative near Chirilagua in 1991, the FENACOA literacy team led a session that was both a literacy circle and a training session for two young women who had volunteered to lead it. The word for the day was *casa*. The participants looked at a photograph of a shack in *Alfabetizando para la paz*, the CIAZO cartilla, which contained photographs illustrating each generative word. Miguel, coordinator of the FENACOA literacy program, asked them what they saw in the picture and what they liked about it. One said, "The trees are nice but the house isn't."

Why don't people have decent houses? "The government doesn't care about poor people." "Sometimes it's because they can't find work, sometimes it's because they don't take care of what they earn—they drink it up." Miguel underlined this point: "Because we're not educated, we don't know how to take care of things. Other people take advantage of us."

They then discussed their own houses: small, with leaky roofs, and not divided into rooms. "We don't take care of the houses because they aren't ours. We live here on the *hacienda* [the farm that had been taken over as a cooperative in the agrarian reform]."

Next Miguel asked how they might get better houses. The idea of a housing cooperative arose; they could make their own adobe bricks, and save money to buy clay tiles or zinc sheets, as they preferred, for the roofs. "The price is about the same," said Miguel, "but if you have to transport them here, tiles are likely to shatter on these roads."

Reading and writing began only after the reflection; they turned to the word *casa* and its syllabic families. Adults learning to write for the first time, especially if they had spent most of their lives working in the fields, found that manipulating a pencil required a manual dexterity quite unlike the heavy physical labor they were used to. Miguel told them, "We're used to holding a sickle. [To hold a pencil] you have to stick just one finger out. Even to stick out only two is difficult." (Others who taught adults confirmed how hard writing was for beginners, like Rosario, whose adult students in Colomoncagua made a fist to pick up a pencil, and Chebo, who said that some of the members of his literacy circle "break the pencil when they pick it up.")

To start, they practiced dexterity exercises with the fingers and the wrist. As they began writing, they were given metaphors for the shapes to produce: first, draw "wheels and mountains." Then form letters: a tortilla for o, a stick of sugarcane for i, a horseshoe for u, and various combinations of these figures for other printed letters.

Later that day the cooperative held a meeting. The participants in the literacy circle joined the cooperative's other members. They discussed work assignments, and then the agenda turned to education. The two women who were to lead the circle had complained that they had signed up twenty-two people, but none had shown up for the first meeting. Miguel decided that the occasion called for a pep talk:

> The disease of illiteracy is suffocating us—not just in El Salvador, but in all of Latin America. Here we made a list of people who can't read, but when the circle started, they didn't show up.
>
> It's important to know how to read and write so you can learn more. Lots of people argue, "I'm old, I can't learn." But it's not true. As long as we are alive, we have to learn. We human beings are born learning and we die learning. Look at compañero Jack [Hammond]. He's a teacher, and he's been working at it for years, but he comes here to learn from us!
>
> An adult who doesn't know how to read feels shy and doesn't want to speak out. He's afraid people will make fun of him. He feels shunted aside, worth less than other people. But it's not true. Look at Guillermo [another member of the FENACOA team who, unlike

LEAMOS Y PLATIQUEMOS

El analfabetismo nos aprieta.

En nuestro país hay injusticia social.

Pocos tienen mucho: grandes casas, haciendas, comida abundante, trabajan cuando quieren, sólo se la pasan ordenando.

En fín, viven como reyes.

La mayoría de nosotros tenemos poco, ni siquiera podemos estudiar.

HAY ANALFABETISMO por que HAY INJUSTICIA SOCIAL

FIGURE 12. "Illiteracy is squeezing us. . . . There is illiteracy because there is social injustice." *Preparémonos para Seguir Aprendiendo.* CIAZO, 1992.

Miguel, had a university education]: he's a teacher. He even knows how to speak English. But give him a sickle or a plow and he won't know what to do with it.

These pep talks were not superfluous. As in the refugee camp, some people protested that they were too old to learn, but teachers and organizers insisted to the contrary. "Education is like love," said Arturo of PADECOMSM. "There's no age for it."

Many campesinos were embarrassed to admit that they needed to learn. Daniel, a member of the executive council of PADECOMSM, said that "the shame of [illiteracy] killed me. That's how I felt." In San Luis de Mariona, on the semirural fringe of San Salvador, a group of people, mostly women, who had volunteered to be health promoters met in 1991 for one of their first training sessions. Emiliano, the president of the community council, sounding very tentative, made a request: "Maybe someone who knows how to read can bring a notebook and write down the most important things." This inspired a young man to offer to "help out" any women who did not know how to read and write. Cecilia, who trained the health promoters, followed this up: "Sometimes people are embarrassed to admit it, and we are embarrassed to ask. But it's important, and we have to trust each other and say it."

To overcome this feeling of shame, organizers tried to demystify literacy by showing that campesinos who lacked it nevertheless had skills that others valued. Julio Portillo, who had been secretary general of ANDES, described the process of organizing a rural community:

> Some may show up who know how to ride horseback, some others may show up who know how to read and write, others who know how to fish with a net, or with a hook and line, others who know how to milk cows. Some will know how to grow vegetables, others know how to grow watermelons, others know how to plant peanuts. You do an inventory. Presumably you're not just thinking about literacy, but organization in general.

In a community under attack, knowing how to fish, ride, and plant were survival skills that could save the lives of educated people. In the guerrilla army, combat skills and ability to live off the land had much more practical use day to day than reading and writing.

Some teachers and organizers encouraged others by their own example. Felipe of PADECOMSM returned to junior high school and graduated more than two decades after finishing grade school. Julio Portillo, who was a professor in a teacher training institute, grew up in a campesino family. Miguel, who worked for FENACOA, a national organization, was a campesino.

Success was a source of pride to the newly literate and to those who recruited and taught them, like Jorge Rivera, who later became president of FENACOA:

> Even my mother said it was impossible for her. A campesino compañero said, "I'm made for the plow but a pencil is different." Nevertheless everyone, 95 percent, so to speak, learned to read and write.

Your mother too?
Yes, my mother too.
In your class?
Yes.

If reflection and concientización were central to motivating people to learn, they also slowed the process down. Well-educated urbanites could not dictate the pace of learning any more than they could speed up organizing efforts. They had to adopt a rhythm that accommodated the campesinos' lack of academic background—and, more generally, the slower pace of rural life. It made some people impatient. Father Rogelio Ponceele thought concientización took too long and that people should just learn to read.

But that would work only for those who were already strongly motivated. Reflection was a necessary warm-up. The discussion of *casa* reported above was a case in point: it started slowly; a few people offered stereotyped responses, and the outsiders from the federation intervened several times to keep the discussion moving. In many circles, people seemed reluctant to join in such discussions. They did not have much experience with, or inclination toward, abstract thinking. Nor were they used to speaking out, especially in formal settings and in the presence of outsiders. With encouragement, more of them spoke up, but the slow start made clear that they had to be loosened up.

Concientización meant identifying problems and their causes. People held the government, the army, and the war responsible for much of the deprivation they suffered. Reflection was not just a hunt for scapegoats, however. They also acknowledged their own responsibility. If they lived in substandard housing, maybe it was because they spent their money on drink or because they failed to take care of their cooperative's property. Other discussions took similar directions, especially those involving relations between men and women. Men who resented women's learning or their activism admitted to their machismo, thereby taking the first step in the very long process of overcoming it.

According to the theory, reflection and consciousness-raising are supposed to go beyond discussing problems and their causes to action aimed at solving them. This principle, however, was honored more in the breach than in the observance. In communities in FMLN-controlled zones, there was followup, but not normally in the context of a literacy circle itself. Adult education was only one of a community's activities, and activism could be channeled into other projects already underway. Elsewhere, literacy circles did not usually lead to action projects, for a variety of reasons. Participation in a circle did not necessarily grow out of activism. In urban areas, where literacy was more of a practical necessity, there were many learners for whom political conviction was not the dominant motive. Those for whom it was might be unwilling to organize publicly for fear of repression.

Adult education generally began in a community after schools were already operating for children; many practical problems had already been solved. If there was a building for a day school, it could be used at night. In government-

controlled territory, organizations sponsoring literacy circles often had good relations with the official school personnel and could use their building. Some
organizations had their own facilities. Popular teachers could be recruited from
among those who had already taught the elementary grades. Those running the
existing schools could bear the administrative burden, and in the case of popular organizations' literacy campaigns, the sponsoring organizations had their own
administrative structures.

The Hidden Curriculum

Grade schools went beyond basic literacy to teach the four subjects of the Salvadoran elementary curriculum: language, mathematics, science, and social studies. They tried to follow the official curriculum (though, as we will see, they
rejected its claim of political neutrality). They hoped the certificates they gave
would be recognized in official schools and allow students to enter higher grades.
Some popular schools even found a friendly official school principal who certified their students' grade completion.

The schools also taught values—as all schools do. Popular schools attempted to instill obedience and conformity, active community participation, and
the revolutionary consciousness that was their communities' political culture—
all at once. This combination might at first glance seem paradoxical. But revolutionary consciousness and obedient behavior were both part of the
communities' norms. Pupils who learned them were socialized to work actively
toward the achievement of community goals. The combination of themes showed
up in illustrations in cartillas, which were as likely to portray illiteracy as a rich
capitalist strangling poor people (page 149) as to show a whole village cooperating on everyday tasks (page 154). That the schools tried to teach these values
simultaneously was another expression of the integration of education and community life that is such an important element of popular education.

Good behavior is part of the meaning of the word *educar*. One can scold
a misbehaving child, "¡*No seás mal educado*!" One purpose of school was to
teach children not to be *mal educados*. Arturo bragged about the popular schools
supported by PADECOMSM: "Lots of people who come are surprised that the
children in our schools are very respectful, very *educados* in comparison to children from the cities." In the repatriated community of Nuevo Gualcho, teachers
gave a talk on good behavior every week, Elia said. They exhorted children to
"take care of the school supplies, how to behave in school, how to behave toward their elders, and everything."

When children misbehaved, the teachers tried to be encouraging rather than
punitive—just as they did with slow learners. They assumed that with understanding, the children would behave properly. I asked Abilio how he handled
mischievous children. "You have to work more with the ones who are more restless," he said. "What I do is, if there is a child who makes a mistake, or who
doesn't pay attention when I'm teaching, I take fifteen minutes or so to explain."

(Though I had asked him about children who were *traviesos* [mischievous], he replied with the word *inquietos* [restless]—giving them the benefit of the doubt.)

Children were taught to come to school bathed and clean, and in some schools younger children were inspected for cleanliness (rather perfunctorily, in my observation). Gabriela said that if they didn't come to school clean and with their hair combed,

> we tell them that if they come looking like that the next day, we're going to bathe them and comb them ourselves.
> *Do you do it?*
> We've never done it, because the next day they come looking different.

If a child misbehaved too often, teachers tried to work with the parents. In San Antonio los Ranchos, Justino said, "If there is any problem, the teacher approaches the parent. The teacher goes to the home, and besides, we always have meetings here [in the school office] at night. So the parents are here, and the teachers are too. Everyone is here, and they discuss the experience of the day. We also have big meetings of parents and teachers."

Some parents did not always cooperate, teachers complained, because they did not see education as necessary. Parent-teacher meetings were frequently occasions for pep talks, like the ones Virgilio gave in Mesa Grande. "We reminded them that in the past, due to the situation of oppression in which we had lived, we hadn't had the opportunity to study, but there we did. So we got them to think about this. Since we had the opportunity, why not take advantage of it?"

Children were also sometimes urged to persuade their parents. The weekly lectures on good behavior in Nuevo Gualcho frequently included such exhortations, Elia said. "They may have to struggle with their parents and tell them, 'I'm going to school,' if the parents don't want them to."

Schools also taught norms of cooperation and community spirit. In Panchimilama, a relocated community near San Salvador, a children's *gremio* (roughly, "union") was formed in 1988. The three school grades were called together to meet with several members of the community council. The adults asked for representatives from each grade (the representatives were actually selected by the teachers), and urged them to take an active part by helping to keep the school neat. Though symbolic, forming a gremio was clearly intended to start children on careers of social and political activism at an early age.

Adult classes also discussed how to live in community, as Rito remembered from Mesa Grande:

> They started explaining to me that education is not just learning to read and write.
> *What else?*
> Education, as far as I understood when they explained it to me, was training people how to live. That's what education is about,

ayuda

ayuda
a | yu | da

todos podemos ayudar
todos necesitamos ayuda
el niño y la niña
ayudan en el trabajo
la mamá ayuda a su hijo
la ayuda agrada

ayote   yegua

yuca   yema

yoyo   yarda

FIGURE 13. "*Ayuda*" (help). *Despertando a mi comunidad: Cartilla Chalateca.* Escuelas Populares CCR and Grupo Maíz, 1993. Artist: Alfredo Burgos.

how to live with your parents, with your family, with your wife and your compañeros—how to treat another human being.

Máximo, who trained teachers for CIAZO, said that education should "make people not be competitive. Instead, they should work for personal and collective improvement, to solve problems of the community, and to create greater feelings of solidarity."

Work was part of the school day. Children planted corn, kept vegetable gardens, and gathered rocks for community projects such as road repair. As with children whose parents kept them out of school to help in the fields, the students' work was not merely symbolic. In communities without roads (or with roads that were impassable during the rainy season), carrying goods in was labor-intensive, and children did their share. Asked if the school gardens produced, Sonia replied, "Yes they do. Children work hard here." On a cooperative near Santa Ana, in an area controlled by the government, children grew corn, beans, and green vegetables. Irma, an ANDES member who advised the popular teachers (and who had grown up in the city), said, "We learned from them. The bigger children knew how to sow, plow, and prepare the fields." Children took home some of the fruits of the school gardens; some they consumed at school parties at the end of the year.

Politics did not have the centrality in grade school that it had for adults, but it was not disregarded. The schools celebrated occasions of social significance. Alfonso described how the schools around Arcatao celebrated the International Day of the Child in 1991:

> All the schools came, and since there are a lot of them, each school could only offer one thing: a poem, a skit, or a song, all of them addressing children's rights.

Popular schools departed from the official curriculum on some topics.

> In social sciences, we teach the situation as it is, not what is in the books. In history, we teach who was Columbus, who were the Spaniards, how they invaded and tricked the Indians. (Marisol)

> They might give you the sentence, "the soldier loves the people," "the soldier defends your country," "the soldier protects the people." As all of us know, the truth is that the soldiers don't protect the people, the soldiers don't respect the people's goods, the soldiers don't respect the people's rights. (Justino)

Some teachers denied that they taught political lessons in the classroom— usually when they were talking about army accusations that they were teaching guerrilla propaganda. These denials often seemed disingenuous; they came up less often after the war ended. Ramón, discussing the choice of generative words, said, "For example, I taught the word *revolu—refugiado* [refugee]." If he was covering up, however, he was not too embarrassed by his slip, because he immediately went on to say, "or the word 'soldier.' 'What do soldiers do? What do they do to us?' And we started motivating people: 'Why? Who? Why did they drive us here [to the refugee camp in Honduras]?'"

The war inevitably intruded on the classroom. It brought the children emotional trauma, Isabel said.

> The environment was too tense, and they didn't assimilate—the fact that one week you were in class and the next week the teacher wasn't there because they had killed him, or a child didn't come any more because they had killed him.
>
> It takes a variety of forms: a child might be aggressive, or fidgety, or distracted; some of them are very distanced from reality.

It also brought practical problems. Orlinda said that teachers had to keep children out of the way of military operations:

> We teach the children how to deal with the soldiers.
> *I would have thought you would tell them to stay away from them.*
> You know that a child is going to go out when you tell him not to. So we tell them not to take anything from them, and not to challenge them.

Some schools chose to suspend classes during military operations. "We told them to stay home and not go out. They were so afraid that they just hid under the beds," said Mercedes. Others, however, were determined not to suspend classes so as "not to remain passive," Virgilio reported. After an operation ended, Marta tried to restore the children's morale. "They were happy because no one had died. And that's when we tried to instill that courage, not to be afraid."

Some, like Justino, thought the best way to help children deal with the war was to minimize it.

> We have seen that tension from the war which prevents the child from being alert and developing his intelligence.
> *And how do you deal with a child so that he can?*
> We try to get the parents to motivate the child and make him interested in studying, and try to forget what happened in the past and think of his future. Because what happened happened, and you have to think of what is coming. But these are things that are deep inside and it's hard to forget them. Maybe that pupil who has suffered the consequences will grow old and still think about what happened, like a nightmare.

Others wanted to offer the children catharsis by dealing with their fears directly. Sonia urged the teachers she trained in Arcatao "always to discuss it with the children, because a lot of the time, what their parents do is just transmit tension to the children, because they have lived through such fierce repression around here. If they don't talk about it and don't see the reasons why, they grow up without a critical attitude. And I believe that the most important thing a teacher should do is create a critical capacity in the child, so the child can question everything that happens."

And Marta, finding young boys playing guerrilla soldiers with sticks for guns, tried to discourage such pastimes. "I tried to teach them that we were not at war on a whim, not because it was good to kill, but there was a need to take up arms. I tried to explain to them not to play that way, and that they saw so many rifles because it was necessary, not because it was fun."

How Well Did They Learn?

The manifest purpose of popular education is to teach people specific skills. But the performance of new learners is highly uneven in quality. Watching them in class, I often wondered how many of them actually learn to read. Some teachers gave wildly optimistic estimates of their success, claiming that learners became literate in three to six months. According to Julio Portillo, former secretary general of ANDES, "there are lots of books that people have been very interested in recently: for example, *One Hundred Years of Solitude*, *One Day of Life*, or *The Forbidden Stories of Tom Thumb*.[2] They're reading books like that after only three months." Others were only slightly less optimistic. According to Jaime, a professional teacher and ANDES activist, "you couldn't be sure because no one has measured how many hours they have been to class. But there have been pupils in the mountains who have learned in four months. Four months."

Rosario said that students in Colomoncagua got through the cartilla in six months. I pointed to a poster in the school office of Segundo Montes City, where we were meeting, and asked if a new learner could read it after six months.

Maybe not the big words, but the small words—a word that is not very demanding, like *niño* [child].
Esperanza *[hope] would be something else.*
Esperanza would be more complicated.

Though I am not trained in educational assessment, I thought long and hard about how I might evaluate reading and writing skills systematically. I concluded that it would be impossible, for two kinds of reasons. The first had to do with my situation as a researcher. I did not have the resources for a formal test or evaluation, and even if I had, my relation with my informants would have suffered. Asking to test learners would have imposed too much formality and inhibited communication.

The second set of reasons is more complex and was intrinsic to what and how people were learning. It is impossible to evaluate the manifest results of popular education comprehensively because neither the outcome to be measured, nor the population exposed, nor an appropriate comparison group is well defined.

The outcome cannot be precisely specified because functional literacy is not a unidimensional concept—it incorporates various kinds and levels of skill. To people in a literate culture who take literacy for granted, it seems obvious what it means to learn to read. But it is not. One man told me, "I know the letters [*yo sé mis letras* is a colloquial way of saying "I know how to read"], but to grasp a whole word at once!" The complex of skills includes recognition of letters, ability to sound out written words, ability to recognize meaning in the words sounded out, and only then ability to read and comprehend sentences; with regard to writing, the ability to trace out letters, to form written words, to write from dictation, and to write whole, original sentences. Materials vary in complexity, and learners vary in their ability to handle material of different lengths and degrees of difficulty, whether in reading or writing.

The population exposed to popular education cannot be defined precisely because the process took place over a long time, for varying lengths of time, in different settings, with different objectives, and gave learners different amounts of exposure. There is no reasonable single expectation of how much anyone should have learned.

It would be necessary to define a comparison group, because any assessment would have to measure whether the population exposed, however defined, achieved a higher level of literacy, however defined, than did some other group that was comparable in background (including especially previous educational opportunity) but had not experienced popular education. Defining such a "control group" is at least as difficult as defining the exposed population.

Though I concluded that a formal evaluation was not possible, I made some nonsystematic observations of people's performance—not on classroom tests but in real-life situations when they read or wrote to meet needs that arose naturally. My observations confirmed the first law of sociology (attributed to Vernon Dibble): some do, some don't. It was obvious that some people who attended classes achieved and maintained a usable level of literacy, while others did not. In much the same way, some people with two or three years of formal schooling as children maintained their skill by force of will, while others who had spent similar amounts of time in school let their skills decay or later said that they had not learned at all. Retention and consolidation depended on use. People who became popular teachers maintained and improved their skills even if those skills were marginal at the beginning. People also consolidated their skills if they were active in popular organizations and had to keep records or communicate in writing.

Even though its results are mixed, popular education may be very cost-effective. Because the work is done by volunteers, and because those volunteers are accustomed to stretching available resources to the limit, the money cost is very low.

Popular educators claimed that because the schools had deep roots in the communities they served, they were more effective than the official schools. Parents felt more closely identified with them, teachers taught on a more accessible level, and the subject matter was more relevant to local needs. Some Salvadoran professional educators, not identified with the popular education movement, share that view. José Luis Guzmán, director of the Institute of Education of the Central American University, said that the main accomplishment of the popular schools was "achieving participation. I believe that that is a key point in the whole pedagogical process. . . . Compared to other rural schools, there's a great emphasis on dealing with the community, the society, and national reality."

Other professionals, conversely, have criticized the official system for its lack of connection. In 1993, after the war, the Ministry of Education, the School of Education of the Central American University, and the Business Foundation for Educational Development cosponsored a national education sector assessment, carried out by the Harvard Institute for International Development (Reimers 1995). In that assessment, rural elementary education comes in for particular criticism as alien to rural communities and imposed on them from without. One participant in the study calls it "education for the community without the community" (Pérez Miguel 1994).[3]

Finally, the conviction that everyone is capable of learning and that many are capable of teaching made it possible to offer popular education to many whom the official system never reached. Though popular education was not widespread throughout the country, in the areas where it was organized there were schools in communities that had never had them under the official system before the war, and others that offered more grade levels than the schools that had existed. Free school supplies, community pressure, and the psychological accessibility afforded by a community-run system persuaded more parents to educate their children.

In any case, popular education cannot be evaluated only by its learning outcomes. It has multiple purposes, and any evaluation must take into account all of its intended effects, both on communities and on individuals. While communities promoted popular education to train members in needed skills, they also saw it as an organizing tool. Running its own schools enhanced a community's overall level of organization and enabled it to pursue its own purposes without interference from the central government.

The effects on individuals also went beyond cognitive achievement. Community organizations promoted education to express the value they attributed to each individual, and to affirm that people deserve education and are capable of benefiting from it. By their very existence, education programs made that affirmation, both for those who learned and for those who did not. The impact of popular education on those most actively involved, the teachers and organizers, was especially strong. Their gains in skill, intellectual accomplishments, and self-confidence were in my view the most important individual effects of popular education.

Education is both an end in itself and a means to other ends. To ask how well it works, therefore, it is necessary to examine much more than how well people learn to read, write, and calculate. The political purposes of popular education were equally important; indeed, they were the major factor motivating those who kept the schools running.

Community Spirit and Moral Incentives

To be a teacher required real sacrifices. Teachers gave their time and labor; they risked capture and harassment; and they risked exposure as incompetent (or so they feared). They overcame these costs by their commitment: commitment to their communities, to the educational process, and to an egalitarian society. Reliance on the work of committed volunteers affected the way the schools were run. Organizations that depend on people's voluntary effort must operate differently from those that offer material rewards, and in this respect most schools and school systems are more like businesses than like popular schools—material rewards can be provided or withheld to guarantee compliance. Value-based organizations, on the other hand, generally offer moral and solidary incentives; they motivate participants by heightening their moral commitment and sense of community (Clark and Wilson 1961; Rothschild-Whitt 1979).

Organizations that operate on this basis reward participants' effort and dedication rather than their technical competence. Affirming the equal value of coparticipants—whether teachers or learners—and invoking ideological commitment leave little room for recognizing professional standing or expertise. Teachers were praised for their unstinting contributions and assured that all they needed to do a good job was conciencia. The importance of their knowledge and skill was correspondingly downplayed. As Máximo of CIAZO told popular teachers in a training session, "the heart counts for more than the brain."

Far from demanding deference to their status and authority, popular teachers did not single themselves out. They were teachers not because they had more education or ability, but because of their community spirit. Teachers in Segundo Montes City (men and women), for example, spent the summer vacation doing construction work on new school buildings. It did not occur to them that, as teachers, they might be exempt from physical labor. They thought of themselves as people who work, just like everyone else. (They also hoped to speed the construction and save themselves from teaching outdoors.)

This incentive system not only affected the way teachers thought of themselves; it influenced the way the schools operated. It made work collaborative. Teachers welcomed—and depended heavily on—every chance to draw on each other's resources. Their modesty about their own talents was genuine, but it was reinforced by the principle that all volunteers were due equal respect. Even when they were singled out, they refused to take credit. "Sometimes," Ramón said, "when someone didn't have the experience to teach third grade, there would be an evaluation, and that compañero would move down, and I would move up. So it was a collective effort. Nobody was concerned to occupy one particular position."

They virtually refused to acknowledge that anyone who enlisted as a teacher could not handle the task. I asked Gabriela, in charge of the school in one of the five settlements of Segundo Montes City, whether teachers had ever been recruited who turned out to be unable to handle the job.

Yes. There are some like that.

And what do you do with them? Do you move them out, or do you help them?

We help them. Someone who is more experienced at giving class goes there. For example, if I see that a compañera has weaknesses, I figure out some way to help her. I even take her class myself for a few days and have her watch how I teach that class.

And does she get better?

Yes, she gets better, because we always teach all the new teachers when they start out.

The popular teachers compared themselves favorably to the teachers of the past who had abused students, or neglected their duties, or treated students and parents with contempt. "Some of them were drunkards," said Jorge, the president of the community of El Carasque in Chalatenango, in a typical complaint. "They went for weeks without giving a class. Or they said they had to go take a course, and they went away for one or two weeks." Esperanza of CRIPDES showed her skepticism toward teachers who had professional training or were not from the countryside. I asked her whether technical ability or conciencia was more important for teachers. "For us, conciencia," she replied. "In those communities you have to take risks: first, repression from the army; second, life is very different, and if a teacher has bourgeois ideas, how will he take the risk of giving a class outdoors, or in a shack where torrents pour in when it rains, or see children sitting on the ground? If teachers are there out of conciencia, what they want is to teach the children, and lots of times the teacher with a degree just does it for money."

Even if these criticisms were exaggerated, it is true that before the war many public school teachers lived elsewhere, eagerly sought to get reassigned closer to home, and hoped to take the advanced courses that would qualify them for the higher pay and status of a secondary school teacher. Whether or not they were committed teachers, they were not committed to the community in which they were working.

Not only were popular schools committed to the communities from which they sprang; they were also explicitly committed to political values. They rejected official education's claim that its curriculum was politically neutral. On the contrary, in their view, it was ideologically compromised by the existing regime's sponsorship. Their own curriculum was avowedly political, as they believed it should be. In this regard, as in rewarding commitment over expertise, they were rejecting the principles of professionalism—in this case, the claim that curriculum could be determined on technical grounds without political implications.

Nor did they acknowledge the right of professionals to prescribe education to local communities and impose administrative decisions from outside. In the official system, the Ministry of Education set the curriculum for the entire country. Popular educators believed that their own curriculum, locally adopted and explicitly value-oriented, was superior both because it motivated learners and because its content was more suited to their needs. They even had occasional conflicts (described in the next chapter) with professionals who supported the popular schools but wanted to uphold standards that conflicted with their own views of community needs.

This rejection of official standards was not complete. Popular educators claimed to follow the official curriculum in most respects and, after the war, demanded official certification of the grades their students had completed. They also hoped that their teachers' experience would be recognized and that, after appropriate further training, the Ministry of Education would hire them as teachers. Yet while they claimed that the education they offered was technically equally competent, they felt that its political distinctiveness made it more valuable to their communities.

If the complaints against traditional teachers and against professionals upholding standards were not exactly the same—the former were accused of being negligent and the latter of being presumptuous and ignorant of community needs—both affirmed that service to the community and its values was worth more than formal certification and technical criteria. (As we have seen, some Salvadoran professional educators agreed.)

It can be argued that relying on the political commitment of poorly educated teachers made a virtue of necessity and ignored the teachers' serious shortcomings. Not only did the popular educators lack professional training; they often presented material in a perfunctory fashion and sometimes with errors, and many of them were barely above the level of the people they were teaching. Yet the prevailing norms required ignoring such deficiencies.

Nevertheless I conclude that facing high expectations while being treated with dignity brought out the best in teachers, as it did in guerrilla soldiers, and made them perform at the top of their abilities. They gave as much as they could because they were supported by cohesive communities in which school and community were closely identified. Dedication to the collective good was part of these communities' tradition and was reinforced by the shared political experiences of organizing, war, and repression. Teachers were recognized for their effort by the whole community, which sustained the schools and chose school occasions for some of its principal celebrations.

Popular education did attempt to turn necessity into a virtue, and succeeded to a significant degree. Communities offered moral incentives because they had no material rewards to offer, and no professionally qualified teachers to whom they might offer them. But moral incentives were also appropriate to the purpose the schools were designed to serve: an education upholding the community's own values rather than conforming to professional and technical criteria. They offered rewards that would be valued by the people who were available, and would elicit precisely the effort required to make the schools work.

CHAPTER 7

Teacher Training

——

$\mathcal{P}$opular education taught more than basic skills. People who were active in community organizations and performed technical functions were trained as organizational leaders and in a variety of specialties. As in the guerrilla army, the most important were popular teachers and health promoters. Catechists received training, and others learned sustainable agriculture, cooperative management, community organizing, human rights monitoring, and other special skills. Popular education provided a pedagogy for training them that recognized their limited formal education but took advantage of their practical experience and their roots in their communities.

Training offered popular teachers some reassurance, helping them to overcome their lack of confidence. It enabled them to formalize the teaching ability they had developed though practice, and to master some of the abstract knowledge that underlay their teaching skills. It improved their mastery of the knowledge and skills they were to convey to their pupils, filling a need that became especially important when the schools began to offer upper primary grades and some popular teachers found themselves teaching grades they had never attended. This chapter will look primarily at the training of teachers, and in some detail at that of health promoters. It will also examine the special role of professional advisors: Salvadorans and foreigners with higher education who trained the volunteers and supervised their work.

Improving Teachers' Skills

In the first years of the war, teachers working in El Salvador had little technical assistance. The FMLN offered training sessions to its own teachers who taught their fellow combatants. Civilian teachers sometimes attended these sessions. The sessions were infrequent and brief, aimed at little more than consolidating the popular teachers' ability to read and write correctly and suggesting a logical order for presentation of the material.

The most intensive training occurred in the refugee camps in Honduras,

Figure 14. "Let's look a bit at the laws of war." *Mi Cuadernito de Derechos Humanos.* CDHES, 1990.

where, as described in chapter 4, all the teachers of a particular grade met for half of each day for training with an international volunteer who was a professional teacher. Segundo Montes City replicated that system of daily training sessions. At first some of the more experienced popular teachers conducted them; then the community hired certified teachers. Training did not reach that level anywhere else; but other communities did get help from churches and nongovernmental organizations. With international financing, these agencies hired Salvadorans and foreigners with professional qualifications to act as advisors and to train teachers for the popular schools.

Training was intended to fortify the teachers' basic skills; to teach methods of presentation; to help teachers plan toward medium- and long-term goals; and to provide political education. Political education was the most variable component. Advisors emphasized it when working with popular teachers who were relatively unpoliticized; in more highly organized communities, they left it up to local leaders.

Teachers were trained using the same methods they were supposed to implement in elementary classes and literacy circles: learning was active and based on concepts relevant to people's lives, and, as much as possible, knowledge was drawn out of people rather than deposited in them. The training was intended to overcome teachers' feelings of inadequacy to the task of teaching itself, and their feelings of inferiority to the advisors, whom they saw as their social and intellectual superiors.

Training programs varied in scope and frequency. I will describe three examples: a community where a foreign teacher sent by the church gave regular training sessions to teachers from surrounding villages; a professional organization, formed to support popular organizations' adult literacy programs, that hired advisors to travel around and train the volunteer teachers from the organizations; and a popular organization that periodically brought teachers from several repopulation communities to its San Salvador headquarters for a three-day meeting.

Sonia, a teacher from Spain, was sent by the diocese of Chalatenango to Arcatao, where she trained the teachers from 1989 to 1992. The teachers from fourteen schools in nearby communities met with her every other Saturday, and every three months they had a three-day workshop. Communities were separated by a few hours' walk; the meeting place was rotated so that the burden of hiking did not fall on the same people every time. (The three-day meetings were held in Arcatao, because the school was large enough for all the teachers to sleep overnight.)

The Saturday sessions began with a discussion of the national political situation. All the teachers present were asked to contribute news they had heard on the radio, and Sonia or a representative of the CCR led a discussion of the latest developments in the war or the peace negotiations, both to keep the teachers informed and to prepare those who taught older children to discuss them in their own classes. When I asked Sonia how she taught teachers to discuss complicated political questions with children, she replied, "The first thing you have to do is have the teachers discuss it among themselves. Everyone gives impressions of what has happened, how they see it, what they hear on the radio, etc. I always urge them to bring it up in class because, really, the children are living through a very tough situation right now."

Throughout the day's training session, major points were recorded on large sheets of newsprint; most people copied them faithfully. The routine was interrupted periodically for recreation. (I discuss the role of games in training below.) During the afternoon, teachers divided into groups according to the grades they taught and planned lessons for the next two weeks. For each of the four subjects (language, mathematics, science, and social studies), they consulted the few textbooks they had and created a "script" that each teacher then copied to use in class.

Some popular teachers had no ongoing training. Advisors from CIAZO visited its member organizations at widespread intervals, like circuit riders. In 1991 Máximo, a Salvadoran who had formerly developed curriculum materials for the Ministry of Education, conducted a two-day session in Torola, beyond Perquín in Morazán, for adult literacy teachers from the nearby communities. In principle, volunteer teachers from the organizations in CIAZO were supposed to come to larger, more frequent training sessions in central locations; but, as Máximo explained, "These people can't go to training in San Salvador or San Miguel. They have too much work, it's too far, and they don't have the right papers." Though the session was intended for teachers of adults, some who taught children in day school showed up and were included. Two teachers had not received the invitation but arrived by coincidence and stayed to attend the session.

On the morning of the first day, only four of the twelve people expected had arrived. To fill the time without beginning the formal lesson, Máximo announced that he would play the role of a teacher, and afterward they would criticize his performance. He always threw himself into his sessions with great enthusiasm and energy. But this time he walked in lackadaisically, sat down, and said, "Let's see what I'm supposed to teach you today, students." He scolded one of the teachers who had not brought the cartilla. After a few minutes, he asked for their criticisms, and they answered eagerly:

"You didn't greet us."

"You didn't call us compañeros, you called us students."

"You criticized us."

He elaborated on some of their comments.

You can't sit down, you have to walk around to keep people's attention. Even though you've been working and are tired, you have to show enthusiasm.

I shouldn't talk about what *I'm* going to teach *you*. We all learn in popular education.

We're forming a new man in El Salvador. The higher up someone is, the more he should serve others.

As more people arrived, Máximo presented the method for conducting a reflection on the word *casa*. Repeatedly throughout the two days he urged that every circle do the reflection seriously and insisted that at least two hours be spent on it for every generative word. He frequently interspersed comments meant not only to arouse the teachers' enthusiasm but to guide them in conducting their own literacy circles: "You have to take account of different abilities, but pay more attention to the slower ones. To keep the faster ones from getting bored, have them help the others." He mentioned "the new man we want in El Salvador" several times, and charged the teachers to act as models and to educate their pupils to be new men.

Pedro, who conducted a circle in the nearby village of San Diego, raised an issue that was troubling his students. "They want to learn the alphabet; why are we teaching syllables and not letters?" Here Máximo stood on his authority and insisted that they stick to syllables, but he also explained that teaching the alphabet would not help. The phonetic method doesn't work because people think that words are written just like they sound, but in fact h is silent, c has various sounds, and it can be confused with s. "If they learn the alphabet, they will learn to pronounce the words faster, but that's not reading." Here and at other points he made clear that there was a method he wanted them to learn and use correctly.

At every turn he emphasized the need to be dynamic and to engage the interest of the members of the literacy circle. He assured them repeatedly that their work was important and urged them to take their responsibility seriously. More than most advisors, he explicitly presented the pedagogical purposes of the methods he was teaching. When he interrupted the session for a game, he explained the use of games: they make people laugh and restore their energy, and physical exercise is a good rest from mental effort. But he was trying to cram a lot into a two-day session, and he did not know when an advisor would come to work with these people again.

The education team of CRIPDES, the Christian Committee for the Displaced, took a different approach. Esperanza, coordinator of education for CRIPDES, and Carmen, a teacher from Spain, assisted teachers from eight repopulations in different departments in the center of the country. New teachers got a six-day course in basic literacy teaching; teachers came to a three-day followup session in San Salvador every two months. Fourteen teachers came to one session in 1990. Most of them knew each other and had worked together before, although there were some new members. Two women brought their babies.

Each three-day meeting was devoted to a particular subject: writing or mathematics, for example. This one was unusual because the topic was literature and the purpose was to introduce the teachers to reading for enjoyment rather than to provide material for immediate use in the classroom. The teachers spent much of the three days reading and discussing brief passages from two Salvadoran books: Argueta's *One Day of Life* and *Miguel Mármol*, the autobiography of a veteran of the 1932 uprising compiled by the poet and revolutionary Roque Dalton. They also looked at an African folktale, *The Eagle that Did Not Want to Fly*, and a pamphlet about the issues of democratization that were being debated in the peace talks between the FMLN and the Salvadoran government. In addition to reading and discussing these works, they discussed organizational problems in the schools.

The passage from *One Day of Life* was about the girlhood of Lupe, the book's main character. She had found school boring and had often stayed home because it was far away. Carmen pointed out the lessons for their own work: when children got bored, teachers had to be lively to hold their interest, and schools should be located where children could get to them easily.

The passages to be read were all short—three or four pages. The teachers studied a passage by reading it several times: first silently and individually, then aloud in the group with each person reading a sentence or paragraph. (Their reading skills varied widely.) They were assigned a series of questions to answer in writing, either individually or after discussion in a small group. Then the whole group met, all the answers were written up on sheets of newsprint, and they discussed them further.

Some of the questions were simply about what the story said; others were more analytical. The question they found most difficult (for *One Day of Life* and again later when dealing with *Miguel Mármol*) asked for a short summary of the passage. Even those who had no difficulty understanding the reading had trouble formulating a summary. Some simply repeated the answers they had given to the preceding questions.

Then each community's teachers met as a group to prepare a report about their school: how many grades, how many pupils, what kind of building the school had, whether they had meetings among themselves or with parents, and what problems they faced. They then presented the report to the whole group and discussed common problems.

Answering the questions not only provided a chance to discuss problems; it was also an exercise in writing, this time not about a text they had read but about their own experience. Some of the teachers had a hard time formulating the answers to the questions and writing them down. Vicente, a middle-aged man, and Martina, a young woman, were the two teachers in Santa Cruz in the department of Usulután. Martina was clearly the more adept at writing, and Vicente, somewhat officiously, dictated the answers to her. Then in the larger group, he read back her written report, hesitating more often while reading it than he had in composing it.

The African folktale was told in an illustrated children's book published in Cuba, which the teachers all read in photocopies. It was about an eagle who had been raised by chickens and never learned to fly until one day he finally took off. Carmen asked them to interpret the story. Most referred to the eagle's achieving his freedom, but one interpreted it as being about all the birds learning to get along together. Nonjudgmentally, Carmen commented that that was a completely different viewpoint.

Activists were used to leaving home for meetings lasting more than a day. They followed an organizational routine with which all were familiar. Some were held at conference centers where a staff prepared meals, but people always washed their own dishes. Sometimes the women joked that the men did not know how to wash dishes; but for those who went to conferences regularly, it became a routine and aroused no comment. Committees were established, usually including a cleanup committee and a discipline committee whose main job was to get everyone to sit down so that sessions could begin on time. At the CRIPDES session, Vicente, who chaired the discipline committee, complained that the babies were distracting. Ten of the fourteen teachers attending were women, and some of them protested. Esperanza said that there was no way to provide day care, and it was better to bring the children than not to come.

Esperanza told me afterward that this was the first training session dedicated to the teachers' enrichment rather than teaching skills. But they planned to do more like this, including one in December just before the new school year, "to send them off, so that they all start out with optimism and know that we're there with them."

Teacher training followed a pedagogical process similar to that used with new learners. Advisors encouraged active participation. They took every opportunity to bolster the participants' confidence that they were up to the very important job they were doing. At the same time they challenged them academically. Within the limits of the teachers' skills, they offered material that drew the teachers beyond immediate classroom techniques to understand more theoretical concepts.

The organization of the sessions depended on how often an advisor met with the group. In settings where they met regularly, a great deal of training time was spent preparing the lessons that the teachers would give between then and the next meeting. Where training sessions were less frequent, they dealt more with pedagogy or general culture, and the teachers were left on their own for day-to-day preparation.

Agencies revised training schedules and programs in response to the teachers' needs and to the availability of funds. When CIAZO was established, the plan was to train not the popular teachers themselves, but organizational representatives who would act as "multipliers" training volunteer teachers in each organization. In some organizations (such as FENACOA) they succeeded, and the multipliers trained their members effectively. But in most organizations, the CIAZO staff decided, the system of "multiplication" was not working, and they had to train the literacy teachers directly. When Sonia left Arcatao (after the war ended), intensive courses were offered to the teachers in Chalatenango that prepared most of them for a ninth-grade equivalency exam and some for a high-school equivalency exam; while most of their training time was now devoted to their own academic education, they also continued to meet to plan the lessons they would offer.

Popular teachers appreciated the training and felt that they depended on it. According to Luisa, the education coordinator of Segundo Montes City, "We find training very important because we come from a low cultural level. We need to be trained so that we can take what we've learned to the children [in the classroom]." But in fact teachers had to rely on themselves to a significant degree. Some received no formal training, some got it only occasionally. And even Sonia, who lived in Arcatao and was available all the time, could not work with all the teachers. They were teaching six different grades, and when their Saturday meetings broke up into grade-level groups, she said, they were on their own. "I set them to do the programming among themselves. At the beginning I worked with them all together, but then, after three years, and as the number [of teachers and grade levels] has grown, the older teachers got pretty advanced, because there has been continuous training." Elsewhere too, teachers did most of their planning in their own groups.

This training was part of an effort to improve the quality of the education offered in the popular schools, a goal pursued more systematically over time. Teachers seized the opportunity eagerly, but it meant that they became specialists. School organizers likewise dedicated themselves full-time to keeping the schools running. As education came to depend on specialized personnel and aimed to meet technical standards, it relied less on political will and the shared involvement of whole communities. Upgrading conflicted implicitly with the principle that schools should rely on political commitment and be integrally tied into community life.

Health Promoter Training

Popular education was used to train people in other practical skills, most importantly as health promoters. Poor rural communities in El Salvador had historically been deprived of health care, as they had of education. Health, like education, became a focus of community organizing in the early 1970s.

Getting treatment could involve a difficult trip to a town and a humiliating encounter with a doctor who looked down on campesinos, as many other educated people did, and thought them incapable of understanding their own health conditions. The doctor examined a patient quickly and perfunctorily, charged a high fee, and wrote a prescription the patient could ill afford to fill. Patients were often too timid to ask for an explanation—although they, too, expected to be given a prescription and had strong faith in the chemical cure. When Enrique, a nurse-practitioner from the United States, trained health promoters, they did a role play in which he played a doctor.

> The task was that they came with an ulcer and they had to ask me what it meant, what an ulcer was. And I said, "You have an ulcer. You need this. You have to take two of these five times a day. Four pills after meals. Here you are," and that's it. And the person had to say, "Excuse me, doctor. I want to know—" "No, quick, quick. The next patient is waiting. Hurry up." They didn't know how to be assertive.
>
> I did the role play with a group from the repopulations, who were very political people, who were outspoken, and they couldn't do it. The one fellow I expected more than anybody would probably be able to, he just got all flustered.

Cost, intimidation, and most doctors' limited understanding of poor people's living conditions conspired to prevent campesinos from taking full advantage of medical care. Consistent with their higher social status, doctors were even more distant than teachers. Besides, health care exposed, more clearly than education, the sharp conflict between people's basic needs and the profit motive.

Community organizing and popular education promoted "alternative medicine." Alternative medicine emphasized prevention over cure. It condemned the overuse of pharmaceutical drugs and called instead for reliance on natural medicines made at low cost from plants that grew wild or were cultivated for the purpose. It encouraged patients to understand the causes of their health conditions, including the political-economic causes of illness and of lack of access to

FIGURE 15. "Two Types of Health Care." From *Donde no hay doctor: Una guía para los campesinos que viven lejos de los centros médicos* by David Werner, published by the Hesperian Foundation, P.O. Box 11577, Berkeley, CA 94712.

health care. It made health care an aspect of community organization. The goal was for people to educate themselves and use locally available medicines so that they could meet their own health needs to the greatest extent possible.

Alternative medicine assumed that basic health care can be provided at little cost by people without professional training. Health promoters working in their own communities played a key role. They were trained to diagnose and treat the most common illnesses and injuries. They also acted as organizers and educators. Health promoters were double participants in popular education. The workshops where they were trained were run according to the popular education principle that training should engage them actively and awaken their critical consciousness; they should not just learn to apply procedures mechanically. The promoters also attempted to apply those principles in educating community members to meet their own health needs. The method is codified in the book *Donde no hay doctor* (Where there is no doctor), by David Werner (1980), which has been widely used throughout Latin America. Werner, a North American, developed the practice while working in community health in Mexico in the 1960s (see also Werner and Bower 1982). The book first appeared in 1973. (It was one of the books that Pedro of San Diego remembered reading before the war; he had received a copy when he was trained as a health promoter by the Red Cross.)

The claims of alternative medicine closely parallel those of popular education, not only in demanding decent health care as a right and protesting against the political forces that deny it, but also in legitimizing the initiatives of local communities, relying on local resources, and opposing professional exclusiveness.

Like literacy, health work was an important activity of Christian base communities starting in the 1970s. Hugo was one of many catechists from northern Morazán who studied health promotion in a series of week-long courses in the church's San Lucas Campesino University in San Miguel. The promoters worked closely with the International Committee of the Red Cross, which supplied them with a *botiquín* (medicine chest), a small supply of medicines to dispense in their communities. The Red Cross did not fully embrace the alternative approach. It encouraged communities to form health councils, but much of the training it offered was focused on the medicines. Elsewhere people were warned away from chemical medicines. Heriberto, a catechist in the parish of Teotepeque, also had a botiquín. Nevertheless, he urged parishioners,

> "Really, for that headache, this aspirin isn't going to help you. What you need is vitamins. For example, you could make a vegetable soup."
> The medicine was not as important as the education. There didn't use to be pills. People got relief from herbs or plants. And we started to get them to grow medicinal plants.

When the war broke out and it became impossible to organize communities openly, alternative health care and health promoter training continued in the guerrilla army and the refugee camps. In the camps in Honduras, promoters worked under the French-based international organization Doctors Without Borders. Alfredo, a health promoter (as well as teacher) in Mesa Grande, said that his job was to

> give classes in environmental sanitation. Because the truth was there wasn't much medicine, and we had to see how to fight some diseases that were very common there.
> They had gotten us used to just taking medicines. If you had a cold, take a medicine. If you had a headache, take a medicine. For a cold, they used a strong medicine, and when you needed that medicine for some other disease, it didn't work any more, because you had gotten used to it. So we had to raise people's consciousness not to take medicine for just anything. For a cold, not to take strong medicines, but vitamins from orange juice, and rest.

During the war the Red Cross continued supplying medicines to some communities. At the same time, the FMLN urged local communities to organize public health campaigns. Delia, an FMLN combatant and health worker in Morazán, said, "there were, and are, people in the communities born to the vocation of serving the community in the area of health. They are natural healers. We in the Frente tried to take advantage of this." The FMLN trained some civilians together with its own medical brigades.

Like popular education in other skills, health promoter training benefited from the increased international support to Salvadoran humanitarian NGOs close

FIGURE 16. Health education class, San Antonio Los Ranchos. *Photo copyright © Donna DeCesare.*

to the FMLN from the late 1980s on. Many NGOs trained health promoters in FMLN-controlled areas, in government-controlled rural areas, and in cities. Promoters who had learned in refugee camps established clinics in repatriated communities.

The work of promoters was community organization as much as treatment: they taught people to build latrines, to dispose of garbage properly, to boil water, and to grow medicinal plants. Speaking about planning for after the war, Delia said, "We want to create the mystique that the health promoter is the health organizer in the community."

But their training was still primarily focused not on organization or education but on treatment of diarrhea, fever, and wounds, the most common health problems. Training programs varied. In San Salvador, some health promoters from the shantytowns met for training sessions for half a day every weekend. Outside the city, where promoters had to travel from their home communities to a central location, the typical session lasted for five very busy days, with classes or other activities morning, afternoon, and evening.

Angela, a North American nurse who trained health promoters in a parish of the diocese of Santiago de María, in government-controlled territory but on the edge of an area of conflict, taught three things in the first course: oral rehydration, reduction of fever without drugs, and use of the book *Where There Is No Doctor*. Because diarrhea can be fatal, and because oral rehydration is so simple and effective, it is an extremely gratifying first measure for health promoters to learn. According to Enrique, the health promoter trainer who role-played the doctor treating a patient's ulcer, "Everybody felt real empowered by being able to save lives."

Promoters varied in educational level from high school students (especially in large towns and cities) to people who could barely read. Their experience with *Where There Is No Doctor* demonstrates not only that literacy is a very complex skill, but that it is basic to further learning. Though the book presents a broad view of health care, emphasizing the political causes of poor health and lack of treatment and the ways in which poor people can improve their basic health conditions, nevertheless most of it explains diagnosis and treatment of specific medical conditions. To use it, a promoter had to be able not only to read the words (itself a task beyond many candidates) but to locate in the book the material that corresponded to a patient's symptoms. Angela said that in the first week of training, "we spent probably two learning sessions on just the mechanics of how to find something in the book. When you say on page such-and-such, people will just page through until they get to the page such-and-such. They don't have any concept that if it's page 200 and it's a book about this thick, it'd probably be—they have none. And alphabetical order even less."

Training used popular education techniques that demanded active participation, both to reinforce what promoters were learning and to overcome their awe of the medical profession and their resulting timidity. Enrique always asked people to put their chairs in a circle to encourage communication; but many hesitated, preferring to sit behind someone else. Discussing natural medicines, advisors encouraged people to name those they knew of, to legitimize their prior knowledge. Training a group of new health promoters in San Luis de Mariona, on the semirural fringe of San Salvador, Inés asked what plants they used for medicines. When a woman mentioned lemon grass tea, Inés said to the others, "I won't teach that topic; she will." Drawing on the promoters' knowledge not only gave them legitimacy but could introduce new, effective folk medicines. Whenever Susana, a North American who trained people to grow and use medicinal plants, learned of new home remedies, she took them to the pharmacy faculty of the University of El Salvador for identification.

The proportion of initial candidates who completed the course, worked as health promoters, and returned for further one-week courses was low. To leave home for a weeklong course was already a significant commitment. But because the knowledge was specialized, one could not begin working as a promoter without the training, so they had to come to a course without having experienced the work or measured their commitment. Some went out of curiosity, and advisors sometimes joked about the people who came just for the free meals. Others without a clear aptitude were pressured to attend by a community leader: the practice of *dedocracia* (rule by [pointing] the finger) meant that candidates were often assigned rather than volunteering.

Health promoters had some of the same assets and liabilities as popular teachers: they had very limited education, but their close relation to their community enabled them to communicate without the barriers of professional status and campesinos' sense of inferiority. But there were differences. Popular teachers, however modest their learning, did know basic reading and writing. Though health training tried to recognize indigenous knowledge, promoters had to acquire some specialized knowledge and undergo rather extensive training before they could begin. Health promoters had no specific constituency comparable to a teacher's students; they were supposed to treat and educate the whole community.

Though the training of teachers and health promoters used similar methods of popular education, and for the same reasons—to draw people out of passivity and to reinforce what they learned—the different situations of the two kinds of practitioners, as well as the different subject matters, made their training differ in significant ways. Popular teachers were almost always already working in front of a class before they came to a teacher training course, so their motivation was very concrete. There were more people who could train teachers than there were people capable of training promoters (in the guerrilla army, anyone with some university education and many who had started high school might work with teachers; civilians near the dividing line between government- and FMLN-controlled territory sometimes got help from sympathetic teachers in official schools). Doctors and nurses in the refugee camps and medical students in San Salvador could train people to do health work, but it was only during the last years of the war that NGOs began to hire trained health educators to offer the training more widely.

Like teachers, health workers were targets of repression—sometimes mild, sometimes severe. During a training session Angela conducted in a village away from the seat of the parish, a platoon of soldiers showed up and grilled the trainees. "'Now this is first aid, right?' And we said, 'No, it's maternal-child health.' He took the list and he wrote 'First Aid' on the top. And first aid implies working with the guerrillas. Then he said, 'You know, when you have these kind of meetings you'd better notify us. It's up to us to see that everything that goes out in these communities is okay. Because you know, when things get out of hand, it's dangerous. Sometimes people have to leave their homes.' He said 'leave their homes' three times. He said, 'Sometimes they have to leave their homes and it's very sad. When you leave your home all of a sudden, sometimes you die from the sadness.'" Though no one had to leave home in this case, the intimidation was clear. Many foreign health workers were deported (or left the country fearing deportation) after the 1989 offensive.

Games

Games are an important part of popular education, for children and adults. They serve a variety of purposes. They are most commonly known in Spanish as dinámicas, because they are intended to shape group dynamics; but some are also called *técnicas* (techniques), a term that emphasizes a specific educational purpose. They are also referred to simply as *juegos* (games).

Most directly, games provide physical relief from mental activity for people who are not used to sitting still for long periods (Máximo told the trainees at Torola that physical exercise offers rest from mental effort). Particularly on a hot, somnolent afternoon, common in El Salvador, vigorous activity may be necessary to snap people to attention. One hot Sunday afternoon in Usulután, Guillermo of FENACOA interrupted a math lesson and began saying that people appeared tired. Not letting him finish, they protested that they did not want to do another dinámica. He had something simpler in mind: he suggested that everyone applaud after each person's contribution. Just to stand up, stretch, and shout a few slogans ("¡*Que viva!*") can raise people's energy level. After seeing games work in popular education, I have often wanted to walk into my own classes, especially at night when people arrive tired from work, and stand everyone up for a few minutes of jumping jacks.

But they serve many other functions as well. People at a workshop, coming from different places, may not know each other. Games can break the ice. Many turn on reflex errors when players move quickly. (The local variant of "Simon Says" is "*El pueblo manda.*" In political circles it is the people who must give permission before one can do anything.) These mistakes make everyone laugh. They also upset the hierarchy of good, bad, and mediocre students, so that people who are less than outstanding in the classroom can excel at something.

Several games were part of the CRIPDES training session. The first was "elephant-giraffe." All stand in a circle, and the person in the middle points to someone who is "it," and says either "giraffe" or "elephant." "It" must raise his arms above his head to represent a giraffe's long neck, or hold them together pointing down to represent an elephant's trunk. Meanwhile, the two people on either side must spread their hands open beside "Its" head to represent an elephant's ears, or by his legs to represent a giraffe's legs. People are supposed to move quickly. Anyone who makes a mistake replaces the person in the center of the circle, to general laughter.

Advisors had explained the use of games to me, but this was the first time I had seen one. Though I am not particularly reticent to jump into such activities, I was not sure whether, as an outsider who did not know the people, I was invited to participate. It was also early in my field work, and I had not decided what balance I wanted to achieve between unobtrusive observation and active participation. (In the end I came down heavily on the side of participation, a choice I discuss in chapter 9.) I hesitated, tempted to hang against the wall and watch. If I had, however, I would have appeared to be refusing to join the group. So I jumped in, and it was fun. It also made others accept me and interact with me without wondering too much who I was or why I was there. Then and on other occasions, I discovered that by playing a game enthusiastically I became integrated into a group. That is of course one of the points, if not for foreign observers then for the regular participants.

Some games have specific educational functions, like learning letters of the alphabet or counting. (To help health promoter trainees cope with page numbers, Angela gave people numbers and had them line themselves up in order—first with consecutive numbers, then with numbers assigned randomly.) Others teach lessons of solidarity and cooperation. Role plays encourage taking other people's points of view. Teachers learn these games in training sessions to use with their own pupils, so an advisor normally introduces a game by explaining its purposes. Roberto, who coordinated the high-school equivalency classes offered to popular teachers in Chalatenango after the war, introduced the orchestra game, in which small groups imitate the sounds of different instruments. It had two purposes, he told them: to make people less timid and to integrate the group.

Many games require people to act somewhat foolishly, but teachers are willing to surrender their dignity when they are learning games to use in their own classes. Though leaders of adult literacy circles are encouraged to use games in the circles, games are probably more common in training sessions conducted by professionals or others with more experience, who are more aware of their various purposes and more confident in their ability to carry them off.

Inhibitions born of lack of self-confidence are a major barrier to learning for popular teachers and adult learners. Many participants are not used to formal learning or the classroom situation, and those experiences may arouse anxiety or anticipation of boredom. Máximo said that popular teachers are "afraid to give answers; afraid, by tradition, to make a mistake, afraid that other people will make fun of them. So games break down that barrier."

Not always, however. Hilario, a Christian base community activist in San Fernando, Morazán, said, "People aren't used to dinámicas. They're too shy." He went on to say that base communities always did them on retreats. "It's good when you're sitting all day long." But at home "people are tired after working all day, and we always have a lot to do. We don't have time." They undoubtedly have reasons to be tired, but tiredness may also be a cover for other inhibitions.

Advisors used games to judge trainees' leadership potential. Roberto discussed the orchestra game with me: "Do you remember those guitars? They really stood out. That way you identify [leaders] and start giving them responsibilities." (Roberto's lively sense of humor made him a master game leader. He once told me that "some researcher" should come to El Salvador and study humor as a weapon of the people.) Advisors took refusal to participate or half-hearted participation as a sign of lack of commitment or reluctance to engage oneself fully.

Trainees knew that they were judged by the way they played games. Chebo said that some who were trained with him by the Ministry of Education to teach adult literacy were not accepted. "There were some who felt too inhibited even to ask questions. They avoided eye contact with the teacher, or they were the last, and even though they were urged to take part in games, they said they had reasons not to."

Heriberto, too, talked about his training as a catechist. "If I didn't want to take part in a game at the beginning, or was the last to enter, then one of the promoters might say, 'If you don't participate, how are you going to teach the community?'"

There are many dinámicas, ranging from the simple to the very complex. Some involve elaborate role plays with a large cast of characters and some take a very long time. They have been collected in books that catalogue them according to their functions (e.g., Vargas 1984). It is possible to use a game mechanically without full understanding of why it works. This can be an advantage, but it can also mean that a game may be used when it is not entirely appropriate. Some practitioners disdain the overuse of games and deride others who identify them as the essence of popular education. (In chapter 8 I return to the relation of these pedagogical techniques to the broader purposes of popular education.)

Games are clearly well suited to many purposes. They integrate physical and mental activities. They can overcome the intimidation that is a heritage of many people's early experiences of schooling. In Máximo's words, they serve "to get away from the idea that learning is ponderous and boring, and to show them that it can be pleasant." Games integrate participants into the process both by making the process more congenial and by making participants more willing to join in.

The Role of the Professional Advisor

Despite the war, community activities—including popular education—became more regular in the war zones as time went on. Community leaders sought to upgrade the quality of their work. Improving teachers' qualifications, as I have noted, implied sacrificing the principle that all politically committed people were equally qualified to teach and that everyone's contribution was equally valuable. As teachers got more training, they became a distinct group with specialized knowledge. Establishing advanced training for popular teachers meant recognizing that not everyone was capable of the task. Even apart from differences of aptitude, specialization would by definition be restricted to a few people—only those who actually expected to use the skills would invest the time and effort.

Advanced training, therefore, potentially undermined the community spirit and volunteer ethos that rewarded conciencia and effort over ability or mastery of skills. As its quality improved, popular education acquired precisely some of the professional traits the popular educators tried to avoid. Nevertheless, they continued to assert that their work was based on conciencia and political commitment. Sometimes conflicts arose on that score with the professionally-trained advisors who worked with them.

NGOs implicitly allied with the FMLN and headquartered in San Salvador developed increasingly close ties with communities in the FMLN-controlled zones and elsewhere, and sponsored humanitarian and development projects for education, health care, agriculture, self-help housing, and other purposes. They hired professionals who acted as technical advisors to the communities. Especially after 1989, they received foreign funding for many projects.

Their staffs included the education advisors who trained popular teachers. These advisors came to play a special role in popular education. Some were foreigners who went to El Salvador as solidarity activists. They were generally young and found themselves thrust into positions of responsibility even though they had little experience, while their counterparts had high expectations of them because of their foreign education. Some were Salvadorans with teaching degrees who worked for the NGOs because they wanted to act on their political commitment while working in their field. Other Salvadorans advised popular education as volunteers. Irma was an ANDES activist and school principal in San Salvador who assisted popular teachers on a cooperative near Santa Ana. When she was asked to help out, she said that "I had been on the executive board [of ANDES] for two years and I thought I should do it." The level of commitment of Salvadoran advisors varied. They shared political goals, but some were members of the FMLN's five organizations while others had almost no history of activism.

The advisors taught popular teachers important technical and organizational lessons. From their higher education they had gotten not only formal knowledge of pedagogy but a sense of organization and so could help teachers master some of the bureaucratic routines necessary even in small popular schools. They taught how to plan classwork to meet medium- and long-term objectives. Jaime, an officer of ANDES who trained popular teachers, when asked what specific contribution the formally trained teacher could bring, replied, "There's a lot in relation to planning. Popular teachers have many abilities, so if you tell them, 'This is the way you can plan how to present this topic,' they're very satisfied, because they didn't know the method, and now they apply it."

They also prepared educational materials. Cartillas were better designed when professional advisors contributed to them. Early cartillas, such as *Caminemos* ("Let's walk" or "Let's go forward"), written by displaced people being sheltered by the Archdiocese of San Salvador, and an untitled one used by the PRTC with its combatants, were not graded to proceed smoothly from simpler to more complex words. They were also produced cheaply, from stencils. Later cartillas, in addition to being more carefully constructed, looked better: they were printed, were produced on better paper, and contained more elaborate drawings or photographs.

Where possible, cartillas were produced collaboratively by the people who would use them. In the early years, collaboration was possible in the protected spaces that favored popular education—the archdiocese's *Caminemos* was the collective product of popular teachers, and the illustrations were chosen from drawings submitted by refugees. But in Chalatenango during the same period, communities were in constant movement to escape the army. It was difficult to hold meetings, and, as Isabel said, writing the cartilla was not very participatory.

The cartilla *Alfabetizando para la paz* (Literacy for peace), which Chebo and his students used in the class described in chapter 1, was the result of collaboration in 1989 and 1990 by more than a dozen popular organizations that were members of CIAZO. Popular teachers from the organizations conducted a linguistic survey in their communities, asking people to name the most common kinds of foods, to describe their houses, to discuss their festivals, and to talk about similar everyday activities. Then the volunteers met with the professional teachers on the CIAZO staff to thrash out the contents.

This made the choice of generative words a committee process. Cristina, a CIAZO staffmember, disagreed with the inclusion of *lluvia* (rain). She preferred a word that represented the result of people's effort. "But the people wanted 'rain,' and we left it. We have to respect their decision." She said that collaborating had been worth the time and effort. "Lots of the words in the cartilla are things some of them thought up. You won't find many unusual words—someone might ask why we spent so much time doing research to find these words! But the important thing is to involve the people, so that they feel this material is *theirs*."

The pleasure of collaboration was not the only reward advisors found in their work. Many valued the chance to go beyond the traditional methods of teaching in which they had been trained. Recognizing the merits of new methods that violated professional canons was a lesson in humility. Julio Portillo of ANDES said that when he was already a normal school graduate with several years' teaching experience, he "trained to become a popular teacher"—acknowledging that a popular teacher was not less of a teacher than a professional, but a different kind of teacher. He realized from working in popular education, he said, that professionals could not meet the country's educational needs by themselves. "I'm now convinced that education is a task not just for educators, but for all the people." Learning from popular educators had changed his view dramatically: "I am a professor of higher education, and I have worked a long time training educators, and my didactic scheme was completely foreign to what I'm telling you about now."

Working with campesinos whose ways of thinking and working were very different from their own, as comandante Javier Castillo said of his work as a seminarian in Aguilares in the 1970s, was "a great learning experience for us." When Jaime of ANDES was asked what professionals contributed to popular education, he turned the question around. "I personally think that more comes from [the popular teachers], because they live in that situation. So they have material to take to explain a lot of things. They teach what is going to be useful to the student."

Advisors did not romanticize the teachers' accomplishments or overlook their deficiencies; sometimes they sounded almost despairing. Anita spoke of the teachers she trained in Colomoncagua (later she returned with the refugee community to Segundo Montes City). "When I realized that the teachers hadn't understood, I took them aside and explained it again. Normally it was only a few. [But] you have to go lower, and lower, and lower, and then you realize that with many things you think they have to understand, but they don't."

In Arcatao, Sonia found, "these teachers have a lot of difficulties. When I came, they didn't separate the words [when they wrote]. It was a bunch of letters joined together. Arithmetic: they could add in their head but you started from scratch. In grammar or spelling, you started at the bottom. Now numbers—addition, subtraction, multiplication, in other words it's been a process and now they know how to multiply and divide, but some of them; not all of them."

They also lacked the habits of bureaucratic compliance that people who have spent long years in formal education take for granted. Advisors were frequently frustrated to arrive at a workshop and discover that most of the participants were late, that some had not even been notified, or that others had not brought information or equipment that they had promised to bring. Máximo gave the group at Torola a half-chiding lecture on punctuality: "If Salvadorans or Latins aren't like that, the new man has to be."

But the teachers' native ability, enthusiasm, and roots in the communities where they worked compensated for these shortcomings, according to several advisors. Sonia added immediately after enumerating their problems with writing and arithmetic, "Now our ideal is for them to get accredited as teachers someday."

The encounter between campesinos and professionals was not just an encounter between people with different levels of schooling, or between people with intellectual skills and others with practical skills. It was also an encounter between cultures with different views of learning, organizing, and the nature of the physical universe. It was an encounter, not a confrontation, because campesinos felt, though with ambivalence, that they had much to gain from learning, and because better-educated city- and townspeople respected—and in many cases shared, to a degree—the indigenous beliefs and knowledge of the campesinos.

Campesino survival skills saved city people's lives and kept them fed in the guerrilla army. Many folk medical practices likewise offered effective remedies that promoters of natural medicine collected and tested. They did so not just to validate the learners' indigenous knowledge and fortify them against being intimidated by the obfuscation of professionals; they also hoped to find treatments as yet unknown to medical science.

Pastoral agents organizing base communities sometimes encouraged popular religious practices, such as penances, devotions to the saints, and the use of medallions and holy water. The agents were often ambivalent because the practices appeared to promote outward observance rather than personal transformation, but they came from a tradition with deep roots and were a genuine and spontaneous expression of faith. Archbishop Romero encouraged some of these devotional practices (Berryman 1987:69–71; Brockman 1982:65–67; Levine 1992:175).

Many campesinos can detect the presence of creatures of Salvadoran and Central American folklore that are invisible to the well-educated eye. (For anthropological accounts of some of these creatures, see Edelman 1994, and Falla 1986:67–72, based on field work in Nicaragua and Guatemala respectively; for their presence in Salvadoran literature, see Argueta 1983:144; Argueta 1990; Sallarué 1980:63–66). During the CRIPDES training session reported earlier in this chapter, someone mentioned the *siguanaba*, a seductive female giant. From the discussion, it was clear that several popular teachers took the siguanaba's reality for granted.

I brought this up with Carlos, one of the popular teachers. He responded by telling me that he had seen a siguanaba and a *cadejo* on different occasions. The cadejo is a small animal that warns people of danger. (He saw a white or good cadejo; there are also black cadejos.) Once when he was walking near a military headquarters in a large town, a cadejo, which he described as an animal something like a dog and something like a cat, crossed in front of him. He immediately turned around and walked the other way. Just then, some shots were fired into the street from the headquarters, but he had escaped. I had chosen to ask Carlos about the siguanaba privately because he was a younger man, had lived in San Salvador, and had worked in a factory, so I thought that I would not offend him if I showed my skepticism. But after telling me how he had been saved by a cadejo, he concluded, "That's why I believe in these things."

During the war, many people in Morazán reported seeing a siguanaba in the Sapo River. She turned out to be a human being, a woman who had escaped the El Mozote massacre but whose daughter had been wounded by shrapnel and died. The distraught mother lived alone in the woods for years afterward. Whenever she emerged, her disheveled appearance frightened those who saw her. Finally she joined the returnees at Segundo Montes City and recovered (Danner 1994:80–81, 160–161; López Vigil 1991:245–248).

On July 7, 1991, El Salvador was witness to a seven-minute solar eclipse, one of the century's best eclipses for viewing. Even for educated people, it was not just a natural event whose meaning was exhausted in the relative positions of the earth, the sun and the moon; it had other dimensions.

The eclipse had been hotly anticipated since the beginning of the year. A few days before, the Ministry of Education announced that schools would be closed throughout the country and parents were encouraged to keep their children indoors as a safety measure. On the Sunday before the eclipse, I went to the health promoters' training session in Mariona with Cecilia and Inés, who were conducting it. Emiliano, the council president, told us that many women who worked in nearby factories would be unable to come. "Because of the phenomenon that is going to happen Thursday," factories would be closed so that women could stay home with their children, but they had to make the day up today, Sunday. He repeated the phrase "the phenomenon that is going to happen Thursday" several times in a tone of awe and mystery.

During the meeting there was a serious discussion of how to prepare for the eclipse. Parents were warned not to let children look directly at it. In both the presentation and the response, the eclipse was represented as a natural phenomenon. Earlier, however, Cecilia had asked Inés, who was pregnant (and a university graduate), if she was going to take any precautions during the eclipse. Inés acknowledged that she would: "The papers say that it doesn't affect pregnant women, but when you're carrying a baby, why take a risk?"

I saw the eclipse in the company of the FENACOA training team and the cooperative members who took part in the reflection on *casa* reported in chapter 6. As the hour approached, we suspended work and went indoors. Though it was midday, the sky darkened to dusk level. Everyone in the house became quiet—not just while the eclipse lasted, but for nearly an hour. The roosters climbed up into the trees. The hogs lay down and went to sleep. So did several people. I was one of the few who stayed outdoors to watch it. (It was spectacular.) After it ended, Juanita, a women's organizer for FENACOA and a university student, said, "Let's hope it symbolizes the fulfillment of the Salvadoran people's desire for peace."

So educational level did not divide people absolutely. Many people had complex and perhaps somewhat inconsistent attitudes. There were campesinos who could ostensibly agree with pep talks intended to persuade them that they needed education, but who were not entirely convinced. We saw in chapter 5 that even as people welcomed education to help them get ahead, they feared it might undermine their traditional culture. Because knowledge was so often used as a form of domination, moreover, adherence to traditional beliefs could correspondingly be a form of resistance to domination. This complexity of views was not a major obstacle to learning, but it did create a tension as people simultaneously held onto traditional beliefs.[1]

Professional advisors working in popular education did not feel that their superior education set them above those who learned from them. Universally, they felt that they got immeasurably more than they gave. Three months after he left a secure job in the Ministry of Education to train popular educators with CIAZO, Máximo said, "one of the selfish reasons I had for accepting this job was wanting to learn from people, learn how the people live in this country, learn different methodologies. We in the formal state system always felt a little jealous to learn what popular education is. I also feel that I have grown because I'm using a new methodology and new forms of communication. And as I see how much the abilities of the compañeros surprise me, I also feel that I've grown in this sense."

The foreigners who trained teachers were also enthusiastic and convinced that they got much more than they gave. They found themselves in jobs far more challenging that any they could have gotten at home, and, as Anita expressed it, they saw the fruits directly:

> You worked because of the community itself. You couldn't be lazy there, or take it easy. It was an atmosphere of hard work—and work that you liked, because those refugees were smart, and they got everything out of you. If you knew something, they got it out of you. And of course you felt that you had to offer something.
>
> I often asked myself if I could work like this someplace else. I don't think so. At a school in Belgium, you're bound by a program, or a report. And when I went home and told people, they said,

"Poor thing, living in such a shabby house, dirt floor, no electricity," and all that, but you went there to work. It's like what they said about the colonialists: people who went to work in the colonies worked really hard. Why? Because it paid off. I think it was the same in Colomoncagua: you felt like you were doing something. Who knows if you would get that at another job?

Cristina felt she was taking part in a movement working toward a transcendent goal, a just society. "Sometimes they say it's a dream that will never come true, but we are in it, working for what we want. And I really do believe there's going to be a better world, or a better society, for El Salvador." Collaborating in large things and small with others who were very different from themselves but who shared a vision for the future gave meaning to their work.

The Contradictions of Professionalism

Professional advisors occupied a paradoxical position. They were from higher-status backgrounds than the people they trained (professional teachers typically came from lower-middle-class or working-class families) and, by definition, they had more education. Yet on political and pedagogical grounds they foreswore any claim to superiority. Rather than impose solutions on learners, they saw their task as encouraging learners' autonomy. Just as in the guerrilla army, however, different backgrounds made for different perspectives and expectations.

People often deferred to them, moreover, even though they urged others to speak out freely and to share responsibility. The high regard in which others held them gave them authority—as when Susana found that being a North American legitimized her workshops in natural medicines among people used to relying on prescription drugs—but they were reluctant to take advantage of it. They struggled against imposing, but often they set the agenda, and sometimes conflicts arose. Their differences with the people they trained could take either of two apparently contradictory directions: at times they defended professional standards, and at other times they urged political content on reluctant popular teachers.

It was rare that they tried to uphold professional standards, because the political process normally took priority. Discussing the collective creation of the CIAZO cartilla, Cristina argued for broad participation even if the result was technically inferior. "I have compañeros who believe that the product is more important. For me it isn't. The important thing is for the people to decide, discuss, and learn to be critical. That's my vision. I don't mean that I discount the other. I believe that when people learn this, the rest will follow."

Some stood their ground, as when Máximo discouraged Pedro from teaching the alphabet even though members of the circle wanted to learn it. Others foreswore their technically correct solutions. Julio Portillo designed a manual for a post-literacy program. "They tore the manual to shreds and we wound up writing a new one together. The popular teachers said, 'The people aren't interested in knowing that blood has various components—blood plasma, platelets, red and white cells—and what the role of each of these components is. They want to know how to stop a hemorrhage. They want to know if they have some problem in the blood when they feel dizzy, for example.' In other words, things that have to do with their lives, their practical experience." Popular education is *popular*, he said, "precisely because it takes off from the concrete needs of the people and their concrete problems."

Though people in poor communities wanted to learn from their professional allies, they sometimes took demands for higher standards as covert criticisms and refusal to recognize their practical skills. "The way we campesinos are," Isabel said, "when we hear new words or meet well-educated people, we think the things we know aren't worth so much. Training has to reaffirm that what we are doing fits within the framework of a scientific context. We often think, 'What I do just popped into my imagination,' and don't call it by the name that a formally educated person would use, but really, the fact is that children have learned from us because we figure out how to reach them."

Those who organized community schools sometimes rejected the professional standards of their advisors, just as they rejected those of the official system. One occasion on which a disagreement erupted was a meeting of CCR education representatives with educators from ANDES and the National University to plan for the postwar period. Like similar organizations elsewhere in the country, the CCR planned to offer the popular teachers of Chalatenango accelerated courses leading to high school equivalency diplomas and, the organization hoped, paving the way for the Ministry of Education to hire them as teachers. In January 1992, just before the ceasefire, university faculty and ANDES members presented the CCR with a program proposal for the equivalency courses.

The CCR leaders found the proposal unsatisfactory and tore into the professionals (though with good humor): Justino of San Antonio los Ranchos exclaimed sarcastically, "We've had training when bombs were falling, and no one from the university was there!" Isabel, education representative on the CCR executive council, "begging Ernesto's pardon," compared the popular teachers' stipend of one hundred fifty colones a month (less than twenty dollars) to the budgeted salary of five thousand colones for the project director.

The problem they saw was that the proposal reduced the time the popular teachers would spend in training from the current three or four days a month to five days every two months. Besides, they complained, the professionals had designed it without consulting them and were presenting it as a fait accompli. Overall, they felt the plan fulfilled the ambitions of the professionals more than the needs of the popular teachers. They demanded that it be rethought. The program that was actually implemented the following year gave the teachers five days of training a month.

When professionals disagreed with political organizers who emphasized community needs, the former did not usually insist on upholding their own standards, because they acknowledged their subordination to political direction. In other circumstances, it was the advisors who emphasized politics. They urged reluctant popular teachers to conduct reflection seriously before teaching reading and writing, on both pedagogical and political grounds. But, as discussed in chapter 6, some volunteer teachers, especially in government-controlled areas, did not encourage reflection, or did so half-heartedly. Some feared repression; others found that reflection taxed their abilities. Reflection "is the most difficult part," Cristina said, "because it requires the most commitment. Most of us haven't been educated to think, but to accept."

Other popular teachers deemphasized reflection because they did not entirely embrace the political line. Some organizations, even though they enlisted NGOs identified with the popular movement to support their literacy programs, were actually rather conservative. Others, though more left-leaning, wanted to use a literacy program as a recruitment device in conservative areas. Máximo complained that one organization "asked to change some of the words in the cartilla. They think that if we go in with the project as it is, which I believe is already a little watered down, people wouldn't get organized."

Advisors also—ambivalently—wanted teachers to direct discussion to the appropriate political conclusion. During the training session in Torola, Máximo told them that they should not be afraid to tell people they are wrong, for example if someone said a problem existed "*por la voluntad de Dios*"—because it is God's will. But on other occasions advisors welcomed all interpretations on the principle that people should be encouraged to think things out for themselves. In the CRIPDES training session, when the teachers interpreted the story of the eagle, one person referred not to the eagle's liberating himself but to his getting along with the chickens. It would have been easy to dismiss that interpretation as missing the point, especially a point so important as the struggle for liberation. But it was simply acknowledged as a different point of view.

Professionals were sometimes tempted to impose technically correct solutions and sometimes to push a political line—they advanced from their right and their left flanks, so to speak. It is not surprising that differences arose between them and their trainees. Even though the advisors shared common political purposes with the organizers and teachers of popular schools, their different backgrounds gave them different perspectives. They struggled over their differences and worked them out.

Nevertheless, the differences that arose reveal the complexities in the role of advisors who come from outside to serve a process whose mainspring, they believe, must be the needs and goals of the group. Communities in FMLN-controlled zones were highly organized and had a strong political direction. In any disagreement, advisors were likely to find themselves defending professional standards. But they acknowledged the ultimate authority of the community councils over the schools. In some places, in fact, a political leader routinely took part in training sessions. In government-controlled zones, on the other hand, where organizations pursued political purposes less consistently, advisors were more likely to push literacy circles to take a clear political direction. But as chapter 6 showed, these were the circles where discussion was most hesitant and bore overtly political fruit least often.

When advisors pushed a political line, in other words, they were not very successful. Popular education can make an important contribution to an existing political practice, providing theoretical underpinning for the consciousness that has already developed. But such consciousness cannot come into being independently of actual struggles. If outsiders attempt to use popular education to recruit, mobilize, and activate a reluctant population, it is unlikely to lead to political action—although even there it may help people to assert themselves and believe that their political views deserve to be heard.

Popular education embodies a paradox that is present at every level, not just between professionally trained advisors and poorly educated campesinos. Anyone who proposes to raise someone else's consciousness presumes to have some privileged knowledge to share. But those who adopt the premises of popular education are convinced that to dictate consciousness would be a contradiction in terms, and that people become genuinely conscious only if they reach their own conclusions. On the whole, popular education was a genuinely collaborative process, in which the professionals' temptation to assume their own superiority was tempered by their respect for the contributions of the popular teachers. The process was marked by contradictions, to be sure, but it was not an imposition by "superiors" upon "inferiors." Professional advisors worked *with* popular teachers. Their methods provided insurance against dictating. As long as they applied participatory principles, they would not lay down a line.

Advisors incorporated the contributions of popular teachers and encouraged them to be creative. They recognized the value of collaboration, and therefore worked toward consensus whether or not the outcome conformed to the prescriptions of their professional training. They strove determinedly to instill confidence in the popular teachers they trained—confidence in their abilities in the classroom, in their right to speak up, and in the value of what they had to say. Advisors strove to draw people out.

The training they offered went beyond specific skills and political orientation. It opened up broader areas of knowledge to popular teachers. The CRIPDES workshop on reading for pleasure, Esperanza said, was "for them," and so were the recreational classes advisors offered once a week to teachers in Colomoncagua. Advisors recognized the teachers' ability and desire to learn, and used the training process not just to improve their teaching skills, but to broaden their horizons.

They learned from the people they worked with (sometimes in spite of themselves, only after overcoming unspoken prejudices against those they intended to "educate"). They discovered the limits of their formal knowledge, and often their collaborators' ideas did work better. The spontaneity and detail with which they described those discoveries betoken their sincerity. The fact that they learned from their trainees was a source of humility and openness, and provided further insurance against dictating from a position of superior knowledge.

Finally, advisors did not set themselves apart from others. A professional, in their view, was one more member of a group. They had something to offer from their particular perspective, education, and background—different from, but not necessarily more valuable than, the contributions of others. They found the process genuinely mutual. The illiterate man who knew how to plow or the barely literate woman whose intimate knowledge of the life circumstances of her pupils made her an effective teacher also brought something essential.

Advisors did not believe that their work was ideologically neutral—they did not believe that education could be. They came with an ideology that they wanted to share with new learners. But my observations have convinced me that with rare exceptions they stopped short of indoctrination. They knew that it would not work, and they genuinely wanted learners to think for themselves. They were certain that the power of popular education lies in learners' finding their own way and speaking with their own voice. Though they sometimes promoted a distinct point of view, to succumb to the temptation to impose would have violated their own goals. Had they tried, moreover, their trainees would have rejected it. The relation between popular teachers and their professional advisors was a collaboration from which everyone got something. In popular education, teaching and learning were mutual.

This chapter and the preceding one have focused on pedagogy in the narrow sense. Even when examining what goes on in the classroom, however, we cannot ignore the influence of community structure and political goals. The content and quality of instruction were affected, for better and for worse, by the teachers' motivations—community spirit and their aspiration to work collectively toward a better life. Teachers and those who trained them learned from each other, but their mutual learning bore latent contradictions: professionals did not entirely renounce the claims of their professional status, nor did teachers or community organizers surrender their political judgment to the advisors' technical superiority. In its pedagogy as in its community setting, popular education is a political practice.

CHAPTER 8

Popular Education in Practice and Theory

――――

*I*nsurgents challenged the Salvadoran government for more than a decade in a struggle that combined military attack and civilian organization. On both fronts, education played a vital role. The combat skill and morale of FMLN combatants and the support that came from organized civilian communities were essential to the FMLN's ability to wage war for twelve years.

Popular education contributed to both of these. It taught people to perform particular tasks; it raised the morale that sustained them in their unequal combat; and it stimulated the creation of an organizational network to hold them together. To be able to fight, combatants and civilians had to be educated not only in military skills, but in political analysis and organizational skills as well. They acquired abilities that served them on the battlefield and in civilian life, they strengthened their ideological conviction, and they developed the self-confidence to work effectively. Popular education also epitomized the beliefs that inspired those who fought and gave them staying power. The learning process was therefore a significant factor in political and military success.

In this chapter I examine the practitioners' vision of popular education, and show that it embodied both the goals for which they fought the war and their aspirations for a new society. I discuss the self-confidence and sense of empowerment people gained as popular educators and learners. Then, returning to the roots of popular education, I compare Salvadoran practice to Paulo Freire's theory. They shared pedagogical assumptions and practices, but understanding the Salvadoran experience requires attention to aspects not highlighted in Freire's theory: its close relation to the communities that promoted it, and the effects of their poverty and their political engagement. Finally, I analyze the specific contributions of popular education to the outcome of the conflict in which the FMLN won relative success. This chapter thus recapitulates, in a different order, the five principal claims about popular education I enumerated in chapter 1.

The insurgency had to cultivate conviction and self-confidence in order to overcome the ideological hegemony of the Salvadoran oligarchy. Though it ruled by force, the oligarchy asserted a monopoly on intellectual and cultural skills, and thereby claimed legitimacy to rule. That claim to hegemony consigned El Salvador's illiterate poor to inferiority, and did so effectively: many not only submitted to the state's coercive power but believed in their own ignorance and incompetence. By practicing popular education, however, they challenged the dominant belief in their inferiority, claimed to formulate a culture for themselves, and asserted their legitimacy to speak out.

Antonio Gramsci (1971:108–110 and passim) distinguishes between war of movement and war of position. The war of movement, translated into political terms, is the attempt to conquer state power by force. The war of position is the struggle for hegemony: the effort to win the allegiance of the people. Guerrilla war is at least as much a struggle for hegemony as it is a direct struggle for power. It is not enough to accumulate forces. An insurgent movement must secure the voluntary recruitment of combatants and the support of a civilian base by combatting ingrained beliefs in both the legitimacy of those in power and the futility of opposing them. By building community institutions and educating at the same time that it fought a war, the FMLN transcended the Gramscian dilemma and combined war of position with war of movement.

Indeed, the war was first fought on the terrain of culture, well before most people contemplated armed struggle. Christian base community activists adopted a new view of themselves—that they were capable of acting and asserting their own interests. Political action followed, and only after peaceful means had been exhausted did militants take up arms. When they did, they first neglected the need to continue mobilizing support. But it proved fruitless to carry on the military struggle without equal attention to the political struggle. In the mid-1980s the insurgents decided to implement both strategies at once, emphasizing community organization and education again.[1]

Not only were organization and education components of military strategy; they also looked forward to the creation of a new society after the expected victory. Education is an essential part of social transformation. It is not sufficient, because the power that exploits and oppresses must be defeated; but people must also learn to be competent and committed members of society. In that sense, popular education was practiced prefiguratively, to inculcate the values that would prevail in the new society after the war. The insurgent forces fought for state power and a total transformation of society. They forsook those goals for a peace settlement that offered much more limited gains, but allowed them to continue the struggle for hegemony on new ground. The return to peace makes the cultural struggle even more important.[2]

The Meaning of Popular Education

The practice of popular education was based on a vision that embodied strong moral commitments. Two were fundamental: to universal access, and to service to one's community. Each of those principles had important implications for education. Access should be universal in two senses: education should be offered everywhere, and it should use teaching methods that allow anyone to learn, whatever their level of knowledge and intellectual skill. The availability of education should be governed by the principle of equality. The norm of community entailed that a major purpose of education is to prepare people to serve their communities, and that schools should therefore teach the skills and values that will move people to act on behalf of their community. Education must get them committed to serve and provide the necessary tools. Embracing these two principles, people idealized the education they offered and justified even its deficiencies as due to them. Determination and dedication would make up for any material or intellectual shortcomings.

To see how participants conceived of popular education, I examined all the occurrences in the interviews of the phrases "popular education," "popular school," and "popular teacher." In most interviews in which informants referred to popular education, I concluded by asking them what they meant by the term. In their answers they emphasized the "popular" nature of those to whom it was offered, of those who taught, and of the teaching itself.

I found, first of all, that the terminology was highly current, coming up in more than half of the interviews. Most people spoke of "popular education" or "popular schools" spontaneously, and it was clearly part of their understanding that the education they were promoting or receiving was in some sense "popular."[3] Sometimes the term simply referred to the education practiced in their communities or organizations, with no specific content: the school was called a popular school and its teachers popular teachers. Often, however, the context gave it added meaning. Eight themes recurred in people's use of the word *popular*:

1) Popular education is for humble people, campesinos like us.

It's popular because it's like here, rural schools, not in urban-type places. So they are simple communities. (Flora)

An education for the people. . . . In the cantons that never had schools, now there are popular schools where they teach up to sixth grade. (Claudio)

2) Popular education is offered to everyone. It is assumed that everyone who wants to learn has the capacity.

Popular education should not just be for a few people. (Luisa)

For us, popular education is that no one should remain behind. Everyone has to learn. (Felipe)

Though poor people are the most important group it embraces, this inclusiveness also extends to people of all ages. Adults who did not learn as children can do so now.

They call it popular because it's for everyone, from little children to big children and adults. (Julia)

3) Popular teachers are themselves campesinos, poorly educated but intimately familiar with their communities.

[In Mesa Grande] we called it popular education: the teachers were from the refugees themselves. (Rito)

The popular educator is one who springs from the people themselves. Someone from right here. (Luisa)

People trusted the popular teachers more. They weren't shy about asking questions, because the teachers lived there. The others didn't; they just came to teach class and they left. (Humberto)

If our teachers are popular in nature [*de carácter popular*], that means they are teachers who have suffered the causes of the war. They know that these pupils in the school have fled the bombs with them. (Justino)

We can't claim to be well prepared, like in traditional schools, where they are well prepared and wear fancy clothes. We don't have that, because we have no resources. (Gabriela)

4) Popular teachers make sacrifices to educate others, because they have a strong sense of social duty and a strong desire to share what they have learned. These compensate for their lack of education.

What we mean by popular education is that we're going to try harder to teach them. It doesn't matter whether we're well prepared, or how we look; what is important is to do our best to teach them the little bit that we know. (Abilio)

[The popular] teacher isn't working just to draw down his 1,500 colones. Here we do it purely out of good will. (Salvador)

Besides working as popular teachers, they have to go on working the fields and providing for their families. (Sonia)

We had one popular educator who had to walk thirteen kilometers, and then come back—he walked thirty kilometers to be able to do popular education. (Osvaldo)

5) Popular education is part of community life. The community supports the schools, and the schools serve the community.

[They are called popular teachers] because they're put there by the community itself. (Jorge)

The popular teacher has paid attention to the needs of the community. (Alfonso)

When we talk about popular education in the communities, we're not exactly talking about a building that we could call a school, but about the organization of the people. (Lorena)

6) In popular education, people learn things that are relevant to their real lives (in striking contrast to the incomprehensible abstractions taught by teachers with credentials and formal training).

It's popular education because it's an education that springs from the people—not using all that methodology, let's say, of strange words, that our people don't understand. (Humberto)

Popular education is different from academic education: the schools didn't talk about the harvest, or the lack of hospitals in the countryside. They told you about things that were very abstract. (Francisco)

The method of popular education is *popular* precisely because it takes off from the concrete needs of the people and their concrete problems. (Julio Portillo)

7) The teaching style is dynamic, active, and engaging, and intended to help people think, not just to learn facts or memorize.

In a popular class, you have to let children participate, express what they feel, and say everything they feel in their souls. In a conservative education, the child doesn't have this participation. (Alfredo)

Traditional teachers don't form you, they inform you. A traditional teacher gives you the recipe to do a mathematical operation, but doesn't explain what it means or why you did it. (Claudio)

Part of the process in training the health promoters was training them in the different methods of teaching, [and showing them that] just straight teaching didn't work. (Susana)

8) Popular education's curriculum emphasizes political content because it is part of a struggle against oppression.

For us popular education has a connotation of commitment, due to working with the popular sectors. (Pablo)

[In] popular education now, at the same time as teaching to read, you do consciousness-raising. (Nacho)

[In official schools] they might say, "Children die of this or that," but in popular education we tell a child, "No, that child died of malnutrition." (Humberto)

For me personally, popular education means a genuine education, an education for the people. Governments don't want people to learn. It's a way to keep people ignorant so that injustice can continue, because if people don't know how to read and write, they are easily dominated by someone who does know how. (Claudio)

This was the participants' vision of popular education, the vision on which their work was grounded. It included a strong moral component: it represented not only their view of what popular education *is*, but also the way education (all education) *ought* to be. Even its deficiencies were taken to prove its virtues. Some, especially teachers, took a perverse pride in its limitations, because they had overcome them to educate. It should nevertheless be clear from the discussion in the preceding chapters that much of this vision represents aspiration more than description. The reality often fell short.

This presentation of the animating vision of popular education is more complex than the summary I offered in chapter 1. I have synthesized the views of many who participated in different capacities. No one of them presented the vision in its entirety; in fact, people in different positions emphasized different things. The topics raised fall into three groups, dealing with who is educated, who teaches, and the content and methodology of education. Each of these associations was most often mentioned by a particular category of person. The people most likely to identify popular education with its constituency—poor people working together in poor communities—were school organizers (but not teachers), new learners, or community people who had no special role in education. Many of those who defined it in terms of participatory teaching methods and political objectives were outsiders—professional advisors and political cadres. Popular teachers were most likely to mention characteristics of teachers, although they frequently invoked the other criteria as well.[4]

There is another, related difference. Some informants used the term "popular education" mainly to refer to the educational practice with which they were familiar, while others were intentionally defining an abstract model that prescribed a particular content and process. (Not everyone, of course, would recognize a distinction between actual practice and the prescriptions of a model.)

Again, this difference corresponded to the degree of community involvement on the one hand, and professional training on the other. Those with more professional training were more likely to discuss popular education in abstract, conceptual terms, while those working in the communities more often emphasized the concrete and practical. These differences may have arisen because the less sophisticated were closer to what was going on in schools and villages, while professionals were more likely to be aware of the theoretical model and to use it as a reference point.

Coping with Shortages and Conquering Self-Doubt

There are two other aspects that did not emerge prominently in people's use of the term popular education but are, I believe, central to its meaning: the material poverty in which it was carried on and the process of empowerment it stimulated. These aspects came up repeatedly in discussions of how it worked, even though informants did not often associate either of them with the term "popular education."

Material conditions took a heavy toll everywhere. People lacked the most rudimentary equipment and supplies, and necessity fostered creative improvisations. I will return to the implications of poverty for the meaning of popular education later when I examine popular education in El Salvador in the light of Freire's theory.

Also important in people's understanding of the process of popular education, even though it was not prominently associated with the term, is that it empowered people by giving them skills and confidence. Learning, teaching, organizing schools and communities gave people a sense of themselves as competent and worthy individuals who are capable of acting and entitled to act. As campesinos, they had been denied that self-confidence, held in disdain by their social superiors and repressed by the forces of order whenever they risked acts of self-assertion. The discovery of their power to act was central to the political impact of popular education.

It was rare for participants to mention this in a context that explicitly invoked the concept of popular education, as Claudio did: "This thing of popular education has been like a discovery that we've made that it is possible to do it."

Many informants nevertheless believed that becoming educated could give people the power to act. "Inside all these projects," Heriberto found, "there's a goal, which is not to be like those people who say that the government can do everything, and we can't do anything; if there's no teacher, we can't study. Instead, we have to let ourselves be worth something—be worth what we are worth."

Conversely, others believed that because they lacked education they were not competent. Daniel, a member of the executive council of PADECOMSM, expressed the pain he felt as an adult who was still trying to learn: "I still don't know enough with this little bit of studying that I've had now—even though I've felt myself improving with the little I've learned. I couldn't even face my own community. The shame of it killed me." Those who did learn continued to feel unsure of themselves, like Ramón, who even as a teacher was afraid that a parent would look at a child's notebook and blame him for a mistake.

Against this background of poignant self-deprecation, achieving education or educating others was a personal triumph. People did not display pride openly, but it came out nevertheless. New learners often seemed astonished at having achieved what they had never thought possible, like the many combatants who mastered new skills. Others took pride in telling the story of how they had learned, because it gave them the chance to tell about all the obstacles they had overcome.

Some were more indirect: Herminio, who learned to read in Colomon-cagua, said that he would persuade someone who was reluctant to learn by telling his own story. When I asked Ovidio, who had also learned to read in the refugee camp, whether he still read, he spoke about a pamphlet about the peace negotiations then going on. After revealing that he did not understand the details of the negotiations very clearly, he nevertheless proceeded, "But on that point, I want to say something about the dialogue [i.e., the negotiations]. Maybe we Salvadorans, who have had ten years of war, would like to see the war end so we could really get to work, and have them find a different way out, not just by force." His views were somewhat awkwardly expressed, and hardly profound, but for a man who did not seem to be very given to political analysis, it struck me as significant that he was determined to voice his opinion.

Those who worked as teachers were also reluctant to claim credit, but they took obvious pride when talking about their students' accomplishments. Severino admired the disabled combatants he taught: "Even on their crutches they always showed up for class." Rosita, active in the base community of Zacamil, taught some women to read. She smiled broadly as she remembered, "Almost two years later, one of them went up to the front during mass and read a lesson from the Bible. When I saw her it was admirable."

Some of Marta's students went on to higher grades in official schools elsewhere. "They told me that they hadn't had any problem, and that they congratulated them when they saw how much they had learned from a popular teacher. It made us very proud and encouraged us to continue, because what we could give them was important, and now they're studying seventh and eighth grade. And it's a big surprise for me that, well, I got to fourth grade, and I *taught* fourth grade. And they asked the students how could it be that someone who had only been to fourth grade had taught them."

Some of Gabriela's adult students in Colomoncagua took on important responsibilities in Segundo Montes City. "They are now at a level that I'm not at," she said. "There are coordinators, doing big jobs, purely mental work, and writing, and they were compañeros who learned to read with me. They thank me, and I say, 'Yes, but I'll never reach the level that you are at now.'"

Some who did not teach took the same pride in the success of students in schools they helped to organize, like Arturo of PADECOMSM. "We feel very proud because there are hundreds and hundreds, thousands of children who know how to read and write. Some of my wife's students, who were with her in first grade, are now going to fifth and sixth grade."

This game of mutual admiration allowed them to show pride while ostensibly remaining humble. I believe that their modesty reflected genuine astonishment that they had gone as far as they had, but they could take pride in their contributions to their community and the fruits of their success in their pupils. Luisa, the coordinator of education in Segundo Montes City, found it "incredible" that 85 percent of the community knew how to read. "There's probably no place else in the country like Segundo Montes."

An assignment as a teacher could be a proving ground. Many who did it well were chosen for higher-level duties. This sometimes disrupted the schooling process (although people were usually moved around only at the end of an academic year) and caused resentment among those running the schools, even though they were proud that popular teachers were tapped for community leadership. Taking on community tasks as teachers or in other leadership positions can be a form of social mobility among people who had relatively few outlets for their creative energy. They had little chance to pursue success as entrepreneurs or get the formal education to qualify themselves for a profession, even though they might be intellectually capable; being a popular teacher or community activist became a channel for their abilities. They throve on it.

Many who proved themselves were women. Salvadoran society did not allow women much scope for creative action, and even women who joined the insurgent struggle generally did so to fight economic injustice and had little consciousness of gender inequality (Gargallo 1987). But they discovered their abilities as they became active. Becoming active could disrupt expectations, especially in their families. When Marta, the popular teacher in Laguna Seca, became the first woman elected to the executive council of PADECOMSM, she said, "Sometimes my husband didn't want to let me, because it's true, you don't take care of the home and the children. So he told me no. Then when I was elected I told them they had to go tell him because I couldn't. So they talked to him and he agreed to let me work here."

Popular education confronted sexism in personal relationships and communities, if only intermittently. Reflections in literacy circles focused on the inequality of traditional gender relations, especially in couples. Women were encouraged to recognize their right to act independently, and men were urged to examine their own sexism. I do not want to exaggerate the concern; Máximo of CIAZO thought that it was mainly lip service. When people discussed the status of women in reflections, he said, "They talk the talk [*el discurso lo manejan*], but it's as if they don't believe it." (He still encouraged the teachers he trained to raise the issue, though.)

More than half the popular teachers were women. Many of them took on administrative and organizing responsibilities for the schools or got the education that prepared them for other responsible roles. Nevertheless, the women I interviewed did not show any strong gender consciousness, or claim recognition as women for their accomplishments. Nor did I detect any major differences between men and women in their views about teaching or in their sense of themselves as teachers. They both expressed a spontaneous warmth and attentiveness to children's needs, of the sort that is generally thought to be more common among women than among men.

It is inconceivable that either popular education or the larger political struggle could have occurred without the participation of women, any more than it could have occurred without the participation of campesinos. There were more women in the refugee camps and in the repopulated communities, to start with; men were more likely to have fallen to repression or to be away in combat. The need to "do a lot with a little," to use all resources to the maximum, evidently required taking advantage of women's abilities as well as men's. And the commitment to equality—even when violated in everyday behavior—entailed recognizing that women could handle new responsibilities.

Women's activism often expressed traditional gender concerns, however. Women formed committees of family members to support the (mainly male) political prisoners. Women combatants received weapons training alongside men, but they often went on to work as nurses. The Christian Mothers for Peace of Morazán organized to provide cover for tasks in which men would have aroused suspicion, but their first concern was to get food for their families' tables. Women who took on community tasks most often worked in education and health, both traditionally women's work. In many countries of Latin America, women have become active precisely around issues made salient by their traditional role (notably, feeding their families and protecting their male family members who suffer repression), but when they do, they go public and reject their traditional relegation to the private sphere (Jelín 1990; Radcliffe and Westwood 1993). The paradox that women's activism simultaneously reaffirms and transcends the sexual division of labor means that it does not easily lead to the assertion and conquest of equal rights (Molyneux 1986; Safa 1990). Nevertheless, by learning and teaching, Salvadoran women began to recognize their abilities and demonstrate them to others, men and women, thereby taking a necessary first step.[5]

Men and women alike came to recognize their abilities and gain the confidence that they could do things they had considered impossible. They acquired a new sense of themselves. They no longer had to submit to the inferiority to which they had always been consigned, as in Rufino's childhood memory: "Once I said to my mother, 'Mama, I dreamed I was a teacher.'" Rufino was a visibly tense man. In 1987, suffering what he described as a mental problem in the refugee camp, he had been told to rest and had stopped teaching for six months. But he glowed with enthusiasm when he talked about his work, and he glowed when he remembered his dream. "My mother said, 'That's like chasing a deer and grabbing it by the tail.' But she smiled, and I still remember my mother's smile. And I stopped and thought, 'It's so far away.' But now I've seen that she wasn't right. What I dreamed came true."

As Severino observed, "The people who studied were the ones who had money, because they could become teachers, they could become lawyers, they could become doctors, but the campesino never studied. I once heard it said that the one who is born to be a doctor will be a doctor, and the one who is born to be a campesino will be a campesino. But in practice we see that it isn't true. It's the lack of opportunity, or poverty itself, that keeps you from going to school."

Literature on social movements has recently pointed to personal growth as an important goal and outcome of social movements (McAdam 1988; Tarrow

1994:147). Participants have to think creatively and act collaboratively in order to work toward an important goal; the goal in turn gives meaning to their mutual relations—so that their activity becomes an expression of themselves and a source of pride in accomplishment. When in popular education people recognized their abilities and won the recognition of others, they achieved a new sense of themselves as competent individuals who could attempt to transform their world rather than resigning themselves to it.

That they achieved confidence in their abilities by putting them to use in popular education does not mean that that is its purpose. There are programs in the United States today that do attempt to promote self-esteem—the "recovery" movement (which seeks to cure many problems by treating them as addictions) and some high school curricula, for example—and assume that people can overcome their defects simply by raising their low opinions of themselves. Such programs make use of the idea of empowerment, but they differ from popular education. They are designed not to spur people to accomplishments worthy of higher self-esteem but to affect their self-esteem directly. These programs also differ from popular education in that they deflect attention from the social causes of problems to the failings of the individual. One U.S. author was criticized by a reviewer for "forcing the radical third-world pedagogy of Mr. Freire into a troubled and unlikely marriage with the quintessentially American language of self-help [and] at times sounding more like Norman Vincent Peale than Nelson Mandela" (Karabel 1994; cf. Mecca, Smelser, and Vasconcellos 1989; Rapping 1996).

Popular education did not pursue self-esteem for its own sake. Rather, participants gained self-confidence because they discovered their abilities, learned new skills, and put them into practice. By working toward goals they valued as part of a political program, participants came to recognize and exercise skills whose lack or denial did in fact constitute part of their oppression; they thought better of themselves because their accomplishments clearly demonstrated that they could do more than they had been allowed to realize.

As they achieved self-confidence, individuals strengthened their communities as well as themselves. The new sense of oneself as a competent person arose in the context of working in concert with others to improve the communities. Before a community could act, it needed a sufficient number of members who had the requisite sense of efficacy. All those who participated in popular education—and by extension, all those who supported it indirectly by taking part in other community projects—asserted the power to act collectively against the forces that oppressed them. This capacity to cooperate became social capital, a resource enabling communities to achieve all their goals more effectively (Coleman 1990; Putnam 1993:167–169; Putnam 1995:67).

Freire Revisited

Because Paulo Freire's theoretical formulation of the processes and purposes of popular education is widely seen as definitive, and because the present study offers one of the few accounts of a popular education process to go beyond the anecdotal, I want to examine the extent to which the Salvadoran experience follows and diverges from the Freirean model.

Salvadoran practice conformed to the Freirean model in many respects. It expressed the same commitment to an egalitarian ideology. Participatory methodology, a commitment to relevance, and a content that exposes the basis of oppression were among the aspects highlighted in the informants' discourse around the term popular education (though, as I have noted, the first and last of these were mentioned more often by professionals than by participants from the local communities). Participation is meant to break down passivity in learning and to develop critical consciousness. Subject matter that derives directly from participants' lives stimulates their interest and makes their education relevant to them. And when participants recognize their oppression, it is assumed, they will struggle for emancipation.

So Salvadoran practice adopted the purposes and the pedagogy of the Freirean model. But it diverged in some respects, and had unique features that were not envisioned by that model but in my view were central to the process. It was significantly determined by social and political conditions, in two ways: practitioners adapted to the limits imposed on their work by material conditions, and they organized education to serve and to express their political struggle. The material and organizational conditions in which education is carried out receive surprisingly little attention from Freire and other theorizers. But they are central to understanding the process in El Salvador. The effect of those conditions on the educational process is one of the distinctive lessons to be learned about popular education from the Salvadoran experience.

Where Salvadoran practice coincided with the Freirean model, it was usually not because practitioners deliberately adopted it. While some who pioneered popular education in El Salvador knew of Freire's approach and consciously sought to apply it, most had little awareness of it. The first popular teachers during the war, whether combatants, refugees, or teachers in villages in the war zones, for the most part began naively, without any conscious methodology. Claudio, a combatant: "We didn't use the term [popular education] in the war. It was more like, 'I'm going to teach you to read and write.'" Marta, who founded the popular school for the children of Laguna Seca: "[We remembered] the little bit we had learned when we were children. . . . So we set out a little group of words. . . . And that's how we taught: the same as we had learned." Nacho, who trained combatant-teachers: "We didn't connect it to political discussion much. It's not like popular education now, where at the same time as teaching to read, you do consciousness-raising."

Proceeding without a model, popular educators discovered emancipatory possibilities and effective methods to foster them. Later they became aware of popular education as a formal practice and discovered that it met their needs, justified what they were already doing, and offered orientations for improvement.

A few were familiar with Freire. Raúl said that he and others employed in the National Literacy Program (PNA), which was created to accompany the 1980 agrarian reform, studied his work directly. "The supporting documents we read were the literature of Paulo Freire: *Education as the Practice of Freedom, Popular Education*, and all that literature. In essence it was the method of Paulo Freire."

Cristina encountered Freire when she was teaching displaced people in San Salvador. "I started working with refugees in the San José de la Montaña Seminary [which was being used as a home for displaced people]. Then we heard about the theories of Freire. We started circles with the same syllabic method that was used with children, but it didn't work because it looked just like it did for children. Then new theories started coming, that the adult doesn't learn something which isn't going to be useful for survival."

Camilo, a law student in the late 1970s, worked with popular teachers in a rural community near the capital. "Paulo Freire's *Pedagogy of the Oppressed* inspired us a lot. At that time it was getting known in university circles around the country, and in Latin America. . . . What helped me a lot back then was Paulo Freire, teaching me that it wasn't just a matter of depositing, but for me to learn from them too."

In the 1980s the Ministry of Education itself produced an elaborate illustrated pamphlet setting out Freire's ideas for in-service training of its teachers (Ministerio de Educación, n.d.).

Others without formal training knew that there was a theory underlying popular education, but were only dimly aware of it. When asked to explain it, some offered abstractions which they seemed to quote as a formula or acknowledged their ignorance. Elena, explaining that she chose words for a cartilla from people's life experience (see chapter 6), said,

> Really, it's the method of that man—I don't remember his name.
> *Freire.*
> Yes.

But despite her confession of ignorance, Elena had just demonstrated her grasp of one of Freire's essential points when she said that she chose words that represented "things people live with to identify and remember the letter better." Others who similarly displayed great skill and self-confidence in their work as teachers nevertheless felt a sense of inferiority because they had not mastered the theory. Five women who taught in Segundo Montes City were invited to present a panel to professionals in San Salvador; Gabriela, though proud of her work as a popular teacher, could hardly imagine claiming credit for it in front of the professionals. "They asked us how we had taught some things, and how we had made a lesson plan, and we answered them all. We felt very shy because they were all university professors, and we were just campesinas. Then they taught us about popular education, and we brought it back here [to Segundo Montes City] to teach it to the compañeros." Ironically, even though professionals had invited Gabriela and her compañeras to describe education in Segundo Montes City, she assumed that they could teach her what popular education was.

Heriberto, describing his activities as a catechist in the parish of Teotepeque, talked about using organizing methods derived from popular education, but when pressed to describe them in more detail he became tongue-tied:

> The goal was for people not just to get the food or the pills [as a handout] or learn to read, but something more.
> *Which was what? What was the something more?*
> A lot. Well, I don't know how to explain it, but to make people—what—I don't know how to explain. In other words, this something more is something that we've completely—we have to get beyond ignorance.

He went on to explain that getting beyond ignorance meant not just learning but, through learning, achieving a sense of one's own importance. But in his initial confusion he appeared to be searching for the formal, correct answer. All of these popular educators had proven their ability in practice, but they still felt uncertain of it. Knowing that there was a theory that they had not mastered became one more reason to feel that because they were poorly educated, they were inadequate.

Nor had all those with some formal knowledge mastered the theory completely. Cristina tried to explain what she saw as a common misconception. "People think that they are doing popular education because they are teaching someone who never went to school, but they are using the same method as an ordinary, everyday, traditional teacher. Popular education is when people take on a different method. It's a daily struggle to change ourselves, all of us. A doctor or a lawyer can be 'popular' because he is working for the majorities." But her view appears contradictory. She says that education is not popular if it uses traditional methods, even when offered to those who have not had it before. But at the same time she views professionals' work as popular by virtue of the groups they are working with—the issue is who is served, not the way the professionals relate to them.

If the Freirean model of popular education was not followed strictly, it was not only because practitioners had not mastered it adequately. The literature does not provide a clear point of reference. It gives multiple, overlapping, and sometimes contradictory meanings to the term "popular education." Freire's own writings are very difficult, as many readers have found; the concreteness and accessibility he calls for in practice do not characterize his own presentation. The model is not clear on the relative importance of various of its elements: it includes political and pedagogical elements in a sometimes uncomfortable mixture (Fink and Arnove 1991), and it does not prescribe the weight to be given to each.

Nor are the texts intended as a blueprint. The model is deliberately pragmatic and open-ended; particular circumstances require adaptations. It is also dialectical: practitioners draw on the prior knowledge of the learners, which becomes an essential part of the material with which practitioners work, and it is necessarily unpredictable which learners, with what knowledge, will be present in a given case. Thus any model of popular education is incomplete by definition.

Few people read the texts in any case. They were more likely to learn teaching methods at conferences and training sessions, and what little written material they had was often locally produced mimeographed summaries and comic books. These channels of diffusion—direct teaching, experience, and rather ephemeral written documents—were used in part because they were available and books were not, but they also made it easy to modify practices in response to local conditions.

Salvadoran practice departed from the theory of popular education in other, more important ways—not because practitioners cut corners or were ignorant of the theory, but because the practice responded creatively to the social conditions it encountered, on which the theory is silent. This response took two important forms: practitioners adapted to the limits imposed on their work by material conditions, and they organized education in close integration with other community activities. Here, as I have emphasized, lies El Salvador's uniqueness among examples of popular education.

Among the limiting material conditions that had to be taken into account, the war's disruptions were the most obvious. As Severino recounted, "You had to have the chalk in one hand, and your knapsack ready, and your rifle right next to you, because if you didn't, the enemy could capture you. You had to be ready for anything." Teachers were captured, villages were bombed, and fear distracted the children.

Education was targeted for repression. Raúl, who learned Freire's theories and methods while being trained for the PNA, had to change plans when the cartilla he used was confiscated as subversive by the National Guard. He described his new technique in Freirean terminology. Illustrations of generative words in cartillas are known as "codifications," and the process of analyzing them is called decodification. (Only those formally trained in popular education used the terms codification and decodification; others talked about "reflection.") Deprived of their cartilla, Raúl and the literacy teachers he trained decided to dispense with codifications in photographs or drawings. Instead they and their circles walked around the community to look for examples and discussed the problems they observed. "If the generative word to study that day was *casa* [house], for example, the first activity that the volunteer teacher organized was to take a walk through the community with all the members of the circle so that they could look closely at everything they passed; and they began to discuss the housing problem, not by decoding a poster but by doing an activity—going out to see them." But they would not have departed from the program if the cartillas had not been confiscated.

If the war caused problems that required creative responses, the impact of poverty was in some ways more pervasive. Many pedagogical practices—the recruitment of teachers with barely more education than their pupils, the reliance on consciousness and good will, the tight integration of education and politics, and group learning activities (justified by Iván as saving paper in Mariona prison)—were responses to necessity, arising from either the lack of material resources or the teachers' limited education. But they were turned into virtues, because they assured that the relevance of the subject matter motivated learners and that commitment to the good of the community motivated teachers.

The same practices were adopted in prisons, refugee camps, war-torn communities, and the guerrilla army. This similarity was probably not due to conscious adoption of a popular education model. Over time, popular teachers in refugee camps and civilian communities got substantial training in popular pedagogy. Guerrilla combatants and political prisoners, however, got very little at best (though some of them had participated in popular education in their previous political work, and brought their knowledge of the model to the front or the prisons). Informants who had taught in prison or the guerrilla army emphasized not past experience or training but pragmatic experimentation as the source of most of their teaching methodology.

This suggests that similar methods arose in response to similar material circumstances more than from application of a model. Popular education is more likely to be a response to necessity than a choice. Those who need it are people with no access to formal education. For the same reason, its personnel are likely to be unschooled and their resources few. They work, so to speak, under circumstances not chosen by themselves. Economic poverty and cultural deprivation were responsible for many of the characteristics of popular education in El Salvador.

It is likely that any teaching process that is popular in the sense that it attempts to reach people previously unreached and is carried out under political auspices will adopt similar practices. In some places they will be adopted by planning or imitation, and elsewhere they will be independently discovered as solutions to similar problems.

The ways these settings differed also affected the educational process. The fact that there were families in refugee camps and repopulated communities made educating children a goal and gave the effort a focus very different from the one it had in prisons and the guerrilla army. Prisons shared with refugee camps the involuntary confinement and excess of free time that made studying an act of defiance and a welcome diversion; these were a mixed blessing at best, but in any case they made these settings different from communities in the war zones. (The situation in the guerrilla army was intermediate; combatants too sometimes had an excess of free time, but education was always strictly subordinated to military necessity.) Both the similarities and the differences between the sites of popular education confirm its dependence on the concrete material conditions and political circumstances in which it is practiced.

Neither the writings of Freire nor other literature on popular education lead us to anticipate that material conditions external to the learning situation should affect the process so strongly. The theory of popular education prescribes taking into account the context in which learning occurs. But while it draws attention to the context of learners' lives—by recognizing that their ignorance does not imply lack of native ability, and by tailoring the content of education to their interests and needs—it pays little heed to the material and organizational context. Those factors, however, explain a great deal about the form popular education took in El Salvador.

Another important feature of Salvadoran practice not clearly anticipated in the literature is its rootedness in the communities where it occurred and the close integration between the communities and the popular schools. Material shortages meant that education could not have been carried out without community resources; it relied on the community spirit and *conciencia* of teachers and others who volunteered to organize it and provide for its needs; it was set up to serve community purposes.

It was also part of their ongoing political mobilization. Politics is central to both the Freirean model and Salvadoran practice, but in different ways. Popular education on the Freirean model is designed both to inculcate critical consciousness and to lead to political action. In El Salvador the relation to both consciousness and action was not so direct as a reading of Freire would suggest.

Adult educators often skimped on critical reflection, despite the insistence of advisors, whether out of fear of repression or the educators' insecurity regarding the part of the lesson they found most difficult. (Critical reflection was also rare in schools for children. Although political content and participatory process did enter into their education, they were too young to exercise critical consciousness to any significant degree.) Nor were adult literacy circles an important impetus to political organization. Only rarely did they directly inspire collective action.

If popular education did not foment consciousness or stimulate political action very directly, it might therefore appear not so closely linked to politics in El Salvador as it is in the model. But if critical reflection was not emphasized, it was because the Salvadoran poor did not need literacy circles to raise their consciousness of oppression. A decade of political activity before the war had already done that. Everyone involved in popular education at any level had lived with repression, and many had taken up arms against it. The political struggle that formed their critical consciousness preceded and paralleled the educational process.

While popular education did not often directly inspire people to organize for political action, moreover, the communities in which it went on were intensely engaged in such activity. The drive to educate people grew out of a political project already underway, which had education as one of its main expressions, along with community improvement projects and military struggle. Literacy circles did not succeed in inspiring political action in communities without that level of political engagement, as illustrated by the discussion of adult literacy circles in chapter 6.

Normally initiated in the context of political action, popular education was also often driven by political considerations. The need to train skilled political cadres was a major motive. Military necessity sometimes dictated the suspension of classes. Both pedagogy and content sometimes responded to political imperatives. When popular organization representatives chose generative words for a cartilla of which she disapproved because they were not conducive to reflection, Cristina nevertheless felt that the collective decision should stand "so that they feel this material is *theirs*."

So popular education most often occurred in communities already politically conscious and organized. But it still contributed to consciousness and organization. Consciousness does not arise fully formed in a single moment; it matures slowly. Even if education was neither the primary nor a sufficient condition for consciousness, it provided both the opportunity and the intellectual tools for sustained reflection.

It gave people something else as well: the opportunity to speak out and to act, and thereby to overcome longstanding inhibitions. People did not have to be told that their society was unjust. Repression left them a legacy, however: a sense of their own inadequacy, which they could only overcome by acting. Popular education provided an opportunity to learn that they were subjects capable of opposing injustice. As learners or as popular educators, they discovered their capabilities and acquired the conviction that they had the power to confront oppression.

Most of the literature assumes that political action is an effect of popular education more than a cause: that educators initiate education in the first instance for its own sake and only incorporate politicized content into their teaching because it motivates students, and that learners become politically engaged because the content of the classes inspires them. But in El Salvador, the reverse was more nearly the case: politicization was a prior condition more than an outcome of education; education was initiated to serve ongoing political practice.

Steering a Narrow Course

Poverty, war, the community setting, and the political context all had a major impact on popular education in El Salvador. As I have said, I believe that the need to take account of their influence is the most important lesson of the Salvadoran experience for the analysis of popular education generally, since most analyses pay more attention to its pedagogical techniques and its political content. The link to the community setting also has important practical consequences. It provides insurance against two equal but opposite dangers that can arise from overemphasis on pedagogy and ideology respectively.

Some practitioners, looking for a clearly specified teaching methodology, focus on the techniques—reflecting on pictures, playing games—and tend to see them as the essence of popular education. The temptation to use these techniques for their own sake is strong. They offer a ready grab bag of activities for the untrained popular teacher who has little theoretical understanding of the process, and they engage participants and produce a lively atmosphere.

But even the best pedagogical tools can be applied mechanically or inappropriately. Educators may use them without taking into account the needs of learners and the conditions in which they are learning. Worse, some critics charge, the techniques lend themselves to cooptation: officially sponsored education programs can place them in the service of political goals completely opposed to those for which they were intended. Ross Kidd and Krishna Kumar (1981) castigate what they call pseudo-Freireanism, which encourages learners to participate and misleads them into thinking that their contributions are heard and valued, when in fact those soliciting their participation are attempting to coopt them rather than to respond to their needs.[6] These self-styled Freireans, Kidd and Kumar argue, rule out any political analysis of the causes of poverty. Like the recovery movement, they attempt to make people blame themselves for their poverty and teach them to cope. As Freire himself says, teaching literacy can be domesticating as well as liberating (1985:101).

The opposite danger, of too much emphasis on political content, arises when educators present received truths rather than drawing out the knowledge learners derive from their own experience. Popular education can become indoctrination. Peter Berger says that the project of concientización is necessarily an elitist one, undertaken by people who presume they have true consciousness and are capable of bringing it to the unenlightened (1973:113–114).[7] According to Majid Rahnema, "activists in charge of other people's conscientization [have often] tried to use conscientization or participatory methods, simply as new and more subtle forms of manipulation" (1992:125). For Rolland G. Paulston, Freire "sees the teacher as a liberator bringing correct ideas to revolutionary struggle—the Leninist model" (1992:199).

There is some warrant for this conclusion in Freire's own writings—for example, when he juxtaposes "the leaders" to "the people" (1970:124). But he has also been criticized for being, in effect, not Leninist enough: according to Frank Youngman, Freire's lack of explicit theoretical analysis "disables his approach as a vehicle for socialist adult education" (1986:179). I do not propose to offer a political evaluation of Freire; I am concerned instead with whether either of these distortions was present in El Salvador. There are tendencies in both directions, but because the process was rooted in a community setting, it enjoyed some protection against going to either extreme.

On the one hand, as I have shown, concientización may become indoctrination when articulate, high-status outsiders offer a fully formed ideology to people lower in status. But I believe that there is a difference between concientización and indoctrination, and that what popular education workers in El Salvador offered was not indoctrination. Outsiders did not go to rural communities to purvey a received truth; they worked to enable learners to reflect and understand. They did not use the term "accompaniment" as clergy and lay people had to describe their option for the poor in the 1970s, but their standpoint was similar. They saw themselves as learners too, and their own minds changed dramatically. Relations were mutual, and the development of new ideas, in a common phrase, "*es todo un proceso*"—it was all part of a process.

Of course the outsiders had a slant. They actively challenged some campesinos' views: the idea that poverty was the will of God or the result of individual failure, for example. But the campesinos themselves were not a blank slate. Some of them would very likely object to the same ideas—not by challenging them for deviating from orthodoxy, but by presenting examples intended to persuade. As I have shown, when learners were reluctant, outsiders did not generally succeed in raising their consciousness.

Some Salvadoran teachers used popular education techniques as a crutch, just as some relied on rote learning methods, and their overuse affected the quality of education. They presented no threat of cooptation or accommodation, however. As long as the war went on, no authority offered to coopt. The postwar period will test whether popular educators can withstand cooptation as they demand financial support from the state while trying to retain the freedom to run their schools (Hammond 1997).

Popular education *also* did what Kidd and Kumar accuse pseudo-Freireans of doing: it taught people to cope and use their own resources, not just to confide in the future overthrow of the oppressive state. Some of their problems were of their own making—sexism, drunkenness, and failure to organize, for example. Others could be solved by mobilizing community work teams. The entire process of popular education was based on the assumption that people could improve themselves by their own efforts.

Addressing these problems, however, did not mean succumbing to the illusion that self-help could solve everything. On the contrary, a community's effort to solve its own problems ("achieve a lot with a little") was part of the battle against oppression, a necessary mobilization of resources for a greater struggle. While they sought to take full advantage of their own resources, the war going on around them left them no chance to forget that they were oppressed.

In most respects popular education in El Salvador followed the Freirean model, but it diverged in some ways. Some of its divergences arose to fill gaps on issues Freire does not discuss; others directly contradicted his prescriptions. The most important differences, to reiterate, derived from the central role of the community in popular education. Community material conditions—specifically, poverty and war—strongly affected the educational process; education was an integral part of community life, and depended on the support the community provided; education grew out of prior community political engagement more than the other way around.

To emphasize these divergences is not to criticize the Freirean model but to recognize that it is necessarily incomplete (cf. Gadotti 1996:112). One cannot expect that an inherently dynamic process will conform strictly to a theoretical model. Differences arose because the model is flexible and adaptive. Salvadoran popular educators took the emancipatory project from the pioneers and gave it new meaning. What they did makes clear in practice what Freire affirms in principle: that popular education depends decisively on material reality and must be understood in terms not only of pedagogical principles but also of the concrete conditions in which it occurs.

Popular Education and the War

On January 16, 1992, the FMLN and the government of El Salvador signed an agreement to end twelve years of war without victory for either side. The FMLN was recognized as a legal political party; the government promised a land distribution program for the soldiers of both armies and for civilians in the formerly FMLN-controlled zones; and constitutional amendments had been negotiated that separated military and police functions and abolished the Treasury Police and National Guard—the principal agents of the massive state-sponsored repression that had prevailed before and during the war.

The FMLN, which had fought for state power and dispossession of the oligarchy, won much less. Now it faced its former opponents on the terrain of electoral democracy, which it had once disdained as hopelessly compromised with bourgeois interests. It would now have to struggle for power in a completely new and still unequal combat. Still, this outcome was one that few would have believed possible at the beginning of the war. The FMLN settled because it was clear that victory remained distant, because its base was exhausted by the long struggle, and because changes in the global political situation had made the Salvadoran government, too, more willing to compromise.

Though the FMLN could not claim victory, it won a stalemate even though the Salvadoran army was much larger and equipped and trained by U.S. money and military personnel. The FMLN succeeded because it cultivated combatants' skills and morale and maintained a close relation to its civilian base. An important element of this success was the education of combatants and civilians, based on the conviction that all people were capable of learning. Education contributed to the war effort in three major ways: it offered training in specific basic skills and intellectual growth; it raised morale; and it stimulated community organization.

Training in basic skills has occupied the most attention in this book, because it was the initial and most often the immediate purpose of education. Classroom instruction also contributed to general intellectual development, something a new political order would require of people who were to be active participants capable of running and organizing society. Only education could foster the needed skills and sense of competence.

Education fortified ideological commitment by putting into practice the conviction that all are equal and deserve equal opportunities. Making that belief a concrete and tangible reality raised the morale and aroused the dedication of all those for whom the struggle was part of their daily lives, in combat or in civilian roles. Those who educated themselves and others mastered new skills. The recognition they won reinforced their confidence in their new capacities.

Finally, because so many felt the need to create schools, education stimulated organization and gave it purpose. Once established, organization became a resource to be applied to other ends. This was especially true in refugee camps and communities in FMLN-controlled zones. Prisoners initially organized for more confrontational ends, but then they adopted education as one of their ongoing collective activities. (Education contributed much less to organization in the guerrilla army, which was already organized to fulfill its primary task—waging the war.)

Popular education bore these results despite its many shortcomings. Beyond the limitations due to material conditions, practitioners did not always live up to their own ideals: despite the ideal of equality, sexism and elitism were only imperfectly overcome; despite the ideal of universal education, some did not learn. Organizational coordination often fell short, and learning frequently gave way to other priorities. Nevertheless, its accomplishments—in learning, personal development, and political gains—were significant, especially since the resources that could be dedicated to it were so scant.

It is difficult to evaluate the contribution of education to the outcome of the struggle. I have discussed the difficulty of evaluating the effectiveness of the teaching of basic skills. It is even harder to evaluate the other outcomes, because they were rarely the objectives of specific learning experiences; rather, they arose as byproducts. But participants felt that they grew in all these areas, and organizers and educators pointed to them as both goals and accomplishments.

These developments in individuals and communities were important weapons for waging the war. The FMLN recognized their strategic importance, especially from 1984 on. The new strategy presumed that the war would continue for a long time and would require deep and stable organization. The actual extent of education programs during seven more years of war demonstrates the seriousness of the FMLN's commitment. The process, scope, and effects of educational practice among combatants and civilians all bear witness to the importance of education as a component of the eventually successful strategy.

Guerrilla warfare is fundamentally a political rather than a military phenomenon, and it was the politics of the Salvadoran insurgency that determined the importance of education. Education nurtured individuals' capabilities and served the broader goals of integral development, ideological affirmation, and organization as well. Learning was a large part of what the combatants were fighting for. Education was a concrete expression of the belief that people are equal by right and of the commitment to make them equal in fact.

CHAPTER 9

The View from City University

I want to conclude by discussing my own encounter with popular education. It has had a tremendous effect on me as an educator. I end this book on a personal note both to amplify the story of popular education and to allow readers to evaluate my account in the light of my perspective. In this second respect, this concluding chapter can be regarded as a methodological appendix, the section of the book in which the author begs the reader's pardon for all the failings of the study—or stubbornly insists on its virtues.

I went to popular education with a Ph.D. in sociology and a lifetime in the formal education system. I had a strong belief in the objectivity of knowledge: I believed that learning meant acquiring knowledge that existed and was waiting to be acquired, and that teaching meant conveying that knowledge in the clearest and most straightforward way possible. The premises of popular education stand in dramatic contrast to my prior assumptions: they presume that knowledge is derived from personal experience, and that what one learns depends on how one learns and in what circumstances; they hold that people learn through activity, and the role of the teacher is to engage students, not to deliver prepackaged knowledge to them.

Both as a political activist and as a teacher, I had often found my positivist, rationalist views inadequate, but they still loomed large in my presuppositions. Popular education offered me an alternative teaching philosophy and teaching style. It has influenced me in two areas: my understanding of how I learn, and my understanding of how I want to teach. On both counts, it has led me to rely less on theory and deduction and more on direct experience. I realized that my understanding of popular education often turned on particular experiences and personal relations, and I observed a teaching style that both draws on learners' past experiences and opens up new experiences for them as part of the learning process. What I learned about teaching met some of the needs I had confronted, and had begun to fulfill intuitively, in my work. Without entirely abandoning my old assumptions and methods, I have begun to incorporate those of popular pedagogy.

Doing Field Work

I came across popular education by accident. My activism in the Central America solidarity movement of the 1980s took me to work for the regional government of war-torn Las Segovias, Nicaragua, in 1985 and 1986. It was there, in resettlements of campesinos displaced by the contra war, that I first encountered popular education. Back in New York I taught a course on Central America, and I wanted to see more of it. So I went for the first time to El Salvador and Honduras (where I visited the camps for Salvadoran refugees in Colomoncagua and San Antonio) in 1988. I spent my second trip to El Salvador, the following year, as a volunteer at the Non-Governmental Human Rights Commission of El Salvador (CDHES).

Though I went to El Salvador out of political commitment and interest, I took with me nearly twenty years' experience as a college teacher. It was a great joy to meet popular educators who placed so much importance on education, struggled with enormous determination to get it and to provide it to others, and showed such pride when they succeeded. Still I did not at first contemplate formal research.

On my first trip, I was determined to see the countryside, and my solidarity contacts enabled me to get to some out-of-the-way places. I felt no dilemma in presenting myself as a solidary visitor; that was what I was. As I became more interested in popular education and began to do formal research, I never made any secret of the fact that I was also a researcher. When I asked to stick very closely to educators and to sit in on their meetings and classes, I simply said that I was interested in education.

I was never sure how people reacted to me. But solidary visitors were a frequent intrusion on the landscape. People took us for granted and had standard interaction routines for us—undoubtedly trying to say things and act in ways that would engage our sympathy and encourage our solidary help. Like me, many visitors carried notebooks and wrote everything down, and some were particularly interested in education. On the other hand, they were not so likely as I was to travel alone, speak Spanish, stay several days, be so focused on getting interviews, use a tape recorder, or ask so many or such specific questions.

A researcher must choose between neutrality toward and identification with people in the field. For this research, coming in solidarity opened up opportunities that I would not have had if I had been primarily labeled a researcher. If I had not identified politically with their project, I would not have gotten in.

Identifying in another way, I am convinced, was even more important for the conduct of the research. Very early on, I made the decision to participate wholeheartedly in the activities I was observing. As I reported in chapter 7, when I watched people play a game, it was clear to me that jumping in not only was appropriate but won the group's acceptance; if I had held back, I would have appeared to be putting myself above them. In some training sessions I became a member of the team coordinating the session; on occasion I freely offered my evaluation of their work. I felt it appropriate to take as much part as I seemed to be asked to.

Taking part in this way did more than create rapport. It helped me to understand the process better. This was the important epistemological lesson I took from this research. I learned a lot about popular education by choosing to throw myself into it rather than to observe it from afar. I experienced the situation more completely, and I watched my own psychodynamics. By doing so I got a much fuller view.

I was surprised that I was occasionally allowed to attend small, closed meetings in which sensitive topics were discussed very frankly. Still my access was not complete. There were questions I could not ask. The most sensitive had to do with the relation of civilian communities to the FMLN. The civilians claimed that they were noncombatants protected by the Geneva Conventions, and that if the army attacked them it was violating international law. If I had inquired too obtrusively I would have aroused suspicion. I can only conclude that the relation was closer than I was usually allowed to see.[1] As time went on and I was trusted more (and compared different observations), and as the war drew closer to its end and the risks decreased, I was shown more.

My being a man affected the way people interacted with me. In general, interviews with men were easier: easier for me and easier for them, easier to get an interview and easier to carry it out. As a result I did not examine the specific role of women—which is one of the exciting aspects of popular education—as deeply as it deserves.

I was surprised that one kind of question turned out to be delicate. As a sociologist I wanted quantitative precision on many questions, such as how many people were in the literacy circles and how many of them actually learned to read. But when I asked for a numerical estimate of anything, people got embarrassed. Gradually I realized that they were not used to thinking quantitatively and my questions made them feel stupid or inadequate. This happened so often that I stopped asking such questions. I tried to phrase questions to produce an answer I thought I could interpret. Even so, when I asked whether something was "*un poco o bastante*" (a little or a lot), someone might answer "*un poco bastante.*" (Hart [1990:17] reports a similar experience in Nicaragua.)

Reflecting on this repeated experience, I realized several things. I understood more about the intellectual development of highly competent but unschooled people who, no matter how competent in other respects, are likely to have trouble with numbers (unless they are market vendors, in which case they can add prices and make change better than any calculator-dependent New York cashier). I also understood relations between people with differing levels of formal education better. Among the ways in which the more educated intimidate the less educated is by unconsciously holding high expectations of them. These expectations are actually a form of unintended flattery, but their effect is often to reinforce the uneducated person's sense of inferiority. The power of knowledge to intimidate suggests that objective truth is not necessarily value-neutral.

In 1989 I had the extraordinary experience of being arrested while working as a volunteer at the CDHES. I had gone with a member of the commission to La Ringlera, a village on the coast of Usulután near El Espino beach, to videotape testimonies of people who had been harassed by the army. An army unit arrived, apparently by coincidence, and said that we were not authorized to be there (though we had come in openly, on the only road, and on the way had passed another army unit that had not stopped us). We were held for two days and nights. I spent the second night in the San Salvador jail of the Treasury Police.

Being alone in a jail cell, even for just one night, focuses the mind. I learned a lot about myself. I also got a greater appreciation of the situation of political prisoners, even though I did not face what they did. Despite feeling real fear, I knew that I was almost certainly safe. The period of the worst repression was long past. Besides, we had been captured by men in uniform, there were dozens of witnesses, and an unwritten international human rights law dictates that one priest is worth one hundred campesinos, one foreigner is worth ten priests. And as I had already learned on the second day, before my night in the custody of the Treasury Police, a villager had walked four hours to the nearest phone and alerted the CDHES, which instantly mounted an international publicity campaign to rescue us. People of privilege enjoy a cumulative advantage, even when they are in trouble, and almost always have the option of leaving. This set me apart from the people I met on other occasions as well. While campesinos always welcomed solidary visitors, our different circumstances undoubtedly affected how they saw us.

To many people, learning through participation comes naturally. I am not one of them. My sociological training taught me that it is necessary to maintain distance to assure scholarly neutrality—that is, to prevent me from either identifying too closely or "contaminating" the research site by my presence. It took an act of will, repeatedly, for me to be more participant than observer. But it confirmed for me the value of popular education's reliance on experiential learning.

Participating often made me tremendously anxious—not because I was violating scholarly canons, but because I was afraid I was falsely claiming to belong and would be shown up as a fraud. (Someone might read my notebook and see that I had made a mistake.) One occasion in particular stands out: I went with Máximo of CIAZO and Hugo of PADECOMSM to a training session in El Carrizal, in the mountains east of Perquín on the Honduran border (now in Honduras, part of the territory El Salvador lost in the 1992 World Court settlement). We went there from the two-day session in Torola where I had observed Máximo's dynamic teaching style and rapport with the popular teachers.

Most of the popular teachers who were to come to El Carrizal had mistakenly been told that the session was scheduled for the following day, so we had a day to kill. The next morning twelve people arrived. Some had walked several hours from neighboring villages to get there. I had merely watched the session in Torola. Máximo now evidently decided that he wanted to make use of me, and he asked me to do several small tasks. The first was to lead a dinámica. Not sure that I could handle it, I said I didn't know any, so he started to do it himself.

Suddenly I wanted very much to lead a dinámica. I offered to do one that we had done in Torola. It required racing an opponent around a circle. Several of the popular teachers there for training were young men in their twenties who were used to running and who perhaps did not mind showing up a middle-aged, highly educated outsider. In my eagerness to keep up I pulled a muscle that hurt for two weeks (in fact, when we left El Carrizal the next day, I had to be carried out by "campesino ambulance"—a mule—down the mountain we had climbed on foot). Still it was fun, and I was exhilarated at having introduced and led a dinámica.

That same day, we divided into three teams, one of which I was to lead. Each team was to present part of a lesson to the larger group. The four young men on my team were to present the concept of setting goals for a lesson. We were working from the very densely written CIAZO teachers' guide. I quickly realized that it was too demanding for them, even though it had been written for popular teachers of limited education working in this very program. (At least one of the four had never been to school; his father had taught him to read. When Máximo said that those who were teaching the second level might get official second-grade certificates along with their pupils, they were very interested.)

When I discovered that none of them knew how to use a table of contents, we practiced finding things with it. Then we talked about the nature of goals. For the lesson we were studying, seven goals were listed—far too many and complex for them to comprehend and present to the whole group clearly. So I reduced them to three. Of the four men, one would present to the whole group the general idea of goals, and each of the others would present one of the specific goals.

I was thoroughly anxious before, during, and after the team's discussion. Were they understanding my explanations? Was it going well? Was I doing a good job? Somehow this task became the measure of my worthiness to participate in popular education. Was I giving them too much? Wasn't it supposed to come from them, and wasn't I being overly directive? In my imagination it felt that my whole value as a teacher, as a compañero, and as a person was being tested. We rehearsed the presentations they were going to make to the larger group.

As the whole group was about to reassemble, I urged the team to show some spirit when they made their presentations. To my surprise this came to me quite naturally. In my own classes I rarely gave much thought to arousing my students' motivation; it seemed to violate scholarly neutrality and the presumption that their interest in the material should be motivation enough. But I have learned to do it more.

I introduced each of their presentations, in too much detail because I was afraid that they would not do a good job. Three of the four, however, did much better before the whole group than they had in our small group.

From this training session, I learned some important things about how popular education actually works. I was critical of the mixup in the dates and of the difficulty of the written material. I felt good about encouraging the team. I realized that I should trust their abilities—and the collaborative process—more.

But at the same time I felt that I was being tested. For days afterward I dwelt on how anxious it had made me. I was convinced that all eyes were on me, censoriously. (I had also been anxious about leading the dinámica, but I felt good about succeeding.) My anxiety arose partly because Máximo's assignment caught me unprepared, and I am used to walking into a teaching situation prepared. But more to the point, in popular education the test is not in the theoretical understanding but in the practical doing. If I failed, perhaps I had no right to impose my presence on them, write about them, or explain popular education to others.

Of course no one there was evaluating me. We were doing a collaborative project that did not depend only on me. However badly I had done, none of them except perhaps Máximo would have evaluated me as failing, because the well-educated gringo (no one actually knew how much education I had, but they surely assumed I had a lot) wears the emperor's new clothes: whatever he does must be right even if it looks funny. But at the same time that I was questioning my political merit, my assumptions about education as a testing process were intruding. As I show in chapter 6, popular educators do not evaluate each other invidiously.

So by examining my own reactions, I learned substantive lessons about popular education.[2] That I could only learn these things by experiencing them directly validated for me popular education's experiential pedagogy. The epistemology in which I was trained insists that learning is a purely intellectual process of amassing knowledge and applying the tools of logic to that knowledge. Sociology is a science, and sociological research is something one does as in a laboratory, in which the researcher is separate from the subject of research. Indeed, subjects are "subjects"—subject to the researcher's handling, not people from whom one can learn something.[3] The epistemology that underlies popular education assumes that knowledge is relational and that for one to know something effectively it must relate to one's prior knowledge and grow out of one's experience.

Learning to Teach

My implicit pedagogy was similar to my epistemology. I assumed that teaching involves the straightforward communication of objective knowledge. My views on teaching were implicit because even though most of my fellow graduate students and I were preparing ourselves to be college teachers, we were taught nothing explicitly about teaching. Our mentors seemed to view it as a necessary evil, something we do to pay for our research habit, not something to take seriously or to try to do well.

If one had such misguided priorities as to want to do it well, however, the way to be a good teacher was to know more—not so different from the way to be a good researcher: master the material and present, in class, an accurate and incisive understanding of the topic to convey knowledge to the receptive students. (If they weren't receptive, it was their own damn fault.) We unwittingly adopted the very "banking" style of education that Freire criticized. No one suggested that the presentation matters or that one can learn to do it better, taking into account the strengths and weaknesses of a known group of students. And certainly no one suggested that one can learn something from schools of education, generally thought to be sinkholes for those who are not smart enough to make it in academic fields.

Popular education insists that learners must participate and engage with the material actively rather than sit and absorb it. Active engagement does not happen by itself; the teacher must make deliberate efforts to draw out students' participation. Their participation must be focused, moreover, or it may degenerate into banality. As I accompanied training sessions, I saw that teaching methods can be learned. One can plan a class by setting goals and choosing the methods that best suit the goals and the group. All of this means focusing on the needs of a class as much as on content. The teacher must not just hope for everyone to take part, but must plan and use specific techniques to present particular points and to draw them out of students. (These revelations will hardly surprise anyone who has taken a first education course.) To reiterate, this emphasis on drawing out participation contrasts dramatically with the teaching style I had adopted unthinkingly.

Research on higher education in the United States has recently focused on learning styles, finding that people vary in the ways in which they learn most effectively (Hutchings and Wutzdorff 1988; Kolb 1984). Researchers have offered several typologies making broader or finer distinctions between cognitive styles, but for present purposes they can be grouped into two types, which I will call the logical-linear and experiential styles. The first emphasizes theoretical exposition and logical deduction, while the second emphasizes direct experience and interpersonal interaction.

This research on learning has evident implications for teaching. A given style of teaching will be more effective with those whose learning style it most closely matches. A logical-linear teaching style is impersonal and assumes that knowledge can be presented as independent of the context in which it is taught or the learners' characteristics. An experiential style, in contrast, draws on personal relations in a learning community and tries to create a nurturing environment to stimulate students' desire to learn.

Higher education in the United States has traditionally emphasized theory and abstraction, appealing primarily to students who prefer the logical-linear style. Recent emphasis on experiential learning has grown out of a desire to serve a broader range of students. Much of it comes from the field of women's studies and seeks to understand women's learning processes and to create learning environments in which they will thrive. Some research has shown that women are likely to prefer the experiential approach, and other research has found the same for members of minority or oppressed groups (Belenky et al. 1986; Clinchy 1993; Collins 1990:208–212).

As universities grow in size and diversity, this research suggests, more students enter the academy who learn better through personal connection and experience. I teach at Hunter College, a branch of the City University of New York, the country's premier urban public university. At a time when higher education is changing rapidly, CUNY continues its proud tradition of offering an education of the highest quality to students most of whom are from poor and working-class families (Kasinitz 1995). Most of them are women, many are nonwhite. Many of these students fit the profile of those sometimes said to have a nonlinear learning style. Exclusively logical-linear teaching puts these new students at a disadvantage.

Some teachers, however—including myself—are skeptical of the essentialist claim that women and members of minority groups are especially likely to benefit from experiential learning. We argue that it belongs in the university curriculum because all students can benefit from diverse styles of teaching to stimulate a variety of learning processes (cf. Elbow 1973:147–191).

Some researchers imply that the experiential style necessarily sacrifices a critical stance toward the object of one's knowledge. Blythe McVicker Clinchy distinguishes between connected and separate knowing (1993:187–190). Connected knowing is based on attachment and the attempt to understand the object being examined on its own terms; separate knowing establishes distance between the knower and the object. Clinchy identifies the latter with critical thinking and the scientific method (1993:187). Connected knowers, she says, rarely make moral judgments because they identify with the objects of their knowledge. Though popular education emphasizes the experiential and pragmatic, it insists on making critical judgments. It encourages an atmosphere of compañerismo within a study circle, but also demands concientización. People name oppression, condemn it, and fight against it.

In popular education I saw experiential teaching in practice. But even before that, I had occasionally experimented with it unwittingly. For several years I had tried to integrate the teaching of writing into my coursework. The linear pedagogy did not seem to offer much, because it presumed mastery of the very skills I was trying to teach. I experimented with ways to present writing as real communication rather than an abstract exercise: free writing, peer editing, small group discussion of writing topics, and other activities in which students communicate in unconventional ways the ideas they will later present formally in writing. Popular education offered another variant of this, so I tried bringing some of its techniques into my classroom.

In a course I taught on Central America for several years, I recognized that the students needed some experiential grounding. We read novels. An occasional Central American student and, more commonly, students from the Caribbean enriched the class by describing their lives before migrating or the lives of relatives whom they visited. I invited guest speakers whenever possible—usually Salvadorans and Nicaraguans who were in the United States at the invitation of solidarity groups; but my students were usually less interested in their political message than in their firsthand accounts. The goal of the course was for all students to understand theoretically the changes in campesino life in recent decades and why those changes had led to revolt in some countries but not others—to understand, that is, a somewhat abstract causal process in a part of the world with which most of them were unfamiliar. But we got there by reconnaissance of the terrain to make it more familiar.

The research on learning styles gave me a framework within which to understand why teaching methods I had observed in basic literacy instruction could work in a college course.[4] Armed with some knowledge of learning styles research, I have more consistently adopted a diversity of methods, while still practicing more traditional, expository teaching.

Meeting students in popular education has made me appreciate the life situation of my college students better. They have, on the whole, weak academic preparation. They grew up with television as their main teacher and socializer. They come from all over the world; the native language of many is not English, and some are studying in English for the first time. They face great economic stress (one CUNY student in eight was on welfare before the 1996 federal legislation); they have to balance the desire for growth through education with the need to make a living and secure a credential.

They are, of course, very different from campesinos learning to read. They are at a much higher academic level, and they are city dwellers aspiring to the middle class. But if in El Salvador the basic dividing line between an educated and an uneducated person is functional literacy, and if in the United States through most of the twentieth century it was a high school diploma, today it is increasingly the college degree that is a basic prerequisite for economic opportunity and respect. Just as with Salvadorans who have never gone to school, my students' poverty and lack of self-confidence affect their ability to learn. They have no sense of entitlement to education as a right. They wonder whether they deserve to be there, and whether they can hack it.

I understand interrupted student careers better, both their necessity and their drawbacks. When I was in school we marched in lockstep progression from kindergarten to graduate school. Many of today's students are adults. They persist admirably to complete their degrees, but they may have lost the habit of studying and they do not go to school full time because they have obligations to work and family.

Coping with Cutbacks

The material poverty of popular education puts the budget cuts at my institution into perspective. When library acquisitions are virtually halted and faculty have to photocopy class material at their own expense, I know that popular educators would still envy my advantages. But I also understand more deeply how right I am to complain. Some may unconsciously think of education as a purely intellectual process—you and Socrates at opposite ends of a log—to which material factors should be irrelevant. We assume a certain baseline of material conditions, however, and it is easy to take their availability for granted. Recently the musical *You're a Good Man, Charlie Brown*, based on the Peanuts comic strip, was revived in New York, and (according to a review in the *New York Times*) as Charlie Brown struggled over a book report, a child in the audience piped up, "Where's his computer?" Notwithstanding popular education's heroic achievements in the face of material poverty, it remains clear that material resources are a real constraint in learning and teaching.

CUNY is facing tremendous pressures to reduce costs. Class size increases and services disappear. In the fall of 1995 I taught the largest class I had ever taught—ninety students in a section of introductory sociology (still small by some colleges' standards), with no teaching assistant and no discussion sections. I took the large class as a challenge, and worked hard to create a small-group discussion-oriented atmosphere. In nearly every session I planned an activity to break down the lecture format and get students to take an active role in discussion and writing. But many of them need individual attention. When the professor only appears as a distant figure on a lecture platform, it is hard for them to seek that attention out.

Today's cutbacks come down precisely on people who, because of their poor preparation, need more, not less. As students pay more to get less, state legislators see education as a commodity that can be measured in credit hours completed and degrees granted. Cost-accounting standards claiming that productivity goes up when there are more students in a class make a travesty of education. Such claims are either a parody of the quantifiability of knowledge or a mere political scam. The ignorance they reveal of the teaching process is a strong recommendation for learning by direct experience. If the only purpose of college is to grant credentials, we could just as well give the degree on admission. But if the purpose is to foster intellectual growth, we must create the right environment.

There has been considerable debate in U.S. higher education about whether a college education should depart from traditional linear pedagogy. To some critics, such adaptations mean pandering to students and watering down the curriculum, leading eventually to the abandonment of a virtually sacred "canon" (Bloom 1987; d'Souza 1991). Some argue against offering remedial education, claiming that many students are too far below college level to benefit from college at all—whether because of genetic endowment, culture, or lack of preparation (cf. MacDonald 1994; Traub 1994).

This is not the place to respond to those critics, except to point out that the canon is a fairly recent invention and that changes in both enrollments and economic opportunities make the academy a very different institution than it was only one or two generations ago. One can, as I do, defend rigorous academic standards and at the same time reject the demand of many critics to exclude. I believe that today's blacks, Latinos, and immigrants are entitled to as good an education as the children of European immigrants were in the first half of the twentieth century.

These students thrive on the education they get and prove that they are capable and deserve an education that respects them and takes their abilities seriously. Though experiential teaching may appear to encourage a laid-back, let-it-all-hang-out style, the fact is that it does not come easily or automatically, either to students or to teachers—certainly not to me, especially since I continue to demand analysis that is logically and empirically sound. Experiential teaching requires careful planning ahead of time and sensitivity to what is going on in the classroom. It is often much easier to lecture; I can have a lecture down cold, and just tell the truth, pre-packaged. It is very difficult, moreover, to measure how effective active learning strategies are; often one must accept them on faith.

Experiential learning does not mean giving students a sugar-coated pill. If they take it seriously, they work harder, grappling with material that is challenging both personally and intellectually. Many students, suffering the pressures of very crowded schedules and a legacy of uninspired teaching in elementary and high school, would just as soon be told what they are supposed to know. For both students and teachers, then, change is demanding as well as stimulating.

I do not propose that teaching should abandon analytic or critical knowledge in favor of an eclectic embrace of whatever is offered. While I have adopted some elements of an experientially-based teaching style, I do not believe experiential learning can become the only goal. I still aim for systematic theoretical understanding. I expect my students to do a lot of reading and to understand phenomena of which they have no direct experience. My approach to teaching is still primarily content-centered, even if less so than when I started teaching. I demand rigorous analysis and attention to evidence. Sociology teaches us that our individual experience is limited and sometimes deceptive. We must go beyond it by making controlled observations and achieving theoretical understanding. At the same time that we take advantage of our students' experience, we want them to transcend it.

In many ways (though not all), teaching at CUNY today is the equivalent of doing popular education in El Salvador. Students who are not adequately served by the public school system get blamed for their deficiencies. They are uncertain of their abilities and have a hard time making ends meet. They are offered increasingly antiquated and inadequate facilities. Yet they come to CUNY for the bachelor's degree that promises to get them across the divide separating the educated from the uneducated.

Though college teachers can profitably learn from popular education, how-ever, what we do is not popular education. We work in large, bureaucratic insti-tutions where people's—students' and teachers'—involvement is partial, unlike the communities where popular education succeeded. By itself, the obligation to impose grades would preclude the relations of equality and mutual exchange presumed by popular education. There are other aspects of popular education that we cannot readily adopt. We can take from it the insistence on open access and the design of a pedagogy that will be relevant; but because the university is not a natural community, I do not think there is much place in it for consciousness-raising.

I make a political analysis central to the content of my sociology courses, because I believe that an adequate understanding of social reality requires it. I hope that that political analysis will awaken in my students a critical attitude and an awareness of alternatives. But I do not try to create a collective conscious-ness. For that, I would have to presume an ideological consensus and a political goal. My students come from a variety of backgrounds. They are not a natural community, and not all of them are poor. They do not share an ideology. Most of them have instrumental goals: they want to get the credential required for material success.

Above all, they are not seeking collective solutions to their problems. How-ever much I wish that they were—and believe that they would be better off if they tried—I have to respect their purposes. I try to give students tools for skep-ticism and awareness of alternatives, but I do not demand any particular politi-cal choice. It would not work, nor would it be appropriate, to presume an ideological consensus as the basis of a course. Nor would it work to try to cre-ate one. It would not work pedagogically, and I do not think it would work po-litically. If a professor promoted a particular line and expected students to reproduce it, some would psych the requirement out and meet it, but forget af-ter the semester ended, retaining no more than they do from a class that requires rote memorization. Others would try to learn it by heart without ever recogniz-ing it as a distinct political position.

I began this book by summarizing the vision of popular education in four principles. Two of these, I believe, commend themselves to college teachers in the United States today: open access for all kinds of students and a curriculum students will see as relevant. Of the remaining principles, one—the integration of educational institution and community—does not match reality; the second—the cultivation of political consciousness—has, I believe, only very limited application.

If I adopt some of Freire's methods for ends different from his, am I coopting him and descending into pseudo-Freireanism? I do not think so. Cooptation implies a *pretense* that education is liberatory. A teacher who uses some of the techniques of popular education not for Freirean liberation but to arouse students' cognitive dispositions, and does not promise them emancipation, is not acting in bad faith. We can recognize that popular education is meant for different conditions, but still learn from it.

Throughout this book I have emphasized that people who come to popular education with backgrounds of higher and lower status nevertheless feel strong bonds of reciprocity; those with advanced education claim that they learn more from their students than they teach. That claim sometimes sounded to me like an exaggeration; I had to learn its truth by experiencing it myself. I have learned a lot from Salvadoran educators and learners, and what I have learned has had a great impact on me—as a college teacher and as a person.

I ask whether I have given anything in return. I hope that the answer I got at a cooperative in San Juan Opico in 1990 is valid. On Teachers' Day, the literacy circles celebrated the Day of the Popular Teacher with a festival, and Mario Solórzano, the president of FENACOA, spoke. (I had arrived at his office the day before after having been away for a year.) After introducing all the Federation's staff, he introduced me as "compañero Jack, a professor from a university in the United States. Every time he comes here he comes to see us in FENACOA and he always asks, 'Where are you going? I want to go to the countryside.' He has been on the coast of Usulután, where the mosquitos bite, and in San Agustín. Now he has come to meet you—so that you can know that you are not alone."

I know that people were encouraged by the solidarity of outsiders in fighting a war and in fighting ignorance. I offer this book in the spirit of repayment for all I have received from the popular educators of El Salvador. The debt cannot be paid, but I hope that it will be worthy of them.

NOTES

Chapter 1 *Introduction*

1. In a translation of his poetry, Ariel Dorfman says that the word *compañero* "stubbornly resisted an English-language equivalent.... *Compañero*, a man, or *compañera*, a woman, could be rendered as *mate, friend, comrade, companion*; but none of these has the unique resonance of the Spanish. If you look at the origins of the word, a *compañero* is one with whom you share bread" (Dorfman 1988:n.p.).

2. Campesinos are disparaged in terms reminiscent of the racist discourse often heard in the United States, although no real or imputed distinction of biological descent separates them from other Salvadorans. The vast majority of the population is taken to be of mixed Indian and European background, in contrast to the small minority who are considered Indian (*indígena*) or of purely European descent. But there is no ethnic term in common use (comparable to *mestizo* or *ladino* in other countries) that applies to them.

3. He was one of six priest-professors at the Central American University who, together with their housekeeper and her daughter, were murdered in their own home by the Salvadoran army during the 1989 offensive.

4. I have generally kept the word *campesino* untranslated when I refer to poor Salvadoran rural dwellers, and in particular to their culture. I use the English word "peasant" when I discuss anthropological literature on peasant wars, which encompasses countries outside the Spanish-speaking world (especially China and Vietnam) as well as within it.

5. It can indeed be a pleasure. I watched an adult man learn the syllable "co." When his teacher told him to double it, he said, "co . . . co," first hesitantly and then, with a gleam of discovery that the syllables formed a word, "¡*Coco*!" (coconut, or, colloquially, head or intelligence).

6. Freire's influence on church workers who embraced the post-Vatican II mission was made evident at several of the Catholic Interamerican Cooperation Program (CICOP) conferences. The CICOP conference was held annually between 1964 and 1973 to introduce U.S. Catholics to new developments in the Latin American church. Freire's talk at the 1970 conference in Washington appears in the conference's proceedings, entitled *Conscientization for Liberation* (Colonnese 1971), and several contributions by other authors reflect his influence. The book is dedicated to six men—five bishops

and archbishops and Freire, the only lay person. The dedication refers to a struggle for "socioeconomic reform and human promotion as [a] moral right," and calls the six dedicatees "embodiments of that struggle."

7. Salvadoran practice also differed by offering primary schooling to children in the war zones as well as adult education. In some countries, "popular education" refers only to adult education. The methods most closely associated with the term were designed for adults.

In recent years some of the pioneers of popular education in Brazil and elsewhere in Latin America have begun to consider its application to public elementary and secondary schools. Popular public education entails not only distinct classroom methods, but also the democratic management of schools with the participation of parents and students as well as teachers and administrators. Freire himself was municipal secretary of education of São Paulo, Brazil, from 1989 to 1991 (Freire 1993; Gadotti 1991 and 1996; Torres 1994).

8. I identify these informants by pseudonyms, with the exception of a few—priests, comandantes, and leaders of national organizations—who can be considered public figures (and who have given me permission to use their real names).

If an informant is identified by first name and surname, the name is the person's own (in the case of guerrilla comandantes, many of whom used pseudonyms, the name is the one by which they were widely known). If an informant is identified by first name only, the name is a pseudonym.

CHAPTER 2 *The Christian Origins of Revolt*

1. "Christian base community" is the usual English term corresponding to the Spanish *comunidad eclesial de base*, literally church base community.
2. Whenever my questions are necessary to provide context for quotations from informants, I include them in italics.
3. Many threatened priests did go into exile, and many foreign priests were expelled. Three priests whom I interviewed left the country for exile: Miguel Ventura (after being captured and tortured), José Alas, and German Montoya. Ventura later returned and spent much of the war in Morazán, but it may be thanks to having escaped when they did that these three survived to tell me the tale.

CHAPTER 3 *Learning on the Front Lines*

1. This chapter is based on forty interviews with guerrilla combatants and informal conversations with many others. They include men and women; foot soldiers, squadron leaders, and comandantes; some who became literate and some who taught literacy; and combatants with a variety of military specialties. The informants represent three of the five political-military organizations that made up the FMLN, including the two largest, the FPL and the ERP; and the most important region each of these organizations controlled—eastern Chalatenango and northern Morazán, respectively.
2. This exchange has often been quoted to explain the FMLN's (and especially the FPL's) choice of a mass-based strategy over the *foco*. Carpio failed to add that there are indeed mountains in El Salvador; nevertheless its small territory was thought not to offer a terrain in which a guerrilla army could hide out for a long period. At one time the founders of the FPL believed that only a Central America-wide revo-

lution was feasible because Salvadoran combatants would have to rely on a rear guard in other countries (Harnecker 1993:77–78).

3. The unstated conclusion to this sentence is "to bomb us."

4. *Compa* is an abbreviation of compañero used in El Salvador exclusively to refer to members of the guerrilla army.

5. The reader may remember that Chebo, the fisherman-teacher whose story opens chapter 1, rejected the word *pala*, because it was not useful for farming. But to combatants, evidently, anything that could be used to "fight the enemy" played a vital role and so provided material for reflection.

6. Some of these guerrilla literary works have been collected in Huezo Mixco 1989, Morel 1993, and (in a bilingual edition) Alegría and Flakoll 1989.

7. As noted earlier, the Spanish *conciencia* incorporates the meanings of "conscience" and "consciousness."

8. Throughout the war, the five organizations continued to operate separately and controlled their respective territories with very little overlap. They were integrated mainly at the level of the General Command. Despite this separation they maintained operational unity for the most part. Their divergent political programs led the FMLN to divide into factions after the war ended (Hammond 1995).

9. In 1989 he was murdered by FMLN urban commandos (*Comisión de la Verdad* 1993:173).

10. Schools and other institutions were named for the FMLN's martyrs. Clelia died in combat in 1983.

11. Compare the observation that many "jobs pegged as 'women's work'" in the United States "have revolved around the telephone. . . . In such jobs the female worker mediates—rather than initiates—communication" (Lupton 1993:29).

12. Although the topics discussed among women combatants were similar to the themes of what the U.S. women's movement called consciousness-raising, I never heard anyone use the term concientización in reference to them.

13. In chapter 1 I put Wickham-Crowley, along with others (notably Goodwin and Skocpol 1989), in the rational-peasant school because that is their explanation of peasant motivation. Their explanation of the outcome of peasant war, however, is structural.

14. Wickham-Crowley also misrepresents the Salvadoran case by the claim—less central to his argument—that "by their own admission" the Salvadoran opposition "systematically executed several thousand Salvadoran civilians" (1989:518). The sources cited, including Freedom House, can in no sense be considered the FMLN's "own admission." One must be cautious about accepting claims about guerrilla atrocities made during the Reagan administration. The U.N.-sponsored Truth Commission created as part of the peace settlement found no such record (*Comisión de la Verdad* 1993).

CHAPTER 4   *Protected Spaces: Refugee Camps and Prisons*

1. This section is based on the interviews reported and on my work as a volunteer with the Non-Governmental Human Rights Commission of El Salvador (CDHES) in 1989. There I talked with or read the testimonies of many former prisoners and visited three prisons. With one exception it was not possible to interview prisoners formally on these visits, but I was able to meet them and observe the physical conditions

of the prisons. While working with the CDHES, I was myself captured and detained, an event I discuss in chapter 9. This experience, though brief, contributed dramatically to my sense of what it is like to be a political prisoner.

2. Those convicted of killing four U.S. marines in the Zona Rosa in 1985 were not released.

3. Though COPPES was a formally constituted organization with an executive board for each chapter, some informants also used the term to refer to the whole collective of political prisoners.

4. Alfredo, the Mesa Grande teacher and health worker, who was imprisoned in Mariona in 1986 after he returned to El Salvador, demonstrated the emotive power of the word *libertad* when he gave that name to his daughter, who was conceived during a conjugal visit and born after his release.

CHAPTER 6 *The Classroom*

1. I hope that Gerardo's explanation conveys his modesty and uncertainty. But I must confess that in reviewing this tape, I hear an assertive astonishment in my own tone of voice that departs considerably from sociological neutrality and nondirectiveness. I might as well have said, "Do you mean to tell me that you sat at home alone doing nothing but practicing adding and multiplying?"

2. In addition to Gabriel García Márquez's well-known novel, Portillo cites two books by Salvadoran authors: Argueta's *One Day of Life* (1983) and *Las Historias Prohibidas del Pulgarcito* by the guerrilla leader Roque Dalton (1974). Because of its small size, El Salvador is known as "*el Pulgarcito*" (literally, "little thumb"), the name of a tiny character in a folk tale.

3. Formal assessments of popular education since the war have been few, but in 1992 officials of the Ministry of Education collaborated with popular teachers of Chalatenango to examine students in the popular schools and issue official certificates to those who passed. While these examinations were not directly comparable to those offered in public schools, the results suggest that most students had mastered the material of the grades they had attended (Guzmán et al. 1993:38).

CHAPTER 7 *Teacher Training*

1. This oppositional quality of indigenous culture leads Scott (1976) to hold that it can be a source of peasant rebellion. I find his view wanting, as I said in the discussion of peasant revolt in chapter 1. While the culture of subordinates often contains elements of opposition to the dominant culture, it is more likely to be a form of passive resistance to domination than a source of direct challenge—unless it is overtly repressed (cf. Nash 1989:199).

CHAPTER 8 *Popular Education in Practice and Theory*

1. Paradoxically, the strategic shift meant a turn to a war of position in the realm of politics—the struggle for the hearts and minds of the base—but in military terms it was a shift to war of movement: the deployment of small, mobile forces and the abandonment of large fixed bases.

2. Popular education is one of the battlefields on which that struggle has continued after the war; see Hammond 1997.

3. Unfortunately, I cannot verify that those who used the term "popular" to describe education did so entirely spontaneously. While most transcripts show that I asked the question only after an informant had already used the phrase, I had often introduced it when I requested an interview.

4. I have not analyzed the interviews quantitatively, because I did not ask the same questions of every respondent. The finding of differences between people with different roles in popular education and in the communities, while fairly clear, was serendipitous. To present it statistically would impute to it a precision it does not have.

5. At least two women who had been popular teachers were among the fifteen FMLN candidates elected mayor in 1994.

6. Participatory management in industry can likewise be coopted and used to oppose genuine worker control. It can create the appearance of consultation and improve work satisfaction by deceiving workers that they have some control over the process (Fantasia, Clawson, and Graham 1988; Jenkins 1974:240–241; Zwerdling 1980:2–3).

7. By Berger's own acknowledgment, however, his criticism is purely theoretical, based on what he understands the word to mean rather than on any knowledge of actual practice (1973:118).

CHAPTER 9   *The View from City University*

1. Civilian informants nevertheless insisted, in remarks I consider unguarded, that they maintained a division of labor that made for operational autonomy. Cf. Isabel's statement of the FMLN's relation to education in the PPLs in chapter 5.

2. I later discovered in analyzing my interviews that I could similarly learn from my reactions. Some informants' comments made me very excited, others made me angry, and others I wanted to dismiss as misperceptions or rationalizations. Any strong reaction, I discovered, was a datum indicating that I should examine a phenomenon more closely. Often there was a meaning I was avoiding.

3. It was important to me to think of people as "informants" rather than "subjects." "Subjects" suggests experimental subjects, responding to an experimenter's stimuli and observed without necessarily realizing that they are being observed. (Portelli [1991:30] challenges the claim that this is even possible.) Though some find the term "informants" pejorative, to me it means people who inform me, people from whom I learn something.

4. For most of my knowledge of this research, I owe thanks to Dr. Lee Knefelkamp of Teachers College, whose course on adult learning I attended.

   The fact that I chose to attend a course at a school of education may be the most dramatic indication of my new appreciation of pedagogy. But I have also tried some other new things, including the workshops of the Theater of the Oppressed, Brazilian director Augusto Boal's project to join Freirean pedagogy with theater, and teaching in a New York City high school under the auspices of CUNY's American Social History Project.

GLOSSARY

campesina, campesino   Peasant, someone from a rural area.

cartilla   Basic reader, primer.

casa   House.

comandante   Guerrilla commander.

compa (abbreviation of *compañero*)   Member of the FMLN guerrilla army.

compañera, compañero   Companion, friend, fellow worker, comrade; (often *compañero de vida*) spouse, intimate partner.

conciencia   Conscience, consciousness.

concientización   Consciousness-raising.

dinámica   Learning game.

doble cara   Double face; strategy of simultaneous open and clandestine organizing.

foco   Central point, focus; small nucleus of guerrilla fighters.

foquismo   Doctrine of guerrilla war relying on a small fighting force, with little attention to cultivating a civilian support base.

frente   Front; *Frente* FMLN.

guinda   Flight through the mountains to escape the army.

matanza   Massacre; specifically, the massacre of 1932.

pala   Shovel.

REFERENCES

Abed-Rabbo, Samir, and Doris Safie, eds. 1990. *The Palestine Uprising: FACTS Information Committee*. Jerusalem: Association of Arab-American University Graduates Press.

Acuerdos hacia una nueva nación. 1992. San Salvador: Frente Farabundo Martí para la Liberación Nacional.

Alegría, Claribel, and D. J. Flakoll. 1984. *Para romper el silencio: Resistencia y lucha en las cárceles salvadoreñas*. Mexico City: Ediciones Era.

———. 1987. *No me agarran viva: La mujer salvadoreña en la lucha*. San Salvador: UCA Editores.

———, eds. 1989. *On The Front Line: Guerrilla Poems of El Salvador*. Willimantic, Conn.: Curbstone Press.

Alvarez Solís, Francisco, and Pauline Martin. 1992. The Role of Salvadoran NGOs in Post-war Reconstruction. *Development in Practice* 2, no. 2:103–113.

Americas Watch. 1986. *Settling Into Routine: Human Rights Abuses in Duarte's Second Year*. New York: Americas Watch.

———. 1987. *The Civilian Toll 1986–87: Ninth Supplement to the Report on Human Rights in El Salvador*. New York: Americas Watch.

———. 1990. *A Year of Reckoning: El Salvador a Decade After the Assassination of Archbishop Romero*. New York: Americas Watch.

———. 1991. *El Salvador's Decade of Terror: Human Rights since the Assassination of Archbishop Romero*. New Haven, Conn.: Yale University Press.

Amnesty International. 1984. *Amnesty International Report 1984*. London: Amnesty International Publications.

———. 1988. *Amnesty International Report 1988*. London: Amnesty International Publications.

———. 1989. *1989 Amnesty International Report*. New York: Amnesty International USA.

———. 1990. *1990 Amnesty International Report*. New York: Amnesty International USA.

Anderson, Thomas P. 1971. *Matanza: El Salvador's Communist Revolt of 1932*. Lincoln: University of Nebraska Press.

Arguedas, José María. 1974. *El Sexto*. Barcelona: Editorial Laia.

Argueta, Manlio. 1983. *One Day of Life*. New York: Vintage Books.

————. 1990. *Magic Dogs of the Volcanoes*. San Francisco: Children's Book Press.

Armstrong, Robert, and Janet Shenk. 1982. *El Salvador: The Face of Revolution*. Boston: South End Press.

Arnove, Robert. 1986. *Education and Revolution in Nicaragua*. New York: Praeger.

Bacavich, A. J., et al. 1988. American Military Policy in Small Wars: The Case of El Salvador. Unpublished paper, John F. Kennedy School of Government, Harvard University.

Bailey, Richard W., and Tom McArthur. 1992. Illiteracy. In *The Oxford Companion to the English Language*, edited by Tom McArthur, 498–499. Oxford: Oxford University Press.

Bam, Fikile. 1989. Life as a Political Prisoner. *Monitor* [South Africa], 49–53.

Barndt, Deborah. 1991. *To Change This House: Popular Education Under the Sandinistas*. Toronto: Between the Lines.

Beisiegel, Celso de Rui. 1974. *Estado e educação popular*. São Paulo: Livraria Pioneira Editora.

Belenky, Mary Field, et al., eds. 1986. *Women's Ways of Knowing: The Development of Self, Voice, and Mind*. New York: Basic Books.

Berger, Peter L. 1973. *Pyramids of Sacrifice: Political Ethics and Social Change*. New York: Basic Books.

Berryman, Phillip. 1984. *The Religious Roots of Rebellion: Christians in Central American Revolutions*. Maryknoll: Orbis Books.

————. 1987. *Liberation Theology: Essential Facts about the Revolutionary Movement in Latin America and Beyond*. New York: Pantheon Books.

————. 1994. *Stubborn Hope: Religion, Politics, and Revolution in Central America*. Maryknoll, N.Y.: Orbis Books.

Binford, Leigh. 1996. *The El Mozote Massacre: Anthropology and Human Rights*. Tucson: University of Arizona Press.

————. 1997. Grassroots Development in Conflict Zones of Northeastern El Salvador. *Latin American Perspectives* 24, no. 2:56–79.

Bloom, Allan David. 1987. *The Closing of the American Mind*. New York: Simon and Schuster.

Braumann, Rony. 1993. When Suffering Makes a Good Story. In *Life, Death and Aid: The Médecins Sans Frontières Report on World Crisis Intervention*, edited by François Jean, 149–158. London: Routledge.

Brockett, Charles D. 1988. *Land, Power, and Poverty: Agrarian Transformation and Political Conflict in Central America*. Boston: Allen & Unwin.

————. 1991. The Structure of Political Opportunities and Peasant Mobilization in Central America. *Comparative Politics* 23, no. 3:253–274.

Brockman, James R. 1982. *The Word Remains: A Life of Oscar Romero*. Maryknoll, N.Y.: Orbis Books.

Burdick, John. 1993. *Looking for God in Brazil: The Progressive Catholic Church in Urban Brazil's Religious Arena*. Berkeley: University of California Press.

Byrne, Hugh. 1996. *El Salvador's Civil War: A Study of Revolution*. Boulder, Colo.: Lynne Rienner Publishers.

Cabarrús P., Carlos Rafael. 1983. *Génesis de una revolución: Análisis del surgimiento y desarrollo de la organización campesina en El Salvador*. Mexico City: Ediciones de la Casa Chata.

Cáceres Prendes, Jorge. 1989. Political Radicalization and Popular Pastoral Practices in

El Salvador, 1969–1985. In *The Progressive Church in Latin America*, edited by Scott Mainwaring and Alexander Wilde, 103–148. Notre Dame, Ind.: University of Notre Dame Press.

Cagan, Beth. 1994. Salvadoran City of Hope: Segundo Montes on the Brink. *Dollars and Sense* (January-February):1–36.

Cagan, Beth, and Steve Cagan. 1991. *This Promised Land, El Salvador: The Refugee Community of Colomoncagua and their Return to Morazán*. New Brunswick, N.J.: Rutgers University Press.

Carnoy, Martin, and Joel Samoff. 1990. *Education and Social Transition in the Third World*. Princeton, N.J.: Princeton University Press.

Castañeda, Jorge G. 1993. *Utopia Unarmed: The Latin American Left after the Cold War*. New York: Alfred A. Knopf.

Chinchilla, Norma Stoltz. 1983. Women in Revolutionary Movements: The Case of Nicaragua. Working Paper #27, Michigan State University.

Clark, Peter B., and James Q. Wilson. 1961. Incentive Systems: A Theory of Organizations. *Administrative Science Quarterly* 6 (June):129–166.

Cleary, Edward L. 1985. *Crisis and Change: The Church in Latin America*. Maryknoll, N.Y.: Orbis Books.

Clinchy, Blythe McVicker. 1993. Ways of Knowing and Ways of Being: Epistemological and Moral Development in Undergraduate Women. In *Approaches to Moral Development: New Research and Emerging Themes*, edited by Andrew Garrod, 180–200. New York: Teachers College Press.

Clippinger, John H. 1976. Who Gains by Communications Development? Studies of Information Technologies in Developing Countries. Working Paper 76–1, Harvard University Program on Information Resources Policy.

Coleman, James S. 1990. *Foundations of Social Theory*. Cambridge: Harvard University Press.

Collins, Patricia Hill. 1990. *Black Feminist Thought: Knowledge, Consciousness, and the Politics of Empowerment*. New York: Routledge.

Colonnese, Louis M., ed. 1971. *Conscientization for Liberation*. Washington, D.C.: Division for Latin America, United States Catholic Conference.

Comisión de Derechos Humanos de El Salvador. 1986. *La tortura en El Salvador*. San Salvador: Comisión de Derechos Humanos de El Salvador.

Comisión de la Verdad para El Salvador. 1993. *De la locura a la esperanza: La guerra de 12 años en El Salvador*. San Salvador and New York: Naciones Unidas.

Consejo Episcopal Latinoamericano. 1979. *Medellín: Conclusiones*. Bogotá: Secretariado General del CELAM.

Crahan, Margaret E. 1992. Religion: Reconstituting Church and Pursuing Change. In *Americas: New Interpretive Essays*, edited by Alfred Stepan, 152–171. New York: Oxford University Press.

Cummins, Eric. 1994. *The Rise and Fall of California's Radical Prison Movement*. Stanford, Calif.: Stanford University Press.

Dalton, Roque. 1974. *Las historias prohibidas del Pulgarcito*. Mexico City: Siglo Veintiuno.

Danner, Mark. 1994. *The Massacre at El Mozote: A Parable of the Cold War*. New York: Vintage.

Daudelin, Jean, and W. E. Hewitt. 1995. Latin American Politics: Exit the Catholic Church? In *Organized Religion in the Political Transformation of Latin America*, edited by Satya R. Pattnayak. Lanham, Md.: University Press of America.

de la Cruz, Miguel. 1983. La educación y la guerra en El Salvador. *Nueva Antropología* 6, no. 21:83–94.

Deere, Carmen Diana. 1984. Agrarian Reform as Revolution and Counter-revolution: Nicaragua and El Salvador. In *The Politics of Intervention*, edited by Roger Burbach and Patricia Flynn, 165–188. New York: Monthly Review Press.

Dewees, Anthony, Elizabeth Evans, Carlos King, and Ernesto Schiefelbein. 1995. Educación básica y parvularia. In *La educación en El Salvador de cara al siglo XXI: Desafíos y oportunidades*, edited by Fernando Reimers, 217–278. San Salvador: UCA Editores.

Díaz, Nidia. 1988. *Nunca estuve sola*. San Salvador: UCA Editores.

Dorfman, Ariel. 1988. *Last Waltz in Santiago and Other Poems of Exile and Disappearance*. New York: Penguin Books.

D'Souza, Dinesh. 1991. *Illiberal Education: The Politics of Race and Sex on Campus*. New York: Free Press.

Dunkerley, James. 1985. *The Long War: Dictatorship and Revolution in El Salvador*. London: Verso Books.

Durham, William H. 1979. *Scarcity and Survival in Central America: Ecological Origins of the Soccer War*. Stanford, Calif.: Stanford University Press.

Edelman, Marc. 1994. Landlords and the Devil: Class, Ethnic, and Gender Dimensions of Central American Peasant Narratives. *Cultural Anthropology* 9 (February):58–93.

Edwards, Beatrice, and Gretta Tovar Siebentritt. 1991. *Places of Origin: The Repopulation of Rural El Salvador*. Boulder, Colo.: Lynne Rienner Publishers.

Elbow, Peter. 1973. *Writing Without Teachers*. London: Oxford University Press.

Escamilla, Manuel Luis. 1981. *Reformas educativas: Historia contemporánea de la educación formal en El Salvador*. San Salvador: Ministerio de Educación, 1981.

Fagen, Richard R. 1969. *The Transformation of Political Culture in Cuba*. Stanford, Calif.: Stanford University Press.

Falla, Ricardo. 1986. *Esa muerte que nos hace vivir: Estudio de la religión popular*. San Salvador: UCA Editores.

Fantasia, Rick, Dan Clawson, and Gregory Graham. 1988. A Critical View of Worker Participation in American Industry. *Work and Occupations* 15, no. 4 (November):468–488.

Fink, Marcy, and Robert F. Arnove. 1991. Issues and Tensions in Popular Education in Latin America. *International Journal of Educational Development* (Fall).

FMLN, Comandancia General. 1985. El Salvador vive una prolongada situación revolucionaria. Unpublished document, June.

FMLN, Reunión Comandancia. 1985. Los 15 principios del combatiente guerrillero. Photocopy.

FMLN. 1987. *El poder popular de doble cara: Lineamientos de organización*. Publicaciones FMLN.

Freire, Paulo. 1970. *Pedagogy of the Oppressed*. New York: Continuum.

———. 1973. *Education for Critical Consciousness*. New York: Continuum.

———. 1985. *The Politics of Education: Culture, Power and Liberation*. New York: Bergin and Garvey.

———. 1993. *Pedagogy of the City*. New York: Continuum.

Gadotti, Moacir. 1991. Educación popular y estado. In *Educación popular en América*

Latina: Crítica y perspectivas, edited by Anke van Dam, Sergio Martinic, and Gerhard Peter, 72–92. The Hague: CESO.

———. 1994. *Reading Paulo Freire: His Life and Work*. Albany: State University of New York Press.

———. 1996. A voz do biógrafo brasileiro: A prática à altura do sonho. In *Paulo Freire: Uma Biobibliografia*, edited by Moacir Gadotti, 69–115. São Paulo: Cortez Editora.

Gargallo, Francesca. 1987. La relación entre participación política y conciencia feminista en las militantes salvadoreñas. *Cuadernos Americanos*, n.s. 2 (April-May):58–76.

Goffman, Erving. 1961. *Asylums: Essays on the Social Situation of Mental Patients and Other Inmates*. Garden City, N.Y.: Anchor Books.

Goodwin, Jeff, and Theda Skocpol. 1989. Explaining Revolutions in the Contemporary Third World. *Politics and Society* 17, no. 4 (December):489–509.

Gordenker, Leon. 1987. *Refugees in International Politics*. New York: Columbia University Press.

Gordon, Leonard A. 1990. *Brothers Against the Raj: A Biography of Indian Nationalists Sarat and Subhas Chandra Bose*. New York: Columbia University Press.

Gramsci, Antonio. 1971. *Selections from the Prison Notebooks of Antonio Gramsci*. New York: International Publishers.

Guzmán, José Luís, et al. 1993. Las escuelas populares de Chalatenango: Un aporte para el desarrollo de la educación en las zonas rurales de El Salvador. Unpublished manuscript, Universidad Centroamericana José Simeón Cañas, San Salvador.

Hamilton, Nora. 1982. *The Limits of State Autonomy: Post-Revolutionary Mexico*. Princeton, N.J.: Princeton University Press.

Hammond, John L. 1995. Politics and Publishing in the New El Salvador. Review essay. *Latin American Research Review* 30, no. 3:210–223.

———. 1997. Popular Education in the Reconstruction of El Salvador. In *Latin American Education: Comparative Perspectives*, edited by Carlos Alberto Torres and Adriana Puiggrós. Boulder, Colo.: Westview Press, 349–371.

Harnecker, Marta. 1993. *Con la mirada en alto: Historia de las FPL Farabundo Martí a través de entrevistas con sus dirigentes*. San Salvador: UCA Editores.

Hart, Dianne Walta. 1990. *Thanks to God and the Revolution: The Oral History of a Nicaraguan Family*. Madison: University of Wisconsin Press.

Hellman, Judith Adler. 1994. *Mexican Lives*. New York: The New Press.

Henríquez Consalvi, Carlos (Santiago). 1992. *La terquedad del izote: El Salvador: Crónica de una victoria*. Mexico City: Editorial Diana.

Huezo Mixco, Miguel, ed. 1989. *Pájaro y volcán*. San Salvador: UCA Editores.

Hutchings, Pat, and Allen Wutzdorff. 1988. *Knowing and Doing: Learning through Experience*. New Directions in Teaching and Learning, vol. 35. San Francisco: Jossey-Bass.

Inter-American Commission on Human Rights. 1979. *Report on the Situation of Human Rights in El Salvador*. Washington, D.C.: Organization of American States.

International Human Rights Law Group. 1987. *Waiting for Justice: Treatment of Political Prisoners under El Salvador's Decree 50*. Washington, D.C.: International Human Rights Law Group.

Jean, François, ed. 1993. *Life, Death and Aid: The Médecins Sans Frontières Report on World Crisis Intervention*. London: Routledge.

Jelín, Elizabeth, ed. 1990. *Women and Social Change in Latin America*. London: Zed Books.

Jenkins, David. 1974. *Job Power: Blue and White Collar Democracy.* Baltimore, Md.: Penguin Books.

Karabel, Jerome. 1994. Review of *Teaching to Transgress: Education as the Practice of Freedom* and *Outlaw Culture: Resisting Representations*, by Bell Hooks. *New York Times Book Review*, 18 December, 27.

Kasinitz, Philip. 1995. Assault on City University. *Dissent* 42 (Fall):441–444.

Keegan, John. 1976. *The Face of Battle: A Study of Agincourt, Waterloo and the Somme.* New York: Vintage Books.

Kidd, Ross, and Krishna Kumar. 1981. Co-opting Freire: A Critical Analysis of Pseudo-Freirean Adult Education. *Economic and Political Weekly* 16, no. 1 (January 3):27–36.

Kincaid, A. Douglas. 1987. Peasants Into Rebels: Community and Class in Rural El Salvador. *Comparative Studies in Society and History* 29, no. 3 (July):466–494.

Kolb, David A. 1984. *Experiential Learning: Experience as the Source of Learning and Development.* Englewood Cliffs, N.J.: Prentice-Hall.

La Belle, Thomas J. 1986. *Nonformal Education in Latin America and the Caribbean: Stability, Reform, or Revolution?* New York: Praeger.

La fe de un pueblo: Historia de una comunidad cristiana en El Salvador (1970–1980). 1983. San Salvador: UCA Editores.

Levine, Daniel H. 1992. *Popular Voices in Latin American Catholicism.* Princeton, N.J.: Princeton University Press.

———. 1995. Religious Change, Empowerment and Power: Reflections on Latin American Experience. In *Organized Religion in the Political Transformation of Latin America*, edited by Satya R. Pattnayak, 15–40. Lanham, Md.: University Press of America.

Levine, Daniel H., and Scott Mainwaring. 1989. Religion and Popular Protest in Latin America: Contrasting Experiences. In *Power and Popular Protest*, edited by Susan Eckstein, 203–240. Berkeley: University of California Press.

Loescher, Gil, and Laila Monahan, eds. 1989. *Refugees and International Relations.* Oxford: Oxford University Press.

López Vigil, José Ignacio. 1991. *Las mil y una historias de Radio Venceremos.* San Salvador: UCA Editores.

López Vigil, María. 1987. *Vida y Muerte en Morazán: Testimonio de un sacerdote.* San Salvador: UCA Editores.

Loveman, Brian, and Thomas S. Davies Jr. 1985. El Salvador. In *Guerrilla Warfare*, by Che Guevara, with an Introduction and Case Studies by Brian Loveman and Thomas S. Davies Jr., 391–417. Lincoln: University of Nebraska Press.

Lungo, Mario. 1987. *La lucha de las masas en El Salvador.* San Salvador: UCA Editores.

Lupton, Ellen. 1993. *Mechanical Brides: Women and Machines from Home to Office.* New York: Cooper-Hewitt National Museum of Design.

Lynn, John A. 1984. *The Bayonets of the Republic: Motivation and Tactics in the Army of Revolutionary France, 1791–94.* Urbana: University of Illinois Press.

MacDonald, Heather. 1994. Downward Mobility: The Failure of Open Admissions at City University. *City Journal* 4, no. 3 (Summer):10–20.

Mandela, Nelson. 1994. *Long Walk to Freedom: The Autobiography of Nelson Mandela.* Boston: Little, Brown.

Martín Baró, Ignacio. 1973. Psicología del campesino salvadoreño. *Estudios Centroamericanos* 28, no. 297:476–495.

Mason, T. David. 1992. Women's Participation in Central American Revolutions: A Theoretical Perspective. *Comparative Political Studies* 25, no. 1 (April):63–89.

Mason, T. David, and Dale A. Krane. 1989. The Political Economy of Death Squads: Toward a Theory of the Impact of State-sanctioned Terror. *International Studies Quarterly* 33:175–198.

Mayo, John K., Robert C. Hornik, and Emile G. McAnany. 1976. *Educational Reform with Television: The El Salvador Experience.* Stanford, Calif.: Stanford University Press.

McAdam, Doug. 1988. *Freedom Summer.* New York: Oxford University Press.

McCarthy, Mary. 1985. *Occasional Prose.* San Diego: Harcourt Brace Jovanovich.

Mecca, Andrew M., Neil J. Smelser, and John Vasconcellos, eds. 1989. *The Social Importance of Self-Esteem.* Berkeley: University of California Press.

Mena Sandoval, Francisco Emilio. 1991. *Del ejército nacional al ejército guerrillero.* San Salvador: Ediciones Arcoiris.

Menchú, Rigoberta. 1984. *I, Rigoberta Menchú: An Indian Woman in Guatemala.* London: Verso.

Metzi, Francisco. 1988. *The People's Remedy: Health Care in El Salvador's War of Liberation.* New York: Monthly Review.

Miles, Sarah. 1986. The Real War: Low-intensity Conflict in Central America. *NACLA Report on the Americas* 20, no. 2:17–48.

Miller, Valerie. 1985. *Between Struggle and Hope: The Nicaraguan Literacy Campaign.* Boulder, Colo.: Westview Press.

Ministerio de Educación. n.d. *El pensamiento de Paulo Freire.* San Salvador: Ministerio de Educación, Programa Perfeccionamiento Permanente de Maestros en Servicio.

Molyneux, Maxine. 1986. Mobilization Without Emancipation? Women's Interests, State, and Revolution. In *Transition and Development: Problems of Third World Socialism,* edited by Richard R. Fagen et al., 280–302. New York: Monthly Review.

Moncada-Davidson, Lillian. 1990. Education and Social Change: The Case of El Salvador. Ph.D. diss., Columbia University.

Montes, Segundo. 1989. *Refugiados y repatriados: El Salvador y Honduras.* San Salvador: Departamento de Sociología y Ciencias Políticas, Instituto de Derechos Humanos, Universidad Centroamericana José Simeón Cañas.

Montes Mozo, Segundo, et al. 1985. *Investigación: Desplazados y refugiados salvadoreños.* San Salvador: Instituto de Investigaciones de la Universidad Centroamericana José Simeón Cañas.

Montgomery, Tommie Sue. 1982. *Revolution in El Salvador: Origins and Evolution.* Boulder, Colo.: Westview Press.

———. 1983. Liberation and Revolution: Christianity as a Subversive Activity in Central America. In *Trouble in Our Backyard: Central America and the United States in the Eighties,* edited by Martin Diskin, 75–100. New York: Pantheon Books.

Moore, Barrington. 1966. *Social Origins of Dictatorship and Democracy.* Boston: Beacon Press.

Morel, Augusto, ed. 1993. *Este lucero chiquito: Poesía y cuentos de la montaña.* San Salvador: Editorial Sombrero Azul.

Nash, June. 1989. Cultural Resistance and Class Consciousness in Bolivian Tin-mining Communities. In *Power and Popular Protest,* edited by Susan Eckstein, 182–202. Berkeley: University of California Press.

Neier, Aryeh. 1989. Drain the Sea, Scorch the Earth: An Outline of the Counterinsurgency

Strategy. In *Forced Out: The Agony of the Refugee in Our Time*, by Carole Kismaric, 66–68. New York: Human Rights Watch and the J. M. Kaplan Fund.

———. 1993. Watching Rights. *The Nation*, 1 March, 259.

Nóchez, Mario, and Luis Pérez Miguel. 1995. Educación no formal. In *La educación en El Salvador de cara al siglo XXI: Desafíos y oportunidades*, edited by Fernando Reimers, 465–515. San Salvador: UCA Editores.

Paige, Jeffery M. 1975. *Agrarian Revolution: Social Movements and Export Agriculture in the Underdeveloped World*. New York: Free Press.

Paulston, Rolland G. 1992. Ways of Seeing Education and Social Change in Latin America: A Phenomenographic Perspective. *Latin America Research Review* 27, no. 3:177–202.

Pearce, Jenny. 1986. *Promised Land: Peasant Rebellion in Chalatenango, El Salvador*. London: Latin America Bureau.

Peretz, Don. 1990. *The Intifada: The Palestinian Uprising*. Boulder, Colo.: Westview Press.

Pérez Brignoli, Héctor. 1995. Indians, Communists, and Peasants: The 1932 Rebellion in El Salvador. In *Coffee, Society, and Power in Latin America*, edited by William Roseberry et al., 232–261. Baltimore, Md.: Johns Hopkins University Press.

Pérez Miguel, Luis. 1994. La escuela rural. Educación para la comunidad sin la comunidad. *Realidad* 40 (July-August):617–652.

Peterson, Anna L. 1997. *Martyrdom and the Politics of Religion: Progressive Catholicism in El Salvador's War*. Albany: State University of New York Press.

Poole, Deborah, and Gerardo Renique. 1992. *Peru: Time of Fear*. London: Latin American Bureau.

Popkin, Samuel. 1979. *The Rational Peasant: The Political Economy of Rural Society in Vietnam*. Berkeley: University of California Press.

Portelli, Alessandro. 1991. *The Death of Luigi Trastulli and Other Stories: Form and Meaning in Oral History*. Albany: State University of New York Press.

Proceso. 1995. Land: Conflict in the Countryside. *Proceso* 684 (November 1). English edition distributed by Peacenet.

Putnam, Robert D. 1993. *Making Democracy Work: Civic Traditions in Modern Italy*. Princeton, N.J.: Princeton University Press.

———. 1995. Bowling Alone: America's Declining Social Capital. *Journal of Democracy* 6, no. 1 (January):65–78.

Radcliffe, Sarah A., and Sallie Westwood, eds. 1993. *"Viva": Women and Popular Protest in Latin America*. London: Routledge.

Rahnema, Majid. 1992. Participation. In *The Development Dictionary: A Guide to Knowledge as Power*, edited by Wolfgang Sachs, 116–131. London: Zed Books.

Randall, Margaret. 1983. *Christians in the Nicaraguan Revolution*. Vancouver: New Star Books.

Rapping, Elayne. 1996. *The Culture of Recovery: Making Sense of the Self-Help Movement in Women's Lives*. Boston: Beacon Press.

Reif, Linda L. 1986. Women in Latin American Guerrilla Movements: A Comparative Perspective. *Comparative Politics* 18, no. 2 (January):147–169.

Reimers, Fernando, ed. 1995. *La educación en El Salvador de cara al siglo XXI: Desafíos y oportunidades*. San Salvador: UCA Editores.

Rénique, José Luís. 1991. The Revolution Behind Bars. *NACLA Report on the Americas* 24, no. 4 (December 1990/January 1991):17–19.

Richard, Pablo, and Sergio Meléndez, eds. 1982. *La iglesia de los pobres en América*

Central: Un análisis socio-político y teológico de la iglesia centroamericana (1960–1982). San José: Departamento Ecuménico de Investigaciones.

Rothschild-Whitt, Joyce. 1979. The Collective Organization: An Alternative to Rational-bureaucratic Models. *American Sociological Review* 44 (August):509–527.

Rueschemeyer, Dietrich, Evelyne Huber Stephens, and John D. Stephens. 1992. *Capitalist Development and Democracy*. Chicago: University of Chicago Press.

Safa, Helen. 1990. Women's Social Movements in Latin America. *Gender and Society* 4, no. 3 (Summer):355–369.

Sallarué. 1980. *Cuentos de barro*. San Salvador: UCA Editores.

Sands, Bobby. 1985. *One Day in My Life*. Chicago: Banner Press.

Schirmer, Jennifer. 1993. The Seeking of Truth and the Gendering of Consciousness: The Comadres of El Salvador and the CONAVIGUA Widows of Guatemala. In *"Viva": Women and Popular Protest in Latin America*, edited by Sarah A. Radcliffe and Sallie Westwood, 30–64. London: Routledge.

Scott, James C. 1976. *The Moral Economy of the Peasant: Rebellion and Subsistence in Southeast Asia*. New Haven, Conn.: Yale University Press.

———. 1985. *Weapons of the Weak: Everyday Forms of Peasant Resistance*. New Haven, Conn.: Yale University Press.

Seligson, Mitchell A. 1995. Thirty Years of Transformation in the Agrarian Structure of El Salvador, 1961–1991. *Latin American Research Review* 30, no. 3:43–74.

Skocpol, Theda. 1982. What Makes Peasants Revolutionary? *Comparative Politics* 14, no. 3 (April):351–375.

Smith, Christian. 1991. *The Emergence of Liberation Theology: Radical Religion and Social Movement Theory*. Chicago: University of Chicago Press.

Spence, Jack, et al. 1994. *A Negotiated Revolution? A Two Year Progress Report on the Salvadoran Peace Accords*. Cambridge: Hemisphere Initiatives.

Spivak, Gayatri Chakravorty. 1988. Can the Subaltern Speak? In *Marxism and the Interpretation of Culture*, edited by Cary Nelson and Lawrence Grossberg. Urbana: University of Illinois Press.

Statistical Abstract of Latin America. 1987. Vol. 25. Los Angeles: University of California at Los Angeles Latin America Center.

Stein, Barry N. 1986. Durable Solutions for Developing Country Refugees. *International Migration Review* 20 (Summer):264–282.

Sykes, Gresham M. 1958. *The Society of Captives: A Study of a Maximum Security Prison*. Princeton, N.J.: Princeton University Press.

Tarrow, Sidney. 1994. *Power in Movement: Social Movements, Collective Action and Politics*. Cambridge: Cambridge University Press.

Thiesenhusen, William C. 1995. *Broken Promises: Agrarian Reform and the Latin American Campesino*. Boulder, Colo.: Westview Press.

Toch, Hans. 1982. Studying and Reducing Stress. In *The Pains of Imprisonment*, edited by Robert Johnson and Hans Toch, 25–44. Beverly Hills, Calif.: Sage Publications.

Torres, Carlos Alberto. 1989. *The Politics of Nonformal Education in Latin America*. New York: Praeger.

———. 1994. Democratic Socialism, Social Movements and Educational Policy in Brazil: The Work of Paulo Freire as Secretary of Education in the Municipality of São Paulo. *Comparative Education Review* 38 (May):181–214.

Traub, James. 1994. *City on a Hill: Testing the American Dream at City College*. Reading, Mass.: Addison-Wesley.

Truscello, David. 1979. Prison under Pinochet. *The Radical Teacher* 16 (December):13–14.

Tula, María Teresa. 1994. *Hear my Testimony: María Teresa Tula, Human Rights Activist of El Salvador*, translated and edited by Lynn Stephen. Boston: South End Press.

van Creveld, Martin. 1991. *The Transformation of War*. New York: The Free Press.

van Dam, Anke, Sergio Martinic, and Gerhard Peter, eds. 1991. *Educación popular en América Latina: Crítica y perspectivas*. The Hague: CESO.

Vargas, Laura. 1984. *Técnicas participativas para la educación popular*. Vol. 1. San José, Costa Rica: Centro de Estudios y Publicaciones Alforja.

Vilas, Carlos. 1995. *Between Earthquakes and Volcanoes: Market, State, and the Revolutions in Central America*. New York: Monthly Review Press.

Walter, Knut, and Philip J. Williams. 1993. The Military and Democratization in El Salvador. *Journal of Interamerican Studies and World Affairs* 35 (Spring):45–73.

Wasserstrom, Robert. 1985. *Grassroots Development in Latin America and the Caribbean: Oral Histories of Social Change*. New York: Praeger.

Weeks, John. 1985. *The Economies of Central America*. New York: Holmes and Meyer.

Weiss Fagen, Patricia, and Joseph Eldridge. 1991. Salvadoran Repatriation from Honduras. In *Repatriation under Conflict in Central America*, edited by Mary Ann Larkin, Frederick C. Cuny, and Barry N. Stein. Washington, D.C.: Hemispheric Migration Project.

Werner, David. 1980. *Donde no hay doctor: Una guía para los campesinos que viven lejos de los centros médicos*. Palo Alto, Calif.: Hesperian Foundation.

Werner, David, and Bill Bower. 1982. *Helping Health Workers Learn*. Palo Alto, Calif.: Hesperian Foundation.

White, Alastair. 1973. *El Salvador*. New York: Praeger Publishers.

Wickham-Crowley, Timothy P. 1987. The Rise (and Sometimes Fall) of Guerrilla Governments in Latin America. *Sociological Forum* 2, no. 3 (Summer):473–499.

———. 1989. Understanding Failed Revolution in El Salvador: A Comparative Analysis of Regime Types and Social Structures. *Politics and Society* 17, no. 4 (December):511–537.

———. 1992. *Guerrillas and Revolution in Latin America: A Comparative Study of Insurgents and Regimes since 1956*. Princeton, N.J.: Princeton University Press.

Williams, Philip J., and Anna L. Peterson. 1996. Evangelicals and Catholics in El Salvador: Evolving Religious Responses to Social Change. *Journal of Church and State* 38 (Autumn):873–897.

Williams, Robert G. 1986. *Export Agriculture and the Crisis in Central America*. Chapel Hill: University of North Carolina Press.

Wolf, Eric R. 1966. *Peasants*. Englewood Cliffs, N.J.: Prentice-Hall.

———. 1969. *Peasant Wars of the Twentieth Century*. New York: Harper and Row.

World University Service et al. 1981. *El Salvador: Education and Repression*. Compiled and introduced by Jon Bevan. London: World University Service.

Youngman, Frank. 1986. *Adult Education and Socialist Pedagogy*. London: Croom Helm.

Zolberg, Aristide R., Astri Suhrke, and Sergio Aguayo. 1989. *Escape from Violence: Conflict and the Refugee Crisis in the Developing World*. Oxford: Oxford University Press.

Zwerdling, Daniel. 1980. *Workplace Democracy: A Guide to Workplace Ownership, Participation, and Self-Management Experiments in the United States and Europe*. New York: Harper and Row.

SUBJECT INDEX

Abilio, 111, 128, 140, 152, 192
access to education, 6, 10, 133–134,
 159, 190–192, 219, 221
accompaniment, 51, 207
Adelinda, 28, 31, 32, 36, 41, 89
Adolfo, 117
advisors to popular teachers, 82–85, 88,
 179–188. *See also* teacher training
agrarian reform, 40, 43, 48, 117, 118
agricultural production, 35, 113, 115,
 120, 123
Aguilares, 31, 41
Alas, José, 26–27, 28, 32, 40–41, 43,
 226n3
Alberto, 63, 65
Alfabetizando para la paz (CIAZO), 1,
 3, 119, 147, 179
Alfonso, 113–114, 124, 128, 131, 139,
 155, 193
Alfredo, 82, 84, 85, 87, 88, 172, 193
alternative medicine, 170–71
Alvarez, José Eduardo (Bishop of San
 Miguel), 34, 35, 109
AMS, 118, 119
ANDES, 37, 42, 60, 97, 107, 145, 150,
 179, 185
Angela, 173, 175, 177
Angelina, 138
Anita, 83, 84, 142–143, 180, 183–184
Antonio, 131, 132–133
Aparicio, Pedro, 46
Armando, 102
army, Salvadoran, 10, 75–76, 118, 214

Arturo, 128, 150, 152, 196
Association of Salvadoran Women. *See*
 AMS
Azucena, 94, 95

banking education, 17, 217
base communities. *See* Christian base
 communities
Béneke, Walter, 11
behavior: schoolchildren's, 152–153
Bible study, 27, 38–39, 85, 109

cadejo, 182
Camilo, 37, 38, 43–44, 201
Caminemos (Archdiocesan Social
 Secretariat), 89, *90–91*, 179
campesinos, 2, 9–12, 225n4; organization
 of, 40, 45. *See also* peasant war
canon, 220
Caritas, 76, 82
Carlos, 182
Carmela, 106, 108, 113, 123
Carmelina, 59
Carmen, 167, 168
Carpio, Salvador Cayetano, 46, 54, 226n2
cartilla, 1, *3*, 18, 79–80, 89, *90–91*, 107–
 108, 145, 152, *154*, 179–180, 201
Castellano, Miguel, 63
Castillo, Javier, 41–42, 51, 180
catechists. *See* delegates of the word
CCR, 114, 116, 124, 185
CDHES, 96, *164*, 214, 227n1
Cecilia, 150, 182

AUTHOR INDEX